Race, Gender, and Sexuality in Post-Apocalyptic TV and Film

Also by Barbara Gurr
*Reproductive Justice: The Politics of Healthcare for
Native American Women*

Race, Gender, and Sexuality in Post-Apocalyptic TV and Film

Edited by
Barbara Gurr

palgrave
macmillan

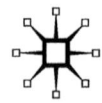

RACE, GENDER, AND SEXUALITY IN POST-APOCALYPTIC TV AND FILM
Selection and editorial content © Barbara Gurr 2015
Individual chapters © their respective contributors 2015

All rights reserved. No reproduction, copy or transmission of this publication may be made without written permission. No portion of this publication may be reproduced, copied or transmitted save with written permission. In accordance with the provisions of the Copyright, Designs and Patents Act 1988, or under the terms of any licence permitting limited copying issued by the Copyright Licensing Agency, Saffron House, 6-10 Kirby Street, London EC1N 8TS.

Any person who does any unauthorized act in relation to this publication may be liable to criminal prosecution and civil claims for damages.

First published 2015 by
PALGRAVE MACMILLAN

The authors have asserted their rights to be identified as the authors of this work in accordance with the Copyright, Designs and Patents Act 1988.

Palgrave Macmillan in the UK is an imprint of Macmillan Publishers Limited, registered in England, company number 785998, of Houndmills, Basingstoke, Hampshire, RG21 6XS.

Palgrave Macmillan in the US is a division of Nature America, Inc., One New York Plaza, Suite 4500, New York, NY 10004-1562.

Palgrave Macmillan is the global academic imprint of the above companies and has companies and representatives throughout the world.

Hardback ISBN: 978-1-137-50150-9
E-PUB ISBN: 978-1-137-49333-0
E-PDF ISBN: 978-1-137-49331-6
DOI: 10.1057/978-1-137-49331-6

Distribution in the UK, Europe and the rest of the world is by Palgrave Macmillan®, a division of Macmillan Publishers Limited, registered in England, company number 785998, of Houndmills, Basingstoke, Hampshire RG21 6XS.

Library of Congress Cataloging-in-Publication Data is available from the Library of Congress.

A catalogue record for the book is available from the British Library.

This book is dedicated to
Mary Shelley, Octavia Butler, Marge Piercy
Han Solo, William Adama, Doctor Who
Dr. Joan Joffe Hall, who first introduced me to feminist science fiction
Morgan Dorm, for (oddly formative) hours and
hours of *Star Trek* and *Cheers*
My mom, the librarian, who never put a book down or told me to
And, always,
To Hailey and Charlie

Proceeds from the sale of this edition go to support Girls Who Code because what they do is important. You would think so too—check 'em out at girlswhocode.com

Contents

Acknowledgments	ix
Introduction: After the World Ends, Again *Barbara Gurr*	1

Part I   The More Things Change, the More They Stay the Same . . .   15

1. Organisms and Human Bodies as Contagions in the Post-Apocalyptic State   17
   Robert A. Booth
2. Masculinity, Race, and the (Re?)Imagined American Frontier   31
   Barbara Gurr
3. Gender in the Aftermath: Starbuck and the Future of Woman in *Battlestar Galactica*   45
   Tracey Raney and Michelle Meagher
4. The Visibility and Invisibility of Class, Race, Gender, and Sexuality in *The Hunger Games*   59
   Mary C. Burke and Maura Kelly
5. Post-Apocalyptic Inequalities: Race, Class, Gender, and Sexualities in *Firefly*   71
   J. Sumerau and Sarah L. Jirek

Part II   The Future in Flux   85

6. Queer Resistance in an Imperfect Allegory: The Politics of Sexuality in *True Blood*   87
   Stacy Missari
7. Woman as Evolution: The Feminist Promise of the *Resident Evil* Film Series   99
   Andrea Harris

8	Cops and Zombies: Hierarchy and Social Location in *The Walking Dead* Melissa F. Lavin and Brian M. Lowe	113
9	"We Don't Do History": Constructing Masculinity in a World of Blood Amanda Hobson	125
10	The Apocalypse Is No-Thing To Wish For: Revisioning Traumatic Masculinities in John Hillcoat's *The Road* Brent Strang	137
11	Propagation and Procreation: The Zombie and the Child James Berger	149

Afterword (Afterward)   165
Barbara Gurr
Appendix: What Else Is Out There?   169
Kirk Lustila
Notes on Contributors   177
Index   181

Acknowledgments

My first thanks, always, go to Creator. My second, always, to my husband, who continues after all these years to listen to me rant when I need to and is kind enough to always tell me I'm perfectly reasonable. In the post-apocalypse you're the one I want by my side, baby. The scholars who contributed to this book are all people I like—it's been a genuine pleasure to meet them, work with them, and get to know them a little better. Their work here and elsewhere is an intellectual turn-on and I'm eager for more. Thank you to each of you who wrote, revised, and revised again, figured out the citation style, met the deadlines, and contributed your thoughtful, insightful, and exciting expertise to this volume. My special thanks to Melissa Lavin for her extra-above-and-beyond efforts from beginning to end. My thanks also go to the editors and production assistants at Palgrave Macmillan for the steady hand, the endless patience, and the support for this project.

This book began in a class I taught for the University of Connecticut's Women's, Gender and Sexuality Studies Program. The class was titled, quite accidentally, "Settler Science Fiction" and it was hands down one of the best classes I've ever been a part of, peopled by sharp, committed feminist students who taught me way more than I could have possibly taught them. They have all since gone on to do their own fabulous and no doubt feminist things, but I hope someday they'll pick this up and know that I still think of them with love and appreciation. Speaking of undergraduate students, my deep appreciation also goes to the Women's, Gender and Sexuality Studies students who helped me edit this manuscript, keeping me as close to deadlines as anyone has ever managed to keep me (which is to say, not terribly close). In alphabetical order: Caroline Alexander, Lucas DeCastro, Austin Heffernan, and Giorgina Paiella. I would be remiss here if I did not also mention Kirk Lustila, who contributed the Appendix—and it's a good thing, as his expertise as a consumer of numerous different media platforms far outshines my own.

I want to close by thanking several people who likely don't even know how they've contributed to this volume, or, perhaps, even to my life: Mike Morris, whose commitment to and knowledge of both the superhero universe and the Star Trek universe are nothing short of inspirational, and whose kindness and wit sustain me from afar; Janessa Wilson, whose righteous rage keeps me on task and who is raising her daughters to define their own lives with power and dignity; Jennifer Clark, whose sheer determination to surround herself with books reminds me over and over that we live our lives—literally and figuratively—through the power of stories; and Dan Miller, for innumerable conversations about the merits of feminist literature over innumerable cappuccinos—who knew, back then, that they would turn into a book indulging my science fiction obsession? Well, they did. I have been so fortunate in my life to have encountered such amazing people.

The contributors and I hope this book is fun. We hope it's insightful. Most of all, we hope it encourages for you, dear reader, a critical analysis not only of popular culture and speculative fiction, but of the raced, gendered, and sexed customs, practices, and institutions which currently define and delimit so much of US society. We know that for many, the apocalypse has come and gone or is ongoing. When the dust settles, the disease is contained, and the zombies are destroyed, we hope that there is cooperation rather than competition, memory that is empowering but not tyrannical, and, somehow, lots of coffee.

So say we all.

Introduction: After the World Ends, Again

Barbara Gurr

Sometimes we envision the end of the world wrought by four demon riders on horseback; at other times humanity's destruction is brought about by our own hubris, at the hands of a human–machine hybrid, through an unnamed and shockingly unexpected epidemic, or simply a random natural catastrophe. Yet despite the many and creative ways we imagine the end of the world, we also imagine that somehow some of us will survive it (although perhaps we don't survive *well*—I, for one, will be a wreck after the apocalypse when the coffee runs out). After all, the story of "how we all died. The end." does not feel very satisfying, but the story of "how most of us died, but some endured . . ." has a certain attraction. Even better, it has *possibilities*. Who survived? Why them, and not others? What did they do to ensure their survival? (Always a question with dark undertones.) And, of course, the all-important questions: Would *I* survive? Would my loved ones? How would I accomplish this? What would I do to save myself, or my family? Would I do the same for strangers? Would they, for me? The details of the apocalypse itself recede in importance as we wonder "what next?" because that is the question that holds our deepest hopes and most existential fears. As speculative fiction (we hope!), post-apocalyptic narratives ask us to consider what it means to be truly human, particularly in the context of survival horror and genocide, by testing not only our physical survival skills, but also our values, our morals, and our beliefs.

The Politics of the Post-Apocalypse

Of course, after the apocalypse – after the eradication of all we know – we who survive will have to build something new out of the ashes. The emerging world may be desperate and dirty; it may be hard and hungry; it may be something completely unexpected. Interestingly, post-apocalyptic narratives, necessarily set after the world ends and the work of rebuilding something new begins, frequently fail to imagine new experiences of race, gender, and sexuality. Instead, the stories created for us in film and television all too often reproduce conservative ideologies which shape how we "read" social constructions of race, gender, and sexuality as natural and inevitable, perhaps even necessary for our survival. Many of the post-apocalyptic films and TV shows under consideration in this book feature survivors scrambling to reestablish the previous order of things, uncritically reinstalling previous hierarchies and race, gender, and sexuality expectations. Perhaps these stories tell us there is enough challenge in simply surviving, and the human imagination cannot extend beyond the terror of constantly fighting off zombies, aliens, or vampires to create a new society, with new social mores and rules of engagement. Or perhaps these stories serve another purpose: to illustrate that our safety and ability to survive as a human collective rely upon the strength of these conservative ideologies; heteropatriarchal gender and race hierarchies survive after the apocalypse not because we are too afraid or too exhausted to create something different, but because they are our best hope, our best strength. To change now would be to weaken our ultimate chances of survival. Or perhaps these stories imply that our previous hierarchies and behaviors are so easily reinstated because they are, after all, "natural," and when the world around us is reduced to a primitive state, we too can drop our social pretensions and return to who we are meant to be. You know: Adam and Eve, not Adam and Steve. Back in the kitchen (or what serves as a kitchen in the post-apocalypse) if we're identified as female, or out in the woods hunting if we're identified as male. Yet despite the general reproduction of race, sex, and gender narratives which simply reinstall the current dominant paradigm, there are also moments of resistance, subversion, and reinvention to be found in even the most conservative of these texts. These moments, and their more frequent absence, reveal our own contemporary desires and anxieties as well as the fears which potentially stifle our abilities to imagine something different, but they also potentially point us toward a new future, shaped by new possibilities. This is what speculative fiction is so very good at: *potentiality*. The very meanings of race, of gender, of sexuality, of labor and reproduction, of power, and of survival itself might not change after the world as we know it comes to an end. But then again, they might.

Race, Gender, and Sexuality in Post-Apocalyptic TV and Film considers these possibilities. For example, what new or renewed significance do we give human reproduction (and thus human sexuality) in the tense matrix of daily survival and the potential annihilation of the human race? For that matter, how can we understand "race" within the context of alien invasion? Will we inevitably resort to violence in our (apparently unavoidably) desperate efforts to survive? What do these televisual stories tell us about kinship and gender roles? About community and alienation? Television shows and films as seemingly diverse as *The Hunger Games, Falling Skies, The Road,* and *True Blood* share both narrative and thematic concerns about the future of humanity, how we know who we are, and what we truly value most but embed these concerns in stories that leave us entertained as well as alternately comforted and perhaps a little bit anxious. Race, gender, and sexuality serve as essential themes in the tense crucible of fear and hope these stories create, though they may not appear prominent to the casual viewer (perhaps particularly if that viewer is white, heterosexual, and cisgender). The authors in this volume bring these social identities and experiences to the forefront of consideration, deepening our appreciation of both the questions asked by speculative fiction and the potential of our collective future as humans.

This is a book, then, about the politics of the post-apocalypse, bringing together scholars from multiple disciplines to mobilize readings of the post-apocalypse through feminist, critical race, and queer lenses in order to theorize both our current politics and our potential future politics. At the same time, we also centralize the cultural politics of televisual storytelling by focusing on the post-apocalyptic stories we produce and consume through television and film, arguably our most popular forms of storytelling in the twenty-first century. The proliferation of mass media throughout the twentieth century changed the landscape of popular culture, but the advent of twenty-first-century viewing practices, which allow whole television seasons or even series to be consumed quickly, without the twentieth century's delayed gratification of weekly installments interrupted by a seasonal hiatus, has been further augmented through transmedia networks relying on websites, fansites, and blogs to carry stories and speculations onward. Similarly, films released in theaters quickly become available in other easily accessed formats. Many of the stories under consideration in this book were originally novels or comics before they were televisual, and many of the stories that started on television or in film continued through webisodes or extended existing video game franchises, attesting to the flexible and transitive nature of our stories; we can now engage with these stories on our phones and on our computers, on airplanes or at the local bar, and we can discuss with virtual strangers what we think will happen next and how we feel about it. The twenty-first century provides us, as story consumers, with a particularly intense and multisensory experience, potentially imbuing the questions that post-apocalyptic fictions ask with an even greater sense of urgency. Importantly, then, this book considers not only the politics of the post-apocalypse (and thus our current politics), but also the politics of TV and film. Ultimately, we argue that the cultural politics of televisual stories are not merely analogous to the larger politics of our world; they are coconstitutive elements vying for and dynamically producing, rejecting, and revising material realities in our broader cultural matrix.

A Brief History of the Post-Apocalyptic Future

Science fiction and popular culture scholars generally agree that the increasing emergence and popularity of post-apocalyptic narratives in popular culture can be traced to the end of World War II and specifically to the dropping of the hydrogen bomb on Hiroshima and Nagasaki by the United States. The world after 1945 was not only a changed landscape physically, politically, and economically, it was also a changed world symbolically. Humans had split the atom. The implications were exhilarating and terrifying, and a brave new world lurched forward, following the machines of death and dragging behind the tattered remains of what came before, unable—perhaps unwilling?—to relinquish entirely the comfortable familiarities of what we thought made us human, before we became like Gods who could destroy life on such a tremendous scale. Through its burgeoning nuclear weapons technology, the United States wielded the power of mass death. But culturally we also sought to return to a nostalgic idea of small-town community, and we were aided in this effort to return to presumably simpler times by the same popular media that at least partially produced the desire in the first place: television shows such as *Father Knows Best* (1954–1960), *Bonanza* (1959–1973), and *My Three Sons* (1960–1972), films such as *It's a Wonderful Life* (1946) and *The Quiet Man* (1952), and even Broadway productions like *Brigadoon* (1947) and *Damn Yankees* (1955) valorized simpler times, the sanctity of (heteropatriarchal) family, and even the dominance of whiteness (if only through the sheer invisibility of people of color in so many of these narratives). Large-scale survival horror similarly relied on the nostalgic and romantic renderings of small-town life in America, highlighting the tension between fear and desire in American popular culture. Films such as *The Day the World Ended* (1955) and *On the Beach* (1959), for example, explored the consequences of total global decimation side by side with small-town stories that revealed a cultural yearning for simplicity and safety, turning nostalgically back to what felt familiar, even if it had never, in fact, been the universal truth.

Narratives and images of annihilation continued through the second half of the twentieth century to organize our cultural hermeneutic. America's fascination with the world after the world's end continued to be fed by, and to feed, our popular culture narratives through films like *Planet of the Apes* (1968), *Escape from New York* (1981) and its sequel *Escape from L.A.* (1996), and the *Terminator* franchise (1984–2015), though post-apocalyptic narratives on TV were less frequent through the 1980s and 1990s (1983's *The Day After* being a notable exception). The first decade and a half of the twenty-first century, however, has witnessed a dramatic popular resurgence of post-apocalyptic narratives, both in print and on the screen; literature such as

James Dashner's Maze Runner series, Justin Cronin's *The Passage*, and Margaret Atwood's MaddAddam series consistently make the New York Times bestseller list, while television and film offer us post-apocalyptic worlds ranging from the graphic violence of AMC's *The Walking Dead* (2010–) and the CW's *The 100* (2014–) to the comedic *Zombieland* (2009) and *This is the End* (2013). Even Disney has entered the post-apocalypse with its relatively benign *Wall-E* (2008).

Although in some ways these twenty-first-century texts continue to rely on previous technologies of destruction—human hubris, environmental devastation, unknown and uncontrollable disease for which we are not prepared—many of them are organized, both obviously and subtly, by a new element: the terrorist attacks on the United States in September 2001, events that were apocalyptic to US citizens and others in the world for the amount of death and grief they wrought, the economic consequences, and the sheer shock of the audacious attack on presumably inviolate land. For many US citizens and others, there is the United States before 9/11 and there is the United States after 9/11, and as numerous scholars have pointed out, TV and film have both responded to this cultural change and helped to mark these two eras as disparate.[1]

Thus the 9/11 terrorist attacks demarcate a new post-apocalypse in which the echoes of the attacks and their ongoing consequences have markedly changed our cultural behaviors and expectations. "America," and the values so frequently associated with it (perhaps most notably freedom and equality, but also democracy and other civil rights) are no longer inviolate, no longer safe, but under constant threat from both outside and possibly inside forces. The United States is engaged in a seemingly endless war on terror, enacted "over there" but with resounding consequences "over here," as the US military commits torture and human rights violations, pulls our soldiers out of military engagements and then reinserts them, maintains prisoner of war camps, and struggles with a precarious economic recovery that is marked by, among other things, a distinct lack of support for returning veterans. We take our shoes off at the airport, are comprehensively surveilled by our own government, and are urged on subways and busses to "say something" if we "see something." Fear has returned to the United States in ways that are reminiscent of the Cold War era, and popular culture reflects this fear in diverse ways.

Cultural theorist Stacy Takacs argues that following the 9/11 attacks, popular culture has promoted a national patriotic agenda. She finds in her analysis of terrorism plots on TV that "tales of apocalyptic terrorist plots prepared national subjects to accept the need for more intrusive surveillance by the state and its agents,"[2] and that films such as *Jarhead* (2005) and *The Great Raid* (2005) as well as TV shows such as *The Grid* (TNT 2004) and *Homeland*

(Showtime 2011–) suggest that "unlimited war . . . is the only cure for national trauma."[3] Her work illustrates the ways in which popular culture and politics intersect and interact; in this case, mass media prepares the populace to accept war, military domination, and to some extent, paranoia and a strong state presence in our lives as the new normal in the post-9/11 (post-apocalypse) era. At the same time, however, popular films and TV have also brought to the forefront a growing concern with the corruption of governments, the increasing power of the military, the growing reach of multinational corporations from the economic to the social worlds, the increasingly unequal distribution of resources, the heavy reliance of the global north on technology and fossil fuels and the increasingly tumultuous and undeniable impacts of this, and, particularly pertinent for US citizens, an undeniable proof that we are perhaps not as safe as we may have thought and a pervasive fear that while the danger may come from within our own borders or from the "others" outside our borders, it will almost certainly come. In the post-9/11 post-apocalypse world, TV and film provide both a cathartic, vicarious resolution of the tensions between a growing nationalist fervor and an increasingly antiauthoritarian ontology, and an opportunity to explore these tensions safely through speculative narratives.

The very same shows and films that reflect these tensions, however, may also ultimately provide reassurance and a subtle—and sometimes not so subtle—epistemology for survival in the post-apocalyptic (post-9/11) world: if we can behave in the right way, we will make it to tomorrow. This new post-apocalyptic era thereby provides the *kairos*, a fruitful and opportune moment to consider the issues of concern to contributors to this volume: race, gender and sexuality, but also socioeconomic upheaval, civil rights, social progress, and conservative backlash. We focus primarily on TV and film produced in the United States and on stories produced after 9/11 to take advantage of this opportunity to mine the popular culture archive as it is unfolding around us.

An Other History of the Post-Apocalyptic Future

Of course, the reality is that this particular timeline of our collective cultural move from "apocalypse" to "post-apocalypse" and from one post-apocalypse to another is deeply marked by cultural amnesia and selective memory, and certainly by race, gender, and sexuality. This is true of both the post–World War II emergence of nuclear-age anxieties and the distinctive tenor of post-9/11 terrorism anxieties. The reliance of scholars on the deployment of nuclear weaponry or advanced terrorist threats to historically mark the move from "apocalypse" to "post-apocalypse" assumes a false universality of experience and avoids consideration of past and current global politics; for example, who has the power to produce an apocalypse and who can only hope to survive it, how this power came to certain hands and how it is (hopefully) constrained, whose survival takes precedence and whose survival is judged unnecessary, or worse dangerous, and how resources get shared or hoarded.

Thus even the question of what, exactly, gets to count as an apocalypse reveals a cultural bias in both scholarship and popular culture as the very idea of "apocalypse" is marked by race, class, gender, and sexual boundaries as well as notions of "ability" and "disability"; not only *who* survives, but *how* they survive and even what the apocalypse looks like may be very different for people of different genders, sexes, and abilities, from different socioeconomic classes, racial/ethnic groups, geopolitical areas, and so on. One can certainly argue, for example, that the indigenous peoples of North America, whose populations likely numbered over twenty million at the critical moment of Columbus's arrival[4] and in the twenty-first century "officially" number less than three million in the United States,[5] have survived an apocalypse and continue today to build a new world in its aftermath. For indigenous peoples in the United States and globally, Europeans and their invasive descendants are the walking death that they must continually evade, accommodate, or fight against. Similarly, the depopulation of West African nations and culture groups during the centuries of the trans-Atlantic slave trade and the devastation wreaked upon African communities and families, followed by over a century of mass colonization of the continent, can be understood as apocalyptic, and the survivors on both sides of the Atlantic can be understood as surviving in a post-apocalyptic world. *An Gorta Mór*, the Great Famine in Ireland between 1845 and 1852, wiped out close to a quarter of the nation's population through starvation, disease, and emigration; many of those who remained and survived lived in desperate poverty under British rule. In the twenty-first century, as we continue to struggle globally with the crisis of HIV and AIDS, it is undeniable that different regions of the world are differently affected, and that the crisis has indeed reached apocalyptic proportions in many communities. Directly linked to the apocalypse of 9/11 on US soil is the ongoing military, social, economic, and political upheaval in parts of the Middle East, images of which frequently resemble Hollywood's best ideas of a post-apocalyptic landscape, with burned out buildings, inhospitable desert, and fleeing refugees highlighted regularly in the news broadcasts of the last ten years.

As historian Ted Steinberg[6] suggests, then, apocalypse is open to interpretation; who we are in terms of our race, gender, sexuality, class, and geopolitical identities shapes our interpretation as well as the stories we tell about what happens afterward. In post-9/11 post-apocalyptic narratives, race, gender, sexuality, power, and hierarchy are the central ancestral artifacts which shape the very nature of our speculative futures, sometimes through their overt presence or absence, and sometimes in the ways in which they are assumed or even ignored. If stories carry meaning—and the contributors to this book agree that they do—then what meanings are carried by our speculations about race, gender, and sexuality after the world as we know it ends? To better examine this question, we must also consider the meanings of race, gender, and sexuality now, before the world ends.

In the mid-twentieth-century United States, even as industry and technology developed at an increasingly rapid rate and the newly formed GI Bill contributed to rising college enrollment and eventually a rising middle class, political and economic backlash against social progress reinvigorated conservative gender and sex roles. Following the end of World War II, women were urged out of the labor force to make jobs available for returning male soldiers, and the government-funded daycare centers that had made many women's paid labor possible were closed. Congress initiated the Lavender Scare, forcing gays and lesbians in civil service to stay closeted or risk persecution. Racial segregation was increasingly resisted, particularly by people of color, but it was also reinforced not only through violence and intimidation, but also the words and actions of formal policy makers such as the 100 members of Congress who drafted and signed the 1956 Southern Manifesto. Those who challenged that return to the home, the closet, and the economic underclass faced not only political and social battles but cultural ones as well, as longstanding American beliefs in heterosexist masculine privilege and white supremacy continued to shape social practice and behavior as much as formal state policy.

The 1960s and 1970s brought progressive change (e.g., President Johnson's War on Poverty, Title IX of the Education Amendments of 1972, and the 1978 Indian Child Welfare Act), but during the 1980s and 1990s, social and political backlash eroded many of the gains made by women, poor people, and people of color. What Richard Goldstein has called the "neo-macho man," the "sexual avenger,"[7] dominated popular culture in the forms of shock jocks, comedians, and musicians. Politically, the era of the Welfare Queen (code for African American single mothers)[8] was inaugurated and, led by President Reagan, many of the social welfare programs which had grown in the 1970s were diminished or even dismantled. Certainly politicians, who have spent the decade and a half since the 9/11 attacks dismantling the Voting Rights Act, filibustering the Violence Against Women Act, and even shutting down the federal government over budget concerns arising largely from the Patient Protection and Affordable Care Act, can be understood as acting in resistance to progressive gains of the last few decades. The United States has embraced progress for some—the 2009 Lilly Ledbetter Act, which is intended to reduce the gender wage gap; the rise of marriage equality; and the increasing visibility of gender and sexuality experiences in the media, for example—but socially and politically we continue to oscillate between conservative and progressive values, as perhaps we always have. Our social and political history since the mid-twentieth century reveals this much at least: race, gender, and sexuality are hotly contested experiences. *Should* they be anything different after the world ends?

Chapter Outlines

This book takes seriously the assertion that popular culture is deeply embroiled in both the reflection and the production of our social desires, fears, and expectations. As cultural theorists argue,[9] meaning is both reflected in and produced by the sounds, sights, and narratives of cultural practice. The post-apocalyptic speculative fiction (PASF) narratives with which this book concerns itself not only participate in cultural meaning-making, they also produce space wherein meaning can be (whether it actually is or not) contested and reformulated. The politics of this space—like the politics of the post-apocalypse—are open to interpretation; how is meaning produced, what meanings are available, and who decides? Further, following anthropologist Anne Norton's argument that meaning occurs within a network of other meanings and has material context and consequence,[10] how does the cultural and political space produced by PASF—or perhaps more accurately, this matrix of spaces— shape our lives in the early twenty-first century? What histories does it entangle, in what directions does it move us, and what directions are potentially foreclosed? How does this matrix of stories participate in our collective meaning-making in the early twenty-first century?

The writers in this volume are interested in the ways in which post-apocalyptic fictions interact with—produce, reflect, interrogate, accommodate, and resist—hegemonic notions of race, gender, and sexuality. Part I considers what happens in the post-apocalyptic world when we fail to imagine something different after the world as we know it ends. What does it mean for our speculative future if conservative ideologies of race, gender, and sexuality are not only mourned after the apocalypse, but passively allowed continuance, actively reconstituted, or briefly resisted only to be triumphantly embraced in the end? Perhaps more important, what does it reveal about our cultural present when we imagine these outcomes in our speculative fictions of the future?

Authors in the first half of the book examine a curious phenomenon in post-apocalyptic stories: sometimes, the more things change, the more they stay the same. For example, in Chapter Three Tracey Raney and Michelle Meagher use the postfeminist lens presented by Starbuck of *Battlestar Galactica (Reimagined)* to interrogate the performance and purpose of gender in the future (past?). *Battlestar Galactica (Reimagined)* is well known for its political and social post-9/11 commentary (see, e.g., Steiff and Tamplin[11]), but despite the show's justly acclaimed willingness to consider a broad array of contemporary issues in a location where gender is presumed unnecessary (a battle-ready spaceship where women's full integration is virtually unquestioned), Raney and Meagher argue that Starbuck's female masculinity, her narrative arc, and her ultimate destiny reveal our own cultural anxieties around gender and, particularly, progressive gender moves such as those initiated by feminists in the late twentieth and early twenty-first centuries.

J. Sumerau and Sarah Jirek (in Chapter Five) also consider the role of gender in the contained and constructed space of a spaceship, this time in the close quarters of Joss Whedon's cult favorite, *Firefly*. Sumerau and Jirek are additionally concerned with understanding not only gender, but also race, class, and sexuality in Whedon's post-apocalyptic future. Although they are fans of the show, they find nonetheless an abject failure on the part of *Firefly*'s creators to imagine something better, instead relying on tropes and stereotypes which fail to offer new possibilities for human relationships and instead reproduce—dangerously—historic and current social inequalities.

Mary Burke and Maura Kelly make a similar argument about *The Hunger Games* in Chapter Four, although they find a more insidious neglect of current social inequalities as they question the embedded race and sexuality politics of the film. Ultimately they draw parallels between the film's narrative techniques around inequality and popular discourses highlighting certain inequalities—and marginalizing others—in the United States, arguing that the film's failure to offer an intersectional understanding of inequality, instead focusing heavily on class inequality to the exclusion of other oppressions, mirrors popular reluctance to engage in dialogues around race and gender discrimination in the United States. In my own chapter (Chapter Two), I also consider the neglect of explicit racial narratives, focusing most closely on the glaring absence of Native Americans in the post-apocalyptic world. However, I argue that this absence, rather than being a result of neglect and a potential weakness in the story, is in fact essential to the meta-narrative of white supremacy found in so many PASF narratives.

I argue that many post-apocalyptic fictions rely on the national cowboy persona of the United States to achieve a white supremacist destiny, but what can zombies, aliens, and Godzilla tell us about US race anxieties? In Chapter One, Robert Booth examines PASF from the mid-twentieth century through the early twenty-first to argue that "contagion" is a common precipitating apocalyptic event in both TV and film. He then links our fears of disease to twenty-first-century US immigration policies, arguing that the chaos engendered by "matter out of place"—things being where they don't belong—is made worse in PASF by the lack of a strong, central authority (such as the military or another hierarchical structure), and may explain the dogged return to conservative ideologies, structures, and institutions we see so frequently in the speculative future.

Authors in Part II offer a less predetermined (though not necessarily less pessimistic) view of the world after the world ends, based on their readings of films and TV shows as diverse as *The Walking Dead*, *The Road*, *Resident Evil*, and *True Blood*. For example, in Chapter Eight, Melissa Lavin and Brian Lowe provide a close textual analysis of *The Walking Dead*'s gender and race hierarchies to illustrate the ways in which the show's creators quickly reinscribed pre-apocalyptic social structures at the beginning of season one. However, by the middle of season five a general opening up of leadership opportunities for various characters prompts the authors to wonder if the post-apocalyptic future may ultimately require more flexibility in our social structures than the show's early seasons led us to believe.

Stacy Missari's analysis of the queer epistemology of *True Blood* in Chapter Six offers us a similar hope that the apocalypse may not compel survivors to embrace conservative race, gender, and sexuality ideologies; instead, precipitating events may require immediate social and political flexibility to survive, and could result in progressive change for queer-identified people and others (such as, perhaps, vampires). Perhaps after the world as we know it ends, our previous social customs and mores will simply no longer make sense; perhaps, as Missari argues, they already do not make sense, and the change is already upon us.

Andrea Harris, however, argues in Chapter Seven that the post-apocalyptic world will not be so subtle (if one can call *True Blood* subtle) and, based on her examination of *Resident Evil*, may very well favor women over men in terms of strength, survival, and opportunity. Her reading of the film's main character offers us a chance to think about the possibilities the apocalypse may bring for women's empowerment, as opposed to the disempowerment that is a more typical narrative arc.

While Harris focuses her analysis on what the post-apocalypse may bring for women, both Amanda Hobson (in Chapter Nine) and Brent Strang (in Chapter Ten) consider what the apocalypse may mean for men or, more specifically, for masculinity. They discover very different things after the end of the world: Hobson finds a world of violence and isolation, fed by religious extremism and what might be a teleological endpoint of current hegemonic masculinity. Nonetheless, she argues that the ending of the film *Stakeland* may offer hope for masculinity's redemption. Strang, on the other hand, instead finds "no-thing" after the apocalypse; his analysis of *The Road* forces us to consider the possibility that all of our angst and struggles to survive the trauma of the apocalypse may, in fact, be meaningless. There may not be any redemption for masculinity or, indeed, for humanity. The post-apocalypse may simply offer . . . nothing.

In Chapter Eleven, James Berger closes our consideration of race, gender, and sexuality in PASF with a less nihilistic, but still uncertain, conclusion. His chapter considers the cultural and social meanings of the zombie figure through a queer lens that interrogates how social and physical reproduction is accomplished, why, and to what purpose. By considering the potential for zombie reproduction—a potential that, as he argues, is quite possibly realized even pre-apocalypse—Berger brings to our attention the essential role of the child in the post-apocalyptic world as both hope for the future and emblem of inescapable decay.

Ultimately, the contributors to this book argue that PASF is in conversation with many societal and cultural nodes: not only race, gender and sexuality discourses, feminist and masculinity studies, and queer and critical race theories, but also the discourses of safety, fear, authority, and resistance that organize our post-9/11 world. Stacy Takacs,[12] following Horace Newcomb and Paul Hirsch[13] among others, points out that television frequently works as a "site for the negotiation of social contradictions and crises."[14] In *After the Apocalypse*, we are interested in not only how TV and film texts provide, produce, reproduce, and resist social discourses of race, gender, and sexuality in the richly potential space of speculative fiction (granted even more potential when it occurs after the end of everything we know); we also consider how PASF narratives interact with and even cocreate broader social and cultural meanings and moments. If, as communication scholar James Carey has argued, mass media communication can be understood as "a process of transmitting messages . . . for the purpose of . . . persuasion, attitude change, behavior modification, socialization" and also as working for the "maintenance of society in time . . . the representation of shared beliefs,"[15] two potentially opposing purposes, then when and how do PASF narratives serve these different functions, if they do? And importantly, which beliefs are shared "for the maintenance" or (re-creation) of society, and why?

It may be true that the more things change, the more they stay the same; it may also be true that the future is uncertain. Post-apocalyptic narratives of the early twenty-first century offer us no definitive answers as to the future of race, gender, and sexuality, but they do give us a space to consider the fears, anxieties, and hopes of the present day. What we will do with those fears, anxieties, and hopes is, of course, still a matter of speculation.

Notes

1. See for example Steffen Hantke, "Bush's America and the Return of Cold War Science Fiction: Alien Invasion in Invasion, Threshold, and Surface," *Journal of Popular Film and Television* 38, no. 3 (2010): 143–151; Stacy Takacs, *Terrorism TV: Popular Entertainment in Post-9/11 America* (Lawrence: University Press of Kansas, 2014); Angela Ndalianis, "Genre, Culture and the Semiosphere: New Horror Cinema and Post-9/11," *International Journal of Cultural Studies* 18, no. 1 (2015): 135–151.
2. Takacs, *Terrorism TV*, 14.
3. Ibid., 13.
4. Lenore Stiffarm and Phil Lane Jr., "The Demography of Native North America: A Question of American Indian Survival," in *The State of Native North American: Genocide, Colonization, and Resistance*, eds. M. Annette Jaimes and Theresa Halsey, 23–54 (Cambridge, MA: South End Press, 1992).
5. Tina Norris, Paula Vines, and Elizabeth Hoeffel, *The American Indian and Alaska Native Population 2010*, US Census Bureau, 2012. Last accessed January 12, 2015, at http://www.census.gov/prod/cen2010/briefs/c2010br-10.pdf
6. Theodore Steinberg, *Acts of God: The Unnatural History of Natural Disasters in America* (Oxford: Oxford University Press, 2000).
7. Richard Goldstein, "Neo-Macho Man: Pop Culture and Post-9/11 Politics," *The Nation*, March 24, 2003, 16–19.
8. Kenneth J. Neubeck and Noel Cazenave, *Welfare Racism: Playing the Race Card against America's Poor* (New York: Routledge, 2001).
9. See for example Patricia Hill Collins, *From Black Power to Hip Hop: Racism, Nationalism, and Feminism* (Philadelphia: Temple University Press, 2006); Diana Crane, *The Production of Culture: Media and the Urban Arts* (Thousand Oaks, CA: Sage, 1992); Jason Dittmer, "Captain America's Empire: Reflections on Identity, Popular Culture, and Post-9/11 Geopolitics," *Annals of the Association of American Geographers* 95, no. 3 (2005): 626–643.
10. Anne Norton, *95 Theses on Politics, Culture and Method* (New Haven: Yale University Press, 2004).
11. Josef Steiff and Tristan Tamplin, eds., *Battlestar Galactica and Philosophy: Mission Accomplished or Mission Frakked Up?* (Chicago: Open Court Publishing, 2008).
12. Takacs, *Terrorism TV*.
13. Horace Newcomb and Paul Hirsch, "Television as a Cultural Forum," in *Television: The Critical View*, ed. Horace Newcomb, 561–573 (New York: Oxford University Press, 2000).
14. Takacs, *Terrorism TV*, 28.
15. James Carey, *Communication as Culture: Essays on Media and Society*, 22 (Boston: Unwin Hyman, 1989).

PART I

*The More Things Change, the More
They Stay the Same . . .*

CHAPTER 1

Organisms and Human Bodies as Contagions in the Post-Apocalyptic State

Robert A. Booth

In this chapter, I show how discourses of contagion and pollution not only imbue many post-apocalyptic cinema and television narratives but also mirror public discourse about immigration. Further, I examine the often-racialized[1] immigrant in post-apocalyptic film and television that is, in essence, a discourse on insider–outsider social divisions and relationships of power. Finally, I elucidate the argument that post-apocalyptic film and television reinforce the primacy of centralized political authority, namely the State, and post-9/11 post-apocalyptic film in particular reinforces the hegemony of the State.

The post-apocalyptic subgenre of science fiction and/or horror has become popular fodder for cinema and television. As Susan Sontag notes, "the science fiction film . . . is concerned with the aesthetics of destruction, with the peculiar beauties to be found in wreaking havoc, making a mess. And it is in the imagery of destruction that the core of a good science fiction film lies."[2] Portrayals of the post-apocalypse often index or echo visual memories of terrible societal traumatic events of the past.[3] With the experience of the social, political, economic, and emotional trauma of the 9/11 attacks, one might reasonably assume that Americans would acquire a distaste for graphic destructive violence. Certainly, after the attacks, filmmakers occasionally felt pressured to remove images of the Twin Towers or to change content that might evoke the tragedy, such as planes crashing into skyscrapers. However, post-apocalyptic genres remain ever popular in American television and cinema. The attacks of 9/11 have changed the tone and timbre of science fiction in the United States, though.[4] Walliss and Aston note that there are "visible markers of how this event has been mapped onto various areas of popular culture" and that the post-9/11 films are decidedly more "pessimistic" than pre-9/11 films.[5]

One common theme in these post-apocalyptic films is that without an orderly, strong, centralized authority, people are reduced to base instincts and criminal behavior. People loot, murder, rape, and cannibalize. Thus films and TV programs such as *The Book of Eli* (2010), the *Falling Skies* series (2011–2015), *The Road* (2009), and *The Walking Dead* series (2010–) often present survivors of the apocalypse as potential threats, where fellow humans may either do unthinkable things in order to survive or embrace base, despicable desires (see for example Hobson, Chapter Nine, this volume). Fellow survivors are now potential Others, to be feared. The philosopher Thomas Hobbes argued for a strong, centralized government and authority, suggesting that without it human life would be "nasty, brutish, and short." This Hobbesian view of human nature presented in post-apocalyptic film and television suggests that humanity needs a strong, centralized authority as protection from humanity's inability to harness and control its "bestial" nature. Without the State, there would be "war by all, against all," as Hobbes said. The Other presents a threat to social order and bodily order. It does so because it cannot be contained or controlled. The disease is incurable, the alien or monster cannot be destroyed, or the zombie horde cannot be held at bay.

Etiologies of the Apocalypse

The post-apocalyptic tale is one that demonstrates a destruction of the social world of humanity, often by humanity's own hubris or callous disregard of itself, the environment, or some other cosmic, natural, or social order. Apocalypse in Western cinema mirrors Judeo-Christian eschatological and cosmological notions of "end times," and several ostensibly secular films have both subtle and, at times, obvious religious themes.[6] Additionally, films that dealt with terror and societal destruction from outer space were popular in the 1950s and 1960s. In American cinema and television, a distinction can be made between catastrophic apocalyptic and post-apocalyptic tales, exemplified by films that document some alien or cosmic disaster such as a meteor strike—*Meteor* (1979), *Armageddon* (1998), and *Deep Impact* (1998)—versus those that deal explicitly or implicitly with the ecological and sociological failings of humanity, such as *Silent Running* (1972), *Logan's Run* (1976), *The Hunger Games* series (2012–), and *Snowpiercer* (2013). Ostwalt notes:

> [C]ommon characteristics of many of these films revise the traditional, western concept of the apocalypse and focus on human ingenuity in avoiding the end rather than on the inevitability of cosmic cataclysm. In these contemporary,

cinematic apocalyptic scenarios, human action (often based on stupidity or greed) directly or indirectly leads to an apocalyptic disaster; therefore, human beings supplant cosmic forces as the initiators of the apocalypse and must take the role of saving the planet from apocalyptic destruction.[7]

The genre of the American post-apocalyptic tale blossomed in the 1950s and 1960s, amid the societal anxieties surrounding the Nuclear Age and the Cold War. The anxieties aroused by dangerous knowledge (e.g., technology and science) have deep historical roots in science fiction. Consider for example Mary Shelley's *Frankenstein* that warns of the dangerous knowledge around the desire to defeat death through reanimation. In these post-apocalyptic films, human technological failure or pursuit of dangerous or forbidden knowledge and morally bankrupt desires are at the root of the problem. Because of the Atomic Age, "radiation" became the etiological foundation of a number of *daikaiju* films[8] that feature giant insects, animals, and monsters. In each of these films, catastrophe was the result of technological and/or environmental hubris.

Beginning in the 1960s and 1970s American cinema also began exploring disease as a mechanism of societal destruction. Anxieties about plague are expressed in apocalyptic and post-apocalyptic narratives like Michael Crichton's *Andromeda Strain* (the novel in 1969 and the film in 1971) and films and television shows such as BBC's *Survivors* (1975–1977, 2008–2010), *Outbreak* (1995), *12 Monkeys* (1995), and *Contagion* (2011). In these tales, the biological agents spread due to human ineptitude or nefariousness. In apocalyptic and post-apocalyptic tales that deal with catastrophic disease, external biological agents (usually viruses or bacteria) invade and violate the human body.

Zombies

One such method of biological contamination is the zombie. Prior to the 1957 film *Zombies of Mora Tau*, zombies were not viewed as pathogenic.[9] Subsequently, particularly due to George Romero's influential *Night of the Living Dead* (1968), zombies are generally conceived of as infected agents of apocalypse. Romero also introduced the ghoul-like aspect of the zombie, namely its incessant hunger for (preferably) human flesh. The zombie becomes a cannibal and revenant, with either a mindless hunger or mindless "rage."[10] The shift to a "zombie by disease" model can be seen in Richard Matheson's 1954 horror novel *I am Legend*, where vampires are a global pathogenic catastrophe. Film adaptations include *The Last Man on Earth* (1964), *Omega Man* (1971), and *I am Legend* (2007). Matheson's novel was influential in envisioning zombies as products of pathogens and for introducing the idea of global zombie apocalypses.[11]

Zombies originally were portrayed in American media as individuals who were automaton-like, mindless, pliant, and nonaggressive, created for the sole purpose of labor.[12] As Chris Vials notes, these stories featured zombie plantation workforces and often involved the threat of a foreign zombie master turning visiting white Americans into zombies as well.[13] In early zombie films, "the true horror in these movies lies in the prospect of a westerner becoming dominated, subjugated, and effectively 'colonized' by a native pagan."[14] The loss of autonomy usually involved the consumption of poisons or elixirs created by the *bokor*, the zombie's master, a transgression of bodily autonomy. The horror in these tales is terror about racial leveling,[15] namely the fear of one's self becoming the Other, but the horror of these early American zombie tales was also rooted in the fear of conversion into mindless workers who toil indefinitely, devoid of any inkling of self, agency, or personal being. Deeply rooted in these fears are themes of transformation, transgression and personal bodily violation, fear of the Other, and fear of becoming the Other.

Pollution and Contagion

The horror of contagion stories, be they supernatural (zombies) or mundane (SARS or Ebola-like diseases), is tied to fear of contamination, physical pollution, and violation of bodily space. This anxiety about contagion may be rooted in "disgust" about our own bodily imperfections and inherent, inescapable "animality" that are themselves projected onto Others through a process of "social-boundary drawing" that projects that disgust outward and is expressed as fears about contagion.[16] Curtis and Biran suggest that "the disgust emotion polices the vulnerable portals of the body, defending them from the ingress of pathogens and parasites" but disgust is also extended to "moral disgust at violations of social norms, and that this may serve to promote the avoidance of social rather than physical parasites."[17] Pathogens have often been explored (and exploited) by the horror film genre.[18] The fear of filth, dirt, contamination, and other pollutants is not simply based in biological, medical pragmatism. Instead, it is the result of epistemological, cosmological categories being violated. "Dirt then, is never a unique, isolated event. Where there is dirt there is a system. Dirt is the by-product of a systematic ordering and classification of matter, in so far as ordering involves rejecting inappropriate elements."[19]

These categories that we, as members of our given society, use to organize our social and cosmic worlds create opportunities for such symbolic contamination. Take the human corpse, for example. In the United States, we have elaborate systems to isolate and control the human corpse from the general populace (embalmment, burial, and cremation). A corpse that moves of its own volition (zombies, vampires, and revenants) is generally considered a supernatural abomination because it violates that very division between living and dead. The horror and terror of the contaminant extend beyond the "practical" fears of contagion; they are deeply rooted in the *symbolic* dimensions of the pollutant and contagion. The anxieties we express are about violations of categorical, symbolic boundaries. Western categorical notions of life and death are supposed to be clearly defined. Either you are alive, or you are not. Ambiguous items that defy neat classification are dangerous due to the very ability to violate categories. In addition, distinct boundaries such as between self and other are assumed to be absolute.

Fears of infestation of the self are fears of losing control over the bodily boundaries between one's self and nonself. Nonhuman agents violate the body through infection. These elements are pollutive and are to be avoided at all costs. Avoidance is the general response to those infected or feared of being infected. The film *Invasion of the Body Snatchers* (1956) may have been a film tasked with exorcising American fears of Communism, but this concern was expressed through fears of loss of bodily agency. Horror and science fiction films have often explored loss of bodily control via parasites—*Alien* (1979), *The Thing* (1982), *Star Trek 2: The Wrath of Khan* (1982), *Slither* (2006), and *Splinter* (2008). Other films rely on viruses and germs as the dangerous element of the tale—*The Last Ship* series (2014–), *Mulberry Street* (2007) and *Quarantine* (2008)—as well as zombies—*Infection* (2004), *Zombie Diaries* (2006) and *World War Z* (2013).

In *District 9* (2009),[20] the main character Wikus van de Merwe is in charge of relocating some large insect-like aliens held in an apartheid-like camp setting. He inadvertently sprays alien chemicals on his face and suffers a slow, painful metamorphosis into an alien. In contagious zombie films, being bitten is considered the beginning of a person's inevitable slip into zombie status, that is if you are not wholly consumed first. In *Falling Skies*, a post-apocalyptic TV series about alien invasion and the collapse of human civilization, children are captured by aliens and "harnessed" with alien life forms that result in docile workers, reminiscent of early portrayals of the zombie. These living harnesses penetrate the human body and removal often results in the death of the host. All of these cases also have the specter of becoming the Other, as is the case with zombie stories since their arrival in the United States. These anxieties are also grounded in fears about personal autonomy and self-control.

Foreign Bodies

The cinematic apocalypse is generally an exclusively white one, insomuch as its protagonists and survivors are usually of European-American descent. That is one reason why Romero's choice of an African American as the rational protagonist in *Night of the Living Dead* was held to subvert this racial order.[21] Most post-apocalyptic narratives continue to have males as primary protagonists. Certainly, there are female protagonists in other genres of science fiction and horror, but post-apocalyptic films that focus on a woman protagonist are in short supply, and where they do occur, the main characters tend to be racially white.

While post-apocalyptic cinema has primarily been one with white survivors, there are a few shows, such as *The Walking Dead*, that have gradually offered a slightly more racially diverse collection of survivors, although that show is not without its share of race issues[22] (see Lavin and Lowe, Chapter Eight, this volume). Early in *The Walking Dead* series, T-Dog, an African American male, expresses concern about post-apocalyptic racism to the elderly Dale character: "I'm the one black guy. Realize how precarious that makes my situation?" (Season 2, episode 2). Screenwriters in *The Walking Dead* have used racial bias both as a critique of racist behavior and attitudes and as an illustration of outdated, pre-apocalyptic thinking. Early in the television series, Sheriff Rick Grimes admonishes Merle Dixon's racist notions, saying: "Look here, Merle. Things are different now. There are no niggers anymore. No dumb-as-shit-inbred-white-trash-fools either. Only dark meat and white meat. There's us and the dead. We survive this by pulling together, not apart" (Season 1, episode 2). Here, the protagonist pronounces that prior, established (if vexing), cultural categories of race have collapsed. Echoing what philosopher Slavoj Žižek has said about capitalism, it seems to be easier to imagine an apocalypse than it is to imagine a racially just and equitable world.[23] Or, perhaps more precisely, it will take an apocalypse to achieve any racial parity.

However, these prejudices are not always addressed in such tales directly. Some post-apocalyptic narratives do feature race more explicitly though. In *The Children of Men* (2006) humanity has become infertile for some unknown reason. As society decays, the white, male protagonist stumbles upon a secret organization's efforts to smuggle a young, pregnant woman, the first woman to become pregnant in many years, out to safety. She is an illegal African immigrant and is essentially humanity's new Eve. This salvation through the body of the Other is mirrored in the television series *The Last Ship* (2014–). In that series, an antidote to a global epidemic exists within the body of a young black Jamaican woman. However, aside from these few examples, immigrants and foreign nationals are usually presented more as threats than as sources of salvation. Indeed, in the case of *The Last Ship*, the primary threats have been a Russian ship's commander and crew, a Central American cartel and its leader, and escaped Guantanamo Bay prisoners who are Al-Qaida terrorists. Clearly, in *The Last Ship*, foreignness is a signifier of threat. This "foreignness" has been used to characterize plagues as foreign in national origin as well. Out-groups may even have their ethnonyms applied to a variety of illnesses like the "Spanish Flu" or "French Pox."[24] These vernacular, common names of epidemics explicitly index the very foreignness of the biological threat.

Much research about bias toward out-groups and links to a fear of illness has been conducted; the research suggests that fear of illness can be a predictor of xenophobia.[25] This connection between the foreign and the diseased shapes not only personal lives; it also shapes and drives collective action. This fear of the Other and anxieties about pandemics potentially manifest in public attitudes toward immigration and immigrants, but those fears appear to be mediated and/or magnified depending on an individual's political ideology.[26] The association of immigrants and other Others with illness, disease, and plague in the West has a long history.[27] These anxieties about the hygiene of immigrants and racialized others extended well into the twentieth century and is often presented as a potential threat in popular media in the twenty-first century.[28]

In 2014, fears of Ebola arriving to the United States were commonly expressed following a large uptick in the number of illegal child immigrants to the United States along its southern border.[29] In popular discourse, the arrival of the immigrant children was characterized as an "immigration crisis." A number of conservative pundits and political leaders expressed concern and alarm. For example, on August 4, 2014, Fox News quoted a letter written by Georgia Rep. Phil Gringrey: "Reports of illegal migrants carrying deadly diseases such as swine flu, dengue fever, Ebola virus and tuberculosis are particularly concerning" and "I have serious concerns that the diseases carried by these children may begin to spread too rapidly to control."[30] Such concerns were not based on the realities on the ground, however.[31]

Increasingly, public discourse represented in mainstream media has focused on threats (real or imagined) from immigration, primarily from Mexico and from the Global South. The fears of immigrants as carriers of disease is itself a form of racialized, racist thinking which categorizes immigrants as contaminants that are "dirty," "disease ridden," and/or morally lacking. Immigrants who "fail to assimilate" are viewed as contaminants, foreign bodies within the American host, infesting the body politic. Thus "uninvited" foreigners are portrayed as invasive to American society. These contaminating bodies are best kept locked away, behind fences, isolated from (other) humans. This is a common image in the television series *The Walking Dead*, where zombies ("walkers") are often kept at bay via chain link fences, such as ones that surround a prison. Returning to the zombie apocalypse trope, more broadly conceived, Comaroff and Comaroff point to the increasingly salient zombie figure in public discourse to critique immigration in parts of Africa.[32] These themes of immigrants and foreign labor overwhelming the State can be envisioned as bodies that "do not belong," and evidence of global patterns of pathologizing the immigrant.

Illegal "Aliens"

In the post-apocalyptic and dystopian film *The Children of Men*, immigrants attempting to come to the last bastion of civilization, the United Kingdom, are fenced into pens and treated like chattel. The images evoke the treatment of the Jews in World War II–era Europe and torture scenes from Abu Ghraib. In *The Children of Men*, large ghettoes are established where foreigners are enclosed and imprisoned. Ghettoes are also created for humans in *Falling Skies* and for aliens in *District 9*. In *District 9*, aliens arrive at Earth seeking refuge or asylum. These aliens are separated and isolated from the general human populace. They are viewed with contempt, disdain, and distrust. They are pollutants to be isolated. In the 1988 film (and subsequent television series) *Alien Nation*, aliens are similarly introduced to the human population. Unlike in *District 9*, these aliens are afforded a limited integration into the human population, mirroring traditional late nineteenth-century and early twentieth-century realities of American immigrants' incorporation into the working classes and gradually into middle- and upper-class positions. In *Alien Nation*, anxieties that humans have about the "newcomers" also mirror the kinds of immigration-centered social anxiety Americans have had, past and present.

Another dystopian film, *Sleep Dealer* (2008), deals with the anxieties of immigration more directly. In this film, foreign workers are walled off from the United States. Instead of entering the United States to work, workers from Mexico and Latin America do their labor remotely, controlling robots that do manual labor in the United States. The technology involves connecting to the neurological pathways of these remote migrant workers, and it slowly kills them. In this film's dystopian world, the labor of the would-be immigrant is extracted from their bodies without the need of having their bodies come in contact with the United States or its citizenry.

The United States has a long history of racialized immigration policy, from mid-nineteenth-century State efforts to limit Chinese immigration to the profiling of Japanese immigrants during World War II.[33] Post-9/11 treatment of Arabs, Muslims, and those mistaken as Muslim is well documented. Local, individual cases of violence targeting Muslim (and those assumed to be Muslim) immigrants, fueled by media-driven panics, occurred immediately after the 9/11 attacks.[34] While not State sanctioned, these types of racialized violence are still forms of political violence. Post-9/11 interrogation, surveillance, and profiling of immigrants and travelers from Muslim countries were, and continue to be, a civil rights issue in the United States.[35] Travel bans, no-fly lists, and scrutiny at ports of entry, ostensibly in order to defend the country, have resulted in a complex system of control over the movement of particular foreign bodies within the United States. Cinematic portrayals of the post-apocalypse often address these themes of attempted (and often failed) efforts of control by the post-apocalyptic state.

The Post-Apocalyptic State

The post-9/11 post-apocalyptic film in many ways remains unchanged by the terrible events of 9/11 and the post-9/11 political realities that have changed (or intensified) the relationship between the individual and the State. However, I suggest that after 9/11 Hollywood's cynicism with state authority and political (and military) excesses offered venues to critique specific government abuses such as the torture techniques used by American soldiers at the prison at Abu Ghraib (*Children of Men*) or drone attacks (*Sleep Dealer*). In post-apocalyptic television and film, it is the very collapse of the Hobbesian central authority and its strong central control that has indeed led to the crisis in the first place and as such, these post-apocalyptic narratives inadvertently and perversely argue instead for the importance of said centralized authority. In the *Walking Dead* series, survivors seek out the remnant of some sort of United States, as do the survivors of the *Falling Skies* series. However, any interactions with the government are unfulfilling, as the government is "impotent" or "incompetent." The true apocalypse is loss of society and social order, things that violate the societal body and pose a threat to a perceived fragile and helpless State. While several post-apocalyptic films pre-9/11 had competent governments, able to eventually deal with the threat (e.g., *Deep Impact*), in post-9/11 apocalypses, the State, if not totalitarian, is portrayed as weak. For example, the fledgling American government (created during the alien occupation) in the *Falling Skies* series is fragile and ineffective at dealing with the aliens. In *The Walking Dead* series, a major story arc was a quest to deliver knowledge to Washington DC, where ideally a government could use the information to do something about the "walker" problem. However, previous contact with the federal government at the Centers for Disease Control was ultimately a failure.

A recurring villain called "the Governor" attempted to rule his tiny settlement as a bloodthirsty dictator. The main protagonist of *The Walking Dead* is a sheriff, thus representing some sort of state authority; however, he oscillates between strength and weakness, ineffectual inaction and self-doubt. In the science fiction series *Battlestar Galactica* (2004–2009), political themes were almost always present, with tensions between the totalitarian-leaning military and the political system which was bureaucratic, prone to in-fighting, and not entirely democratic.

Following the terrorist attacks of 9/11, post-apocalyptic films tend toward either dystopian totalitarian regimes (as in *The Hunger Games*) or ineffectual governments (specifically) and governance (more generally). These films dwell on the State's inability to protect its citizenry, echoing societal anxieties about terrorism. Thus, a radical anti-authoritarianism arises in many post-apocalyptic films that, on the surface, is critical of centralized authority (see Gurr, Introduction, this volume). However, in these post-apocalyptic tales, there is no lack of "governance" or control of the personal body. Control is instead even more closely inscribed on the body through the violent threat posed by the Other. The Other (e.g., alien, zombie, or pathogen) dictates what appropriate human behavior must be in order to survive. Characters are forced into certain behaviors because of the threats presented by the Other. Thus, the State may enact violence and/or control though the State's very inaction. For example, in the film *Red Dawn* (1984, 2012), the government's inability to defend itself compels the protagonists to defend the State by themselves. Of course, the centralized authority of the State may also affect individuals directly. For example, the Disney Pixar film *Wall-E* (2008) portrayed humanity's escape from a global catastrophe. Subsequently, humanity finds itself continually coddled, fattened, and infantilized by an automated consumerist society where all labor is provided by robots and even movement of the human body is technologically mediated. In their spaceship, they float among the stars until Earth can sustain life again. Here, the post-apocalypse represents an even greater amount of authoritarian control over the human body: the ontological crises presented to humanity are resolved through even stricter control of the human body, its movement, and its social space.

In these films, it is the absence of the State that is the ultimate sign of apocalypse, for the presence of the State implies stability, which is usually the opposite of post-apocalypses. Indeed, most post-apocalyptic films with totalitarian regimes feature regimes that arise in response to the instability of a post-apocalypse (such as in *The Hunger Games*). Even films that target social class and inequality in turn seek some maintenance of societal order. At the end of *Snowpiercer*, the result of social upheaval is the destruction of civilization (or at least its remnants). Only two out of the entirety of the human race are shown to survive, in a freezing, inhospitable world. Thus, while the film critiques the draconian methods of social control used, it again argues that lack of social hierarchy is the true source of final apocalypse. Even in the post-apocalyptic world, at least cinematically, one cannot escape the hegemony of the State.

Conclusion

Films that pathologize the Other are nothing new; however, in post-apocalyptic films, these pathologized Others are the result of failures of the State and central authority. Indeed, the pathologized Other is a threat to the State and its citizenry. This anxiety about the Other is always tied to fears of compromise of the self. This is most explicit in films about zombies, but the fear also exists in other contagion films and television programs. Contact with fellow human beings (dead or alive) or aliens is dangerous and usually results in disaster in these sorts of tales. This fosters a fear of the Other that can be further compounded by pre-apocalyptic attitudes regarding difference (race, gender, class, sexuality, etc.). The categorical violations that induce anxiety in these post-apocalyptic narratives are ones that were not effectively contained, controlled, or policed. The boundaries between self and Other are threatened, as are those between the State as a body and the local foreign bodies that threaten it. It is certainly reminiscent of the anti-Muslim public discourse that followed 9/11 (and sadly continues). Common in certain public discourse arenas have been the expressions of fear of the domestic presence of the *orientalized* Muslim, both racialized and essentialized, "violating" the boundaries of the United States.[36] The agents of apocalypse are rarely other nations; instead, the agents of destruction are bodies that cannot be controlled: zombies, monsters, aliens, pathogens, unruly mobs. It is the body and presence of the Other that presents itself as the ultimate threat. It is the presence of foreign matter, of foreign bodies, that becomes the spark that ignites apocalyptic destruction. It is in this way that post-apocalyptic media continues to market racialized and essentialized Others to fear, and it is fear that is the ultimate contagion.

Notes

1. Racialization, according to Silverstein, "refers to the processes through which any diacritic of social personhood—including class, ethnicity, generation, kinship/affinity, and positions within fields of power—comes to be essentialized, naturalized, and/or biologized." Paul A. Silverstein, "Immigrant Racialization and the New Savage Slot: Race, Migration, and Immigration in the New Europe," *Annual Review of Anthropology* 34, no. 1 (2005): 363.

2. Susan Sontag, "The Imagination of Disaster," in *The Science Fiction Film Reader*, ed. Gregg Rickman, 102 (New York: Proscenium Publishers, 2004).
3. Adam Lowenstein, *Shocking Representations: Historical Trauma, National Cinema and the Modern Horror Film* (New York: Columbia University Press, 2005).
4. Lynn Spigel, "Entertainment Wars: Television Culture after 9/11," *American Quarterly* 56, no. 2 (2004): 235–270.
5. John Walliss and James Aston, "Doomsday America: The Pessimistic Turn of Post-9/11 Apocalyptic Cinema," *Journal of Religion and Popular Culture* 23, no. 1 (2011): 53–64.
6. Some recent post-apocalyptic films dealing either directly or indirectly with religion include *The Book of Eli* (2010), *Left Behind* (2014), HBO's *Leftovers* (2014–); however, Ostwalt contends that there has been an overall decline in religiously themed apocalypses. Conrad Ostwalt, "Visions of the End: Secular Apocalypse in Recent Hollywood Film," *Journal of Religion and Film* 2, no. 1 (1998), http://avalon.unomaha.edu/jrf/OstwaltC.htm
7. Ibid.
8. *Daikaiju*, translating roughly as "giant monster" is a genre of Japanese monster films where giant monsters threaten civilization. The best known of this genre in the United States are the *Godzilla* films.
9. Stephanie Boluk and Wylie Lenz, "Introduction," to *Generation Zombie: Essays on the Living Dead in Modern Culture*, eds. Stephanie Boluk and Wylie Lenz, 1–17 (Jefferson, NC: McFarland, 2011).
10. In the films *28 Days* and *28 Weeks Later*, a virus called "the Rage" turns humans into inhumanly violent living zombies.
11. Deborah Christie, "A Dead New World: Richard Matheson and the Modern Zombie," in *Better Off Dead: The Evolution of the Zombie as Post-human*, eds. Deborah Christie and Sarah Juliet Lauro, 67–80 (New York: Fordham University Press, 2011).
12. As Ann Kordas notes: "In many ways, zombies were the perfect laborers. Although zombies were capable of performing physical labor, they lacked all traces of intellect, volition, or self-awareness. They could not think or speak, and they felt no pain. Completely lacking in emotion, they felt no anger or resentment and had no desires of their own." Ann Kordas, "New South, New Immigrants, New Women, New Zombies: The Historical Development of the Zombie in American Popular Culture," in *Race, Oppression and the Zombie: Essays on Cross-Cultural Appropriations of the Caribbean Tradition*, eds. Christopher M. Moreman and Cory James Rushton, 19–20 (Jefferson, NC: McFarland, 2011).
13. Chris Vials, "The Origin of the Zombie in American Radio and Film: B-Horror, U.S. Empire, and the Politics of Disavowal," in *Generation Zombie: Essays on the Living Dead in Modern Culture*, eds. Stephanie Boluk and Wylie Lenz, 41–53 (Jefferson, NC: McFarland, 2011).
14. Kyle W. Bishop, "The Sub-subaltern Monster: Imperialist Hegemony and the Cinematic Vodoun Zombie," *Journal of American Culture* 31, no. 2 (2008): 141–152.
15. Vials, "The Origin of the Zombie in American Radio and Film," 41–53.

16. Martha C. Nussbaum, *Hiding from Humanity: Disgust, Shame, and the Law* (Princeton, NJ: Princeton University Press, 2004), 94.
17. Valerie Curtis and Adam Biran, "Dirt, Disgust, and Disease: Is Hygiene in Our Genes?" *Perspectives in Biology and Medicine* 44, no. 1 (2001): 29.
18. Richard Smith, "Battle Inside: Infection and the Modern Horror Film," *Cineaste* (Winter 2009): 42–46.
19. Mary Douglas, *Purity and Danger* (London: Routledge and Kegan Paul, 1966), 36.
20. The film is technically not a post-apocalyptic film, at least from the perspective of the humans.
21. Elizabeth McAlister, "Slaves, Cannibals, and Infected Hyper-Whites: The Race and Religion of Zombies," *Anthropological Quarterly* 85, no. 2 (2012): 457–486.
22. Gerry Canavan, "'We are the Walking Dead': Race, Time, and Survival in Zombie Narrative," *Extrapolation* 51, no. 3 (2010): 431–453.
23. Slavoj Žižek, *First as Tragedy, Then as Farce* (London: Verso, 2009).
24. Eva G. T. Green et al., "Keeping the Vermin Out: Perceived Disease Threat and Ideological Orientations as Predictors of Exclusionary Immigration Attitudes," *Journal of Community & Applied Social Psychology* 20 (2010): 299–316.
25. Ibid. See also: Jason Faulkner et al., "Evolved Disease-Avoidance Mechanisms and Contemporary Xenophobic Attitudes," *Group Processes and Intergroup Relations* 7, no. 4 (2004): 333–353. See also and Ingrid Gilles et al., "Collective Symbolic Coping with Disease Threat and Othering: A Case Study of Avian Influenza," *British Journal of Social Psychology* 52, no. 1 (2013): 83–102.
26. Green et al., "Keeping the Vermin Out," 299–316.
27. Howard Markel and Adriana Minna Stern, "The Foreignness of Germs: The Persistent Association of Immigrants and Disease in American Society," *Milbank Quarterly* 80, no. 4 (2002): 757–788.
28. Ibid. See also: Carlos David Navarrete and Daniel M. T. Fessler, "Disease Avoidance and Ethnocentrism: The Effects of Disease Vulnerability and Disgust Sensitivity on Intergroup Attitudes," *Evolution and Human Behavior* 27, no. 4 (2006): 270–282.
29. Maggie Fox, "Vectors or Victims? Docs Slam Rumors That Migrants Carry Disease," *NBCnews.com*, last modified on July 9, 2014, http://www.nbcnews.com/storyline/immigration-border-crisis/vectors-or-victims-docs-slam-rumors-migrants-carry-disease-n152216
30. "Ebola Outbreak Fuels Concerns Over Health Risks along US-Mexico Border," *Foxnews.com*, last modified on August 5, 2014, http://www.foxnews.com/politics/2014/08/05/ebola-outbreak-fuels-concerns-over-health-risks-along-us-mexico-border
31. See Laura Murphy, "The Mexican 'Germ Invasion' is Just the Right's Latest Anti-immigration Myth," *theguardian.com*, last modified Wednesday July 2, 2014, http://www.theguardian.com/commentisfree/2014/jul/02/border-patrol-diseases-anti-immigration-myth. See also Linda Poon, "The Immigrant Kids have Health Issues—But Not the Ones You'd Think," *npr.org*, last modified on July 22, 2014, http://www.npr.org/blogs/goatsandsoda/2014/07/22/332598798/the-immigrant-kids-have-health-issues-but-not-the-ones-youd-think

32. Jean Comaroff and John L. Comaroff, "Alien-Nation: Zombies, Immigrants, and Millennial Capitalism," *The South Atlantic Quarterly* 101, no. 4 (2002): 779–805.
33. Gordon H. Chang, "China and the Pursuit of America's Destiny: Nineteenth-Century Imagining and Why Immigration Restriction Took So Long," *Journal of Asian American Studies* 15, no. 2 (2012): 145–169.
34. Muneer Ahmad, "Homeland Insecurities: Racial Violence the Day after September 11," *Social Text* 72, no. 3 (2002): 101–115.
35. Louise Cainkar, "Post 9/11 Domestic Policies Affecting U.S. Arabs and Muslims: A Brief Review," *Comparative Studies of South Asia, Africa, and the Middle East* 24, no. 1 (2004): 245–248.
36. Edward Said, *Orientalism* (New York: Vintage, 1978).

CHAPTER 2

Masculinity, Race, and the (Re?)Imagined American Frontier

Barbara Gurr

The Old West provides a much-beloved and often-used framework for American popular culture. Consider the TV classic *Gunsmoke* (1955–1975) or one of the many Westerns that defined Hollywood cinema for so long, probably something by John Ford, preferably starring John Wayne (you could substitute Clint Eastwood). Or . . . maybe it's the far, far away galaxy of the original *Star Wars* trilogy (1977, 1980, and 1983). It could be the post-apocalyptic setting of Joss Whedon's cult classic *Firefly* (2002–2003), which was not subtle in its reliance on the Western genre (see Sumerau and Jirek, Chapter Five, this volume). It could easily be the USS Enterprise hurtling through space, "the final frontier"; the original *Star Trek* series (1966–1969), *The Next Generation* (1987–1994), and *Enterprise* (2001–2005) all featured episodes which specifically recreated the Old West—*The Specter of the Gun* (Season 3, episode 6), *A Fistful of Datas* (Season 6, episode 8), and *North Star* (Season 3, episode 9) respectively—and other *Star Trek* spin-offs followed similar character and narrative recipes. Wherever and whenever the Old West shows up, however, it is a masculine space, and the triumphalism of that masculinity is primarily racialized as white.

This chapter examines the reimagination of the American frontier in the television shows *Falling Skies* (TNT 2011–2015) and *Jericho* (CBS 2006–2008). In these post-apocalyptic stories, a cowboy brand of masculinity provides the hope (and shape) of the future, echoing, reproducing, and validating the mytho-history of nineteenth-century manifest destiny doctrine. These narratives thus open the frontier once again for white, heterosexual, able-bodied men to carve out the future of the human race in a political, social, and military reiteration of nineteenth-century desire. In this way, these twenty-first-century stories continue the centuries-old practice of settler colonialism in what is now known as the United States, producing a white collective nation through the disappearance of Native America. I offer a close textual analysis of just a few key scenes and characters in order to illustrate how the popular American imagination of the frontier as a place where white men (the heroes) displace Native American men (the "others") serves as a master narrative which continues to inform even our speculations of post-apocalyptic survival. The frontier is a powerful trope; the American frontier is the dominant trope in these narratives (and many other post-apocalyptic fictions, as mentioned in several chapters in this volume; see for example Hobson, Chapter Nine and Strang, Chapter Ten), and its dominance requires both the violent and the subtle erasure and containment of certain race and gender identities in order for others—namely hegemonically gendered white men—to narratively triumph. Women are rarely the makers of history in these stories, even when that history occurs in a speculative future where virtually anything could potentially happen, and Native American men serve as little more than plot devices. But what purpose does this triumph of white masculinity serve, ultimately, in our collective post-9/11 cultural conscious?

The American Frontier and America's Identity

Literary critic David Mogen argues that "American frontier mythology continues to be reworked in popular culture because our conceptions of the American frontier experience are deeply identified with problems of cultural self-definition, the American preoccupation with defining 'American-ness.'"[1] The frequent reliance of post-apocalyptic science fiction on the mythohistory of the American past reveals a cultural yearning for a collective identity of American-ness that has been only incompletely realized. The intense desire to belong (and specifically to belong to the side of righteous triumph), so often enacted in human history by determining who does *not* belong, is arguably a defining cultural urge in the twenty-first-century United States, but it is also typical of all settler colonialist societies (which after all are made up of displaced immigrants). This urge produces an anxious drive toward homogeneity; the social and physical diversity which in fact constitutes the origin stories of settler colonialist nations threatens this drive toward collective identity and, like the bodies of indigenous peoples, must be contained, controlled, and eventually made to disappear in order for a collective (white, hegemonically masculine) identity to emerge and belong.

Ultimately, as it serves to define American-ness, the frontier signifies not only American identity but also Americans' own sense of exceptionalism: Didn't the United States spread from sea to shining sea by triumphing over tremendous adversities because its people—pioneers, farmers, cowboys—struggled and endured, thrived and survived? Their stories of building a nation one sod house, and then one cattle ranch, and then one small town at a time reverberate throughout our popular consciousness, until fact and fiction merge together in the production of a truly remarkable origin story. That story begins with a ragtag band of farmers and merchants—the militiamen of the American Revolution—defeating the greatest military power on Earth and continues through wars with Indians, France, Spain, Indians again, and Mexico (populated largely by *indios* and their descendants), mass immigration, sheep ranching, cattle ranching, more Indian Wars, the Industrial Revolution, the Great Depression, and two world wars. It is a history rich with the genuinely inspirational and the genuinely exaggerated, and it forms the backbone of America's self-identity. Importantly, the hand of God is essential to this sense of exceptionalism, ensuring that the destiny of the United States is made manifest: the nation is exceptional not only because its people are exceptional but also because God has ordained that it be so.

Scholars have long noted that "America" has produced the frontier as much as the frontier has produced popular notions of "America," and popular fiction from the pulp stories of Louis L'Amour to the television Westerns of the mid-twentieth century and the enduring popularity of the Western as a narrative structure in twenty-first-century film reflect this interactive relationship between storytellers and story consumers in the production of the American mythos. The speculative future continues to rely on and define the very shape and function of the frontier: a vast and violent place that provides men with the freedom to determine their own destinies and carve out a new (better?) world. And who are these brave, indomitable men? They're the cowboys. Nothing says "America" like cowboys.

Cowboys and Indians in the Post-Apocalypse

Of course there are still cowboys. And of course plenty of cowboys, both today and in years past, were men of color. Some of them were even women, and some of these women were women of color. Not all cowboys were heterosexual, and those who were may not have been heterosexual all the time. But the *mythic* cowboy is another matter. The cowboy in American popular culture is hegemonically masculine, and this means that he is white, able-bodied, heterosexual, strong, taciturn, rugged, and fiercely independent. The cowboy has become synthesized to this fairly narrow conceptualization in part because he has come to represent American identity *against* America's enemies, and these enemies have historically been raced, gendered, and sexed as "other"—not white, not male, not heterosexual: not American. In fact, America's enemies continue to be understood in the same ways, although the boundaries of the "frontier" have perhaps expanded through the twenty-first-century geopolitics of a seemingly unendable war on terror which itself is increasingly apocalyptic in scope and consequences.

In its search for identity on the frontier, a landscape which has become synonymous with the cowboy, the United States has adopted the cowboy persona as a national personality type.[2] From presidents (such as Theodore Roosevelt, Ronald Reagan, and George W. Bush) and movies (ranging from Bruce Willis's *Die Hard* series to Pixar's *Toy Story* series) to television shows, country western music, the continuing popularity of rodeos, and even Disney's Frontierland (where you can "test your gunnin' skills at the rootin', tootin' wild west shooting gallery," but please remember that "a good cowboy is a safe cowboy"[3]), America loves its cowboys.

And as everyone knows, cowboys fight Indians (leaving aside for the moment the fact that many cowboys were and are Native American). The settler colonialist logic embedded in the mytho-history of the American frontier requires not only that Native Americans be relegated to a shadow narrative via their absence from the land (and the stories told about the nation), but that they be kept there by the cowboy's dominance. The cowboy, in effect, replaces the Native American in the name of progress and in fulfillment of America's destiny, and thus as settlers seek to become authentically indigenous—to belong to the land they inhabit—they must, to some degree, adopt the cowboy's habits, including his race and gender performances. Indians are a part of the nation's history, but the cowboy is the harbinger of the future.

However, one of the essential nuances of settler colonialism is that the original indigenous in fact never completely disappear; their physical, political, economic, and narrative displacement makes room for newer inhabitants to stake their claim to belonging, but those who belonged previously continue to exist in the margins of the great American narrative. They are removed from the contemporary story that settlers tell, as they must be if the settlers are to justify their status as rightfully belonging to the landscape they now occupy, having earned it through their own hard work and perseverance (and the blessings of a righteous God); but the original indigenous persist on the fringes of that story as a reminder of the triumph of the settlers. The relationships between the original indigenous, the new indigenous, the land they share (and don't share), the histories they narrate both explicitly and implicitly, and the meanings of all of these are organized and informed by the ongoing presence/nonpresence of indigeneity in the shared physical and metaphorical landscapes of nation-building. However, although race remains the central theme in scholarly studies of colonialism, post-colonialism, and settler colonialism, gender and sexuality are equally and inextricably bound up with these historical facts and fictions, as they are indeed inextricably bound up with notions of race. In the popular imagination of the American frontier, it is not simply white people who boldly penetrate the unknown frontier; it is white *men*, followed eventually by white women, who will bring domesticity and the arts of civilization. The very meaning of the frontier relies on the constant displacement of its original inhabitants so that white men can tame the wilderness and make it safe for white women, thereby creating the heterodomestic architecture of nation-building. Thus can (white) people (re)populate the frontier in their image through a constant retelling of what Krista Comer calls "one of the most entrenched master narratives of the broader geocultural imaginary": the "wilderness plot" which centralizes "exoticized and depopulated imagery" and the "great unpeopled outdoors."[4]

It is the popular imagination of empty land waiting to be explored and mastered that situates the wilderness plot within the myth of the American frontier; the frontier, both physical and metaphorical, uses the promise of independence, redemption, and freedom conveyed by the wilderness plot to provide the physical and metaphorical space in which American identity can be produced. Of course, this requires that the land must first be empty of human lives and civilizations. If there are already (nonwhite) others in the space of the frontier (or the "new world"), they must be removed, either physically through death and relocation or ideologically through gradual assimilation. Although a sanitized and romanticized version of the original indigenous may still echo through the soon-to-be-mastered wilderness, it serves the purpose of highlighting the American exceptionalism which (seemingly) triumphed over it. In the twenty-first century, the United States has still not quite accomplished this white masculine supremacy, as revealed by our cultural discomfort with immigration, Native sovereignty, and civil rights for women, queer people, and people of color. The work to make the nation's destiny manifest is still not complete and is in fact challenged by the persistent existence of those who do not fit neatly into the collective identity. But one simple apocalypse can fix all that.

The narratives of *Jericho* and *Falling Skies* validate white heterosexual masculinity as centrally indigenous to the land of the United States, displacing prior race, gender, and sexuality claims. They do so both overtly through their central characters and major plots and implicitly as these speculative futures revel in a nostalgic past when the United States was peopled by loyal patriots and skilled frontiersmen. In this mytho-history, white men triumphed over the adversities of a new world through the strength of their will and intellect and the skill of their marksmanship. They triumphed because they were supposed to; after all, God ordained it, and their exceptionalism is the central tenet of the collective American identity. *Jericho* and *Falling Skies* offer us this imagined American frontier reimagined, affirming conservative gender role expectations and producing a conscious absence or carefully narrated presence of Native America in these future histories. The post-apocalyptic landscape of these shows thereby provides the wilderness plot in which white, heterosexual, able-bodied masculinity can finally, and completely, claim an indisputable belonging, indivisible from the land it occupies.

Tipis and Aliens

The very first scene of *Jericho* showcases snow-capped mountains tumbling down to a wide, meandering river. The camera then cuts to a train chugging along beside the river and we see our protagonist Jake Green, whose very name evokes newness and a fresh start, sitting at a table inside a railcar with what looks to be a gas lamp throwing shadows around his melancholy face. A brief stop in Denver and Jake is on the open road, driving through the wide open plains of Kansas (a state whose name is derived from a Native American word) to his hometown of Jericho (a town most likely named after the biblical Jericho, located in the now-occupied West Bank, another site of settler colonialism and indigenous displacement). The camera sweeps across open plains and we see raw nature, "the great unpeopled outdoors."[5] The visual sequence is literally that of majestic purple mountains and fruited plains, not so much a Garden of Eden as an awesome and isolating landscape. The viewer has no sense of people inhabiting this land other than a rushing glimpse of a school bus, but that school bus is parked by a tourist tipi and the story of this tipi—relic of a bygone era, the home of a people shoved to the edges of the frontier by the irresistible force of manifest destiny—is the central metaphor I want to consider for what it tells us about Jake, his unexplained anxiety, and his muscular blue Mustang. The tourist tipi in the wide open plains, which we never see again, is a key to unlocking the metanarrative of *Jericho*.

TNT's post-apocalyptic drama *Falling Skies*, on the other hand, opens with a backstory told to us in children's voices, and then immediately jumps to a burnt-out, twisted urban landscape where a (white) father and son run for their lives from the terrifying alien force that seeks their land and their destruction (we will learn as the episode and the season progress that this was Boston, and the father was a professor of American history at Boston University with a specialization in colonial history and the American Revolution; herein lies the key to *this* story's metanarrative). Thus in the first ten minutes we are told of humanity's fall from grace: the innocence of childhood and the sanctity of family brutally ripped away and replaced by the horror of invasion and a constant, violent struggle for survival. Whereas

Jericho opens with a nostalgic reminder of simpler times before the onslaught of malls, parking lots, and movie theaters, presaging a forced relocation to a pre-technological Garden of Eden, the wilderness plot of *Falling Skies* offers us the hellscape after the fall of Adam and Eve, peopled by demons and the desperate remains of humanity. Yet both visions evoke the American frontier: *Falling Skies* is the frontier of early colonization, when European men struggled to survive the New World with its alien landscape and its alien inhabitants (in a curious inversion of what many Native people must have experienced centuries ago that firmly places white settlers as the indigenous of this story). *Jericho*'s is the more idyllic landscape of the imagined Old West frontier town, where life was hard but folks pulled together and worked through their problems for the common good (we've seen this Western trope in *Bonanza* [1959–1973], *Little House on the Prairie* [1974–1983], and even 2011's special effects spectacular *Cowboys and Aliens*). Native Americans are curiously missing from both of these frontiers.

Or are they? I argue that through their absence, Native Americans actually become what Carol Adams[6] refers to as the "absent referent," the presence which is signified by its narrative lack. The fact that Native people are *not* there is actually what brings them into the story and produces a metanarrative of settler colonialism. This is why that tipi in the opening sequence of *Jericho* is so important; it reminds us that other people were here before the cowboys at the same time that it constructs Native America as little more than a tourist destination in the twenty-first century, the presumably teleological conclusion to America's great destiny. The tourist tipi signifies the hidden but always-already presence of Native America: the people who have always inhabited the seemingly empty landscape, the people who were already here and fought those who threatened their communities, as Jake Green and his posse soon will. The tipi is our one brief acknowledgement that the uninhabited emptiness of the American wilderness plot was never in fact unpeopled, despite the blinding absence of Native people in *Jericho*'s narrative. It reminds the viewer that the empty land we see unfolding before the camera (in the sweeping camera work so typical of Hollywood Westerns, meant to evoke the vast unpeopled wilderness) and the twenty-first-century cowboys who are about to emerge from that barren landscape to protect their town are a repeat of history. But this is not the messy, factual history of diverse communities learning to survive together or, alternatively, threatening each other's survival; this is the history of desire, writ large upon a landscape that must be emptied in order for white men to inscribe their destinies on it. In *Jericho* the visually empty land is virtually emptied via the devastation of nuclear bombs so that the history of manifest destiny can repeat itself and ultimately secure the triumph of all that is good in America.

However, whereas nineteenth-century US expansion did not succeed in completely displacing the nonwhite other, resulting in ongoing and unresolved racial tensions into the twenty-first century, in *Jericho* the defenders of home and hearth are white men, and not only do they ultimately succeed in defending their community, they also defeat the grand enemy and restore justice to a broken, nuclear-ravaged nation. The tipi thus also serves as a cautionary tale: because it is so clearly a tourist trap (as indicated by the school field trip as well as its inauthentic design and presentation) we understand that those who oppose America will ultimately be worse than defeated; they will be consigned to a chapter in history, to be revisited in the popular imagination as nothing more than entertainment and historical fantasy. This is what happens to those who stand against America's destiny, because (so the story goes) defeat is inevitable against the indomitable spirit and strength of the exceptional nation. The tipi thus prepares us for the show's reinvigoration of hegemonic (white, male, heterosexual, able-bodied, etc.) American manhood by recalling the historic closing of the frontier, made possible by yesteryear's (presumably white, male, heterosexual, and able-bodied) cowboy.

The most direct reference to Native America in *Falling Skies* takes a slightly less abstract form through the humans' first alien ally, a Volm warrior whose multisyllabic name the humans shorten (apparently with no sense of irony) to Cochise. The historical Cochise was an Apache warrior who fought the US invaders first at his father's side and then, after his father was murdered by the Americans during what he was told would be a peaceful parley, as a leader in his own right. The Volm Cochise has a similar biography, his own land (planet) and people having been decimated by the Espheni (the same aliens who have now invaded and nearly destroyed Earth), leading him and his father to a life of war. Cochise the alien is strong but largely silent, a skilled warrior who is emotionally stoic, patient, and wise. He is even tall and physically intimidating, as the historical Chochise is reported to have been. His near-perfect reproduction of a stereotypical Native American warrior (even better than that produced by Whorf of *Star Trek: The Next Generation*) provides the show's most obvious reference to the role of Native peoples as American allies in the Revolutionary War (through the somewhat awkward transference of alliances from occupying settlers in the fight for independence from the British Empire to indigenous humans in the fight for independence from the invading Espheni Empire). The narrative decision to name a sympathetic alien after a Native American resistance leader discharges Native America's claim to resistance against settler colonialism—it is something that happened long ago and has no bearing on the present (future) struggle—while simultaneously presenting Native America as sympathetic to the plight of the struggling (past and post-apocalyptic future) nation. Cochise is *Falling*

Skies' tipi, evoking a future which has already been written. Don't worry, dear viewer: America's victory over its enemies (domestic, global, interstellar) is, ultimately, inevitable.

Cowboys and Colonists

Jericho begins with the dropping of several nuclear bombs across the United States, and then details both the struggle to survive the devastating aftermath and the unraveling of the "whodunit" mystery (spoiler alert: it was us). At its most obvious, the show cynically reflects growing American distrust of State authority in the wake of the 2001 Patriot Act and untruths regarding weapons of mass destruction in Iraq, calling rather obviously on post-9/11 sensibilities; the bombs even become known as "the September attacks." At its next obvious, it is a good Western: because the nukes took out all the power sources, the folks of Jericho must ride on horseback, read by candlelight, and distill their own liquor (which they figure out how to do right away). The town's survival depends on the bounty of the surrounding farms, but it also depends on the good sense and the good shootin' skills of its menfolk (and, at times, the womenfolk who stand by them). Jericho's protection against interlopers and thieves is accomplished by a posse of men—Jake, his brother, and their childhood friends—riding into the wild frontier of nuclear-ravaged Kansas to confront their enemies and protect their people. Occasionally the fight is brought to them, and we find the townspeople huddled in indoor safety while a few brave men—covered surreptitiously by posse members hidden in the library, the town hall, a nearby store—broker a peace settlement.

At the same time that the show is a post-apocalyptic Western, it also concerns itself centrally with Jake Green's search for identity. We learn in early episodes that the cause of Jake's anxiety is his own checkered past; apparently he was a heavy-drinking ne'er-do-well who could not even be trusted to meet his responsibilities as best man at his brother's wedding. After fleeing town years ago, a disappointment to his family and his girlfriend, he became a drifter who worked as a mercenary in Afghanistan and eventually (through bad luck and despite his efforts to avoid it, of course) became involved with shady dealings back in the United States. His return to Jericho is prompted by his need for cash and he is in fact once again fleeing the town—once again fleeing his own roots—when the bombs drop, forcing his return. Throughout the show Jake struggles to reconcile his own sense of failure and his yearning to belong; having once abandoned the town and its people in search of a better self, he resists, at first, finding that identity in the very homeland he left. By the end of season one, however, Jake has found redemption in his destined role as a leader in the town and embraces his roots as a citizen of Jericho.

He may have begun the story as an ambiguous hero, but it quickly becomes clear that he is a genuine good guy as other men in the town, from police officers to local farmers, follow his guidance, although at times they argue about it (this is a democracy, after all). Jake, through his exceptional skills, knowledge, and courage, is installed at the top of the leadership hierarchy (taking his primogeniture place beside his father and brother), and the fulfillment of his narrative of belonging not coincidentally restores patriarchal order to the town.

Robert Hawkins and Emily Sullivan are the only two, and deeply qualified, exceptions to the literal rule of white men in this renarrated frontier tale. It is unclear until the second season whether or not Hawkins, an African American, can be trusted, and the viewer knows almost from the beginning that he had something to do with the nuclear bombs. He is a suspicious character to say the least, although in the end he is the courageous and capable sidekick to Jake Green's heroism. Sullivan is the former/current/we're-not-sure love interest of Jake Green; she is a sharp-shootin' and sharp-talkin' tall, curvaceous blonde whose daddy is a side villain and whose past with Jake is both torrid and, perhaps, typical. Her courage is unquestionable, as are her general survival skills, but she is also the bad-girl-turned-good, a teenage rebel who grew up to become a school teacher devoted to the good of her hometown even before the bombs dropped. She is the one girl-with-a-gun in the posse, embodying what cultural critic Katha Pollitt calls the "Smurfette Principle," "a group of male buddies . . . accented by a lone female, stereotypically defined." Pollit argues that the Smurfette Principle sends a clear message: "Boys define the group, its story and its code of values. Girls exist only in relation to boys."[7] This is, after all, Jake's story, his search for identity, and it is his code of values (which stand in for America's code of values: hard work, courage, loyalty, redemption . . .) that define the group. Sullivan's eventual sexual accessibility ensures that these values are tested and proven and that they remain properly heteronormative, but *Jericho* is a masculine story; most of the characters are men, most of the dialogue is between men, most of the action is precipitated by men, and it is men who make the decisions and save the day.

The protagonist of *Falling Skies* is a soft-spoken American history professor named Tom Mason, perhaps named after Thomson Mason, a militiaman in the American Revolutionary War, or Thomson's son Thomson Francis Mason, a lawyer, judge, and later mayor of Alexandria. Or perhaps our protagonist is named after Thomson Francis's brother Thomas Mason, a businessman and planter who entered politics as a member of the Virginia House of Delegates. Their grandfather George Mason was one of the coauthors of the American Bill of Rights and is considered one of the founding fathers of the United States. The Mason family of early US history has a proud tradition of oratory, patriotism, and courage; the Mason family of the post-apocalyptic future continues this tradition, and as in *Jericho* this recollection of history evokes the mytho-history of America's origins and the collective identity it so tantalizingly offers.[8]

Tom loses his wife during the initial invasion by the alien Espheni force, signifying the destruction of domesticity and the safety it represents. But there are other women, and Tom will eventually fall in love with one and father a fourth child (a daughter who will come to embody the dangers of hybridity, but will, of course, eventually be offered redemption). His oldest son and potentially his youngest two by the end of the third season are also heterosexually partnered, thus ensuring the continuation of hegemonic, heterosexual masculinity as the dominant order (the partnerships will be disrupted in the fourth season, but not the heterosexuality). However, despite the women's presence, Tom and his three sons form a phalanx of masculinity organized by an unfailing loyalty and often tender love for each other. Their family unit remains inviolable as over and over again two Mason men, or three, or sometimes all four, ride off into the sunset in posse formation, reluctantly leaving behind the women who offer them the safety of their domesticating love. This is, after all, the frontier, where men protect and provide and women, despite their demonstrated skills and courage, provide a home front to protect and provide for. Maggie, the fiercely independent, gun-toting girlfriend of Tom's oldest son Hal, potentially disrupts this conservatively gendered narrative as she resists Hal's efforts to create a domestic arrangement (largely because she is afraid of rejection), but Maggie, too, is repeatedly left behind when the Masons ride off to war. The fourth season finds Tom's partner Anne taking a much more aggressive leadership role, but this is prompted by her role as a mother and at the end of the season, she accedes to Tom's wishes and kisses him goodbye once again.

Throughout the series the Mason men play increasingly important leadership roles in the Second Massachusetts Regiment (a ragtag regiment of resistance fighters) until Tom is eventually elected president of what remains of the United States, a tenure that is marked by moments of great public oratory and great public courage. His election signifies the restoration of a sense of order, as the beleaguered but occasionally victorious humans seek not only to survive but also to reestablish the proper order of things: the way things were on the eve of the United States' greatest military triumph, signified by the narrative resurrection of the young United States and its militiamen, who fought the British Empire to a victory the world celebrated. It is no coincidence that they are led by a man with extensive knowledge of how that happened, or that he and his family hail from Boston, the birthplace of the American Revolution, and that the survivors they join refer to themselves as the Second Massachusetts Regiment.[9] This is unmistakably the story of the land's "proper" inhabitants staking and defending their claim to belonging; it is the tale of the underdog (Revolutionary-era militiamen or twenty-first-century human guerillas) fighting for their lives and their freedom from a vastly superior force (the British Empire or the invading alien Espheni).

The absence of Native Americans in this retelling of history clears the way for the humans of *Falling Skies*, predominantly white, to claim an identity rooted in *this* land and no other. For example, when Tom offers their alien allies insights from "an indigenous point of view," he is informed that the Volm intend to relocate the Second Mass. to Brazil, ostensibly for their own safety. Tom and his second-in-command Colonel Weaver scoff in disbelief at the thought of removal and relocation from their homeland and assert their right to determine their own destiny based on longstanding occupation.[10] As Tom argues at the close of the third season, "Our planet, our fight . . . this is our home." One of his greatest oratorical moments in the series occurs at the close of season three's finale when he invokes American Revolution–era patriots, proclaiming, "We [humans? Americans?] are . . . passionate about our right to exist, and we adamantly oppose those who would oppress or deny us our freedoms . . . we would rather die than have those rights taken away."[11] Their refusal to leave the now largely defunct United States for the relative safety of what remains of Brazil tells us that the fight is, in fact, not only for Earth, but also for the nation, and that nation is rooted in the land.

The Cowboy Rides into the Post-Apocalyptic Sunset

In *Jericho* and *Falling Skies* the cowboy, in all his dusty, mythic glory, rides again as over and over Jake and his fellow townsmen and Tom Mason and his boys saddle up and ride into the dangerous post-apocalyptic wilderness in posse formation to save the day, the town, and the human race. Their unfailing defense of homeland is an assertion of belonging—"Our planet, our fight . . . this is our home"; it is equally an assertion of *who* belongs—the white, able-bodied, properly heterosexual cowboy, the white, able-bodied, properly heterosexual patriot. The man on the horse, with the gun. The (new) indigenous.

Ultimately, both of these shows assert the right of *some* to be here, in Kansas or on Earth. This right is asserted *against* the rights of others to be here. Both television shows rely on a narrative of settler colonialism which works to disappear the indigenous peoples who originally inhabited what is now the United States and replaces them with the settler's most powerful oppositional persona: the cowboy. Close textual analysis of these television shows reveals the conscious absence or carefully narrated presence of Native

America in these future histories and the use of the post-apocalypse to affirm dominant-culture gender expectations at the same time, revealing a metanarrative which relies on and justifies settler colonialist ideologies. Both *Jericho* and *Falling Skies* take place in the twenty-first century, but they express a yearning for a storied past of glory days when men were men and they protected what was theirs—land, women, freedom—reflecting, perhaps, a growing cultural uncertainty about the safety of the nation or even the efficacy of our national values post-9/11. At the same time, these shows work to reassure the viewer that yes, in fact, America is on the right path and will overcome our current hardships (economic, social, geopolitical), just as the nation always has. The United States, after all, is exceptional.

The absence of Native Americans in the post-apocalyptic landscape—indeed, the tiny minority of people of color in either show—reassuringly signifies the yearned-for conclusion of settler colonialism in the midst of our twenty-first-century uncertainties: the dominance of white masculinity over those who would resist its God-ordained triumph. Apparently, having survived five hundred years of their own apocalypse (brought on by mass migration of Europeans, their diseases, their weapons, and their patriarchy), no Native Americans will survive the global or even regional apocalypse to challenge white masculine authority[12] (as apparently will very few people of color and no queer-identifying people whatsoever). After the nuclear bombs drop or the aliens invade, emptying the landscape, Native Americans truly become a narrative shadow and America's (white, able-bodied, heterosexual, masculine) manifest destiny is finally fulfilled.

Notes

1. David Mogen, *Wilderness Visions: The Western Theme in Science Fiction Literature* (San Bernadino: Borgo Press, 1993): 17.
2. For a discussion on masculinity in American popular culture see Michael Kimmel, "The Cult of Masculinity: American Social Character and the Legacy of the Cowboy," in *Beyond Patriarchy*, ed. Michael Kaufman, 235–249 (New York: Oxford University Press, 1987).
3. "Frontierland Shootin' Arcade" at https://disneyworld.disney.go.com/attractions/magic-kingdom/frontierland-shootin-arcade/
4. Comer, *Landscapes of the New West*, 124–125.
5. Ibid., 125.
6. Carol Adams, *The Sexual Politics of Meat: A Feminist Vegetarian Critical Theory* (New York: Continuum International Publishing, 1990).
7. Katha Pollitt, "Hers: The Smurfette Principle," *The New York Times*, April 7, 1991. No pn. Last accessed January 29, 2015, from http://www.nytimes.com/1991/04/07/magazine/hers the-smurfette-principle.html

8. Tom Mason's human nemesis is John Pope, an untrustworthy but charismatic former convict who is likely named after a Union general in the Civil War who later fought the Apache and the Sioux in the Indian Wars (the Apache are particularly salient here, given the role of Cochise). Or he could be named after an earlier patriot, born on the eve of the American Revolution, who served as a Jeffersonian Republican to the US Senate and later the House of Representatives.
9. The first Second Massachusetts Regiment was formed from the twenty-third Continental Regiment of 1776; the next Second Massachusetts Regiment was a volunteer infantry regiment on the Union side of the Civil War. The Second Mass. of *Falling Skies* is, then, the third to defend its homeland.
10. Here, of course, one cannot help but be reminded of both Thomas Jefferson's and Andrew Jackson's machinations to forcibly remove thousands of indigenous peoples, ostensibly for their own well-being, from land the US coveted.
11. It was Patrick Henry who famously proclaimed in 1775 "Give me liberty or give me death!"
12. Although I nod here to Graham Greene, who plays a Native American business leader in TNT's drama *Defiance*, and to Tahmoh Penikett, who was central to the casts of the reimagined *Battlestar Galactica* and the Syfy channel's *Continuum* and whose mother is aboriginal from the White River Nation in Canada.

CHAPTER 3

Gender in the Aftermath: Starbuck and the Future of Woman in *Battlestar Galactica*

Tracey Raney and *Michelle Meagher*

Introduction

In this chapter we read the post-apocalyptic speculative fiction television show *Battlestar Galactica (2004–2009)* as a critical metanarrative within which contemporary anxieties around gender, gendered identities, feminism, and post-feminism cohere. Originally conceived for television in 1978, *Battlestar Galactica* was a science fiction series that followed the human survivors of a 1,000-year war with the Cylons, a race of warrior robots. Though there have been several spin-offs, the most successful reiteration of the franchise is the 2004–2009 Syfy Channel television series called *Battlestar Galactica* (or *BSG*, as it is commonly referred to by fans). The series begins with a devastating attack by the Cylons on the human fleet; it is an attack that results in mass casualties, the destruction of the human home planet, Caprica, and the displacement of survivors onto several spaceships—one of which is the Battlestar Galactica.

Broadly, post-apocalyptic speculative fiction (PASF) narratives unfold after a cataclysmic or apocalyptic end, which of course, is not really an end, but rather a time in which the unspeakable and the unimaginable have already happened.[1] Despite being severed from the world that its characters once knew, post-apocalyptic stories are not detached from the past. Rather, they are, like other forms of science fiction, "*in [their] very nature a symbolic meditation on history itself.*"[2] Indeed, representations of otherwise unimaginable post-disaster worlds meditate on those past injustices, current anxieties, and ongoing tensions that mark the human condition in everyday life. In this sense, stories of what we refer to as "the Aftermath" are inherently reflexive and symptomatic: they reveal our current paths and suggest the destinations toward which we are heading, and, in so doing, they attempt to unveil to us the true order of things in the present.[3] Accordingly, PASF stories can be read as allegorical narratives of modern cultural anxieties, induced as they are by the tensions, ambiguities, differences, and uncertainties of the world in which we live.[4]

In the case of *BSG*, the vast majority of the storyline occurs during the Aftermath, during which the remaining human and Cylon fleets struggle for survival after a nuclear bomb detonation that leaves behind approximately 50,000 human survivors. For our purposes, one of the most intriguing aspects of this Aftermath story is its depiction of gendered social relations and identities. In effect, Galactica itself—the battlestar ship where most of the human drama plays out—serves as an imaginary space within which the social structures and constraints of gender and patriarchy are rarely experienced and gender-based inequalities seem to be resolved. The women of *BSG* share bathrooms and sleeping quarters with men, they fight alongside men in battle, they assume positions of high political and military power, and many possess the mental acuity, emotional toughness, and physical prowess generally reserved for male characters on prime-time television. Human relationships, social interactions, and the military and political organizations that are central to *BSG* all appear to exist beyond the bounds of traditional gender assumptions of how women and men ought to behave, think, and feel.

In this chapter, our goal is to investigate the extent to which the post-apocalyptic narrative of *BSG* imagines a liberated, post-gendered space for women. We read gender "in" to the post-apocalypse and interrogate both how gender representations serve to advance the Aftermath plot, and how the show uses gender to resolve and move out of the post-apocalyptic period in order to achieve its final revelation. To do so, we rely on post-feminist analyses and consider *BSG* as a futuristic allegory that resonates with, and ultimately reproduces, contemporary anxieties over shifting gender roles—in the military, in politics, and in culture more generally.

Our analyses focus on the central female protagonist, Lieutenant Kara "Starbuck" Thrace, and we show how the progressive nature of this heroic female character is contained within the post-apocalyptic moment—a strategy that is especially evidenced in the final few episodes of the series. More importantly, in our view, any gender parity that seems to be enjoyed by Starbuck is liminal and conditional; it is contained within the time and space of the Aftermath, and it is eventually set aside as obsolete as the story (and series) resolves itself. Starbuck as a post-feminist hero demonstrates the inherently conservative portrayal of gender and gender identity in the show, and we argue that this conservatism is facilitated and enhanced by the narrative strategies of post-apocalyptic storytelling.

We begin with an analysis of Galactica as a post-gendered setting. On the surface, Galactica is characterized by a rough gender equality: men and women work together to run the ship, both men and women hold positions of power, and both men and women are trained to be viper pilots. Next, we position *BSG* as a post-apocalyptic text and show how the wider PASF story it offers can be read as a metanarrative through which gender and gender relations can be interpreted. Finally, we expose a retreatist message at work in the final season of *BSG* and argue that the program's transformative, progressive, and even feminist potential is undermined by an ending that requires the disappearance and allegorical disavowal of Starbuck. Throughout, we argue that the character of Starbuck signals a warning of the inevitable consequences—particularly for women—of leaving the existing social and political orders behind: anomie, self-estrangement, sacrifice, and death. Rather than imagining transformative spaces for women, *BSG*'s futuristic allegory is one in which the limitations of gender are reimposed, where human bodies are remapped as traditionally gendered, and where female power is once again relegated to the limited spaces of family and home.

Post-Feminism and the Female Hero

As critics, fans, and scholars have pointed out, among the most dramatic—and controversial—changes made by the *BSG* production team was the decision to cast the character of Starbuck as a woman portrayed by Katee Sackoff. It is a move that dramatically transforms the landscape of *BSG*. As the main protagonist of the series, Starbuck is the top fighter pilot in the human fleet. At times reckless and shrewd, her military skill and prowess is matched by her physical and emotional demeanor. Starbuck's behavior and actions repeatedly defy traditional gendered stereotypes of femininity: she smokes cigars, drinks heavily, gambles, and engages in several short-lived and purely physical sexual affairs with men. In one of the first images we see in the series, Starbuck is seen jogging onboard Galactica wearing grey and black gender-neutral military fatigues that reveal her muscular shoulders and arms. Her performance of what Judith Halberstam describes as "female masculinity" is on full display.[5] Shortly thereafter, in the midst of a heated card game, Starbuck insults a much older superior male officer, Colonel Tigh. In this remarkable scene, we are presented with an act of unfamiliar female aggression and violence: Starbuck punches him in the face, an act for which she is sent to a military holding pen as punishment. The show has quickly established that she is a tough woman who steps outside the normal bounds of femininity and thus seems to represent a feminist disruption of the status quo.[6]

Although Starbuck is the toughest woman (and maybe the toughest person) on the Galactica, she is not the only tough woman. The Galactica, as many have noted, is a site where men and women seem to interact on an equal footing. Apparently unfettered by the conventions of gender distinction, women take on major positions in government, in training, and in battle. The commissioned men and women aboard Galactica share sleeping quarters and bathroom facilities, they work out, play sports, drink and smoke together, and they wear the same military uniforms. For feminist viewers, there is something refreshing about being offered a universe in which gender doesn't seem to matter. Indeed, Ewan Kirkland suggests that some might read the program as a "post-gender utopia," a universe in which sexism is absent, an answer, of sorts, to a (liberal) feminist critique of the structural and institutional limitations placed upon women.[7]

In our reading we observe not a post-gendered environment, but one that is, to use Kirkland's terms, structured around a "default masculinity" represented by "traditionally male codes of behavior, values, and aesthetics."[8] Rather than offer a post-gender social order in which women and men alike are free from the constraints of masculinity and femininity, *Battlestar Galactica*—even reimagined with women at the center—remains a hyper-masculine environment. Within this gendered space, Starbuck stands out as the toughest, most masculine fighter pilot—as masculine as and often more masculine than her male colleagues. Though she seems on the surface to function allegorically as a feminist figure—that is, the embodiment of second-wave liberal feminist demands for the inclusion of women in male-dominated work and culture—Starbuck is not, ultimately, at odds with what Kirkland describes as the "often-conservative ideologies with inform *Battlestar Galactica*."[9] Like us, Kirkland suggests that excitement over the nontraditional behavior of this character ought to be tempered by situating her within the broader social universe in which she exists. For us, this means attending to the ways in which Starbuck's apparent resistances to conventional patterns of gender are embedded in a post-apocalyptic narrative frame.

Gendering the Post-Apocalypse

An absolutely central element of the *BSG* social universe is the broader post-apocalyptic setting of the show, a context that we argue is highly relevant from a gendered perspective. In fact, the reimagined series begins with a nuclear attack by the Cylons that results in the near holocaust of the human population—a moment that makes explicit reference to gender through the character of a female Cylon, Number Six. In one of the opening scenes of the series we discover that Six is responsible for detonating a nuclear bomb, and that she has achieved this goal by using her feminine wiles to dupe two men.[10] Six is presented to us as a highly sexualized femme fatale: white, blonde, tall, busty, and often wearing a tight, red dress and stiletto heels. She is also offered to viewers as an evil seductress, manipulating the weaknesses of man in order to plot the downfall of humanity. Bent on the total annihilation of the human race, Six can be read as a "pathological cyborg," a common representation of the female cyborg in film and television; she is "hyper-sexualized, dangerous and disruptive."[11] The beginning of the end, it seems, was brought about by a woman whose powerful femininity is performed in a highly dangerous, and ultimately deadly, way.

While the origins of the *BSG* catastrophe are themselves highly feminized, the Aftermath is a decidedly masculinized space, characterized by violence, aggression, war, and chaos. Even the central female protagonist in the human fleet, Starbuck, is portrayed as a masculine hero who fights tirelessly for the survival of the human species. In addition to all of her tough woman characteristics described above, however, Starbuck's hypermasculinity is presented to us as unfulfilling and even destructive. In several instances, her masculinity is overperformed and excessive, to the point where her actions are sometimes called into question, and ultimately regulated, by other male characters, many of whom outrank her. Her physical aggression and recklessness result in the torture of the Cylon Leoben, her brawling with Colonel Tigh, and her unwillingness to cede defeat in the boxing ring against a male competitor, Lee Adama. She has meaningless, emotionless sex that is often unsatisfying; she drinks and gambles to excess; she flies her plane expertly, but sometimes recklessly (in one instance, almost to the point of suicide); she is prone to physical violence that often inflicts extreme physical pain upon herself. Though Starbuck appears to be a tough woman who shrugs off the patriarchal ascription of femininity to her female body, the anguish and pain that accompanies her inhabitation of this masculine, post-disaster space speaks to her discomfort with this role. Her portrayal as a liberated woman is thus undermined by her uneasiness with a hypermasculine identity that she has adopted while living in the Aftermath.

Moreover, Starbuck's gendered identity is a classic post-feminist characterization: although she enacts a masculinized role of power and authority, her inhabitation of this position is rendered problematic, tormenting, and even, deep-down, undesired. This serves to normalize the conventional gender identities and relations that Starbuck appears to disturb. The normalization of conventional gender identities is further supported by the program's frequent suggestion that under different circumstances, Starbuck is inclined toward conventional feminine behaviors and desires, such as being a wife and mother. Indications of her inclinations toward conventional femininity are drawn out by Leoben, a Cylon, in Season three. Leoben imprisons Starbuck in a superficial world of domesticity, which she, at least initially, rejects vigorously. Though confronted with a child that Leoben tells her is her own, Starbuck rejects the child and focuses her attention on escape. But when the child (Kacey) has an accidental fall, Starbuck's capacity to care for and nurture "her" child bubble to the surface. Later on, when Starbuck is faced with the realization that Kacey is not in fact her daughter, she comes to realize the depth of her desire for a child.

This is not the only instance in which Starbuck is positioned as experiencing the contradictions of her Aftermath identity. In blurred and often drunken flashbacks of the past, viewers observe Starbuck as a gentler Kara Thrace. In these flashbacks, portrayed as memories that torment her, we are offered glimpses of Starbuck's more emotional and more feminine side. They reveal her love for a now dead fiancé, her vulnerability to a mother who inflicted upon her both psychological and physical pain, and her deep and genuine feelings for Lee Adama, a fellow Viper pilot and central figure in the *BSG* narrative. These glimpses of Starbuck's other side are often mapped onto a more feminine body than the one we have seen on present-day Galactica. During a break from the war action, she is portrayed off Galactica wearing a revealing, feminine dress with dangling earrings, and during the brief armistice with the Cylons on New Caprica, her blonde hair has grown long as she nurses her husband, Sam Anders, back to health. These images cast uncertainty about the true nature of her character as it might exist beyond the boundaries of the disorder of chaos and war, and provoke audiences to wonder who the real Starbuck is: the blonde, long-haired nursemaid to her husband on New Caprica, or the cigar-smoking Viper pilot who swears, boxes, and uses men for her own sexual gratification. These representations of a feminized Starbuck function to question the authenticity of her Aftermath identity; they also suggest a wistful yearning for a time before (or other than) the apocalypse. Ultimately, Starbuck's representation aligns with other post-feminist cultural narratives, in which women who have "made it" in a man's world are depicted as unhappy, unsatisfied, and, ultimately, nostalgic for a time in their lives or a cultural moment when their roles were more traditionally defined.

Kirkland observes that these representations of Starbuck's femininity all occur in spaces and times separate from the present day on the Galactica. We take this argument one step further, and argue that the wider post-apocalyptic narrative serves as a boundary that marks Starbuck's masculinity as exceptional, as something that exists only within the disruptive space of the Aftermath. The Starbuck we see in the "present" day Aftermath setting is a hypermasculinized Viper pilot, and the fleeting images of her femininity remind us that her performance of female masculinity is just that, a performance. Here, Starbuck is placed in a familiar post-feminist position—she is cast at once as a figure who has refused traditional femininity, but who suffers deeply from the "choices" that she makes. Moreover, insofar as her masculinity is contained within the Aftermath, we begin to question whether she ever made a choice at all—the absence of her femininity begins to seem as though it were a consequence of the catastrophe itself, rather than as a freely chosen set of liberating behaviors. It is through her gender that Starbuck appears to be yoked to the disastrous event and the Aftermath. The consequence of occupying this traditionally masculinized space is that she must navigate her own internal apocalypse as her subjective sense of gender identity remains fractured, "frakked," and perpetually elusive.

It is on this point in particular that we believe Starbuck functions allegorically to respond to cultural anxieties over shifting gender roles. Attending to this allegorical reading means to recognize that though *BSG* offers, at least on the surface, an exciting post-gender environment that, to borrow a phrase from the show, "fraks with" conventional gender hierarchies and patterns; it in fact advocates a post-feminist message. Here, we draw on the work of cultural critic Angela McRobbie, who suggests that post-feminist cultural texts function by offering the appearance of feminism—in the case of *BSG*, a universe in which gender does not seem to be a factor, in which characters like Starbuck can take on conventional male social roles—while undermining feminism as a political project intended to transform hetero-gendered social contracts.[12]

Further to the point, there's an important and troubling double movement in a post-feminist cultural text like *BSG*. It offers a vision of world in which familiar and long-standing assumptions about gender no longer guide behavior and structure social orders. But Starbuck's malaise, her self-destruction, and her duplicity suggest to viewers that there may be a lot to lose in a future in which women compete on even footing with men. Indeed, Starbuck's suffering is a commentary on all that has been lost: the certitude of gendered identities, and the security that comes with adopting the prescribed gender identity assigned on the basis of one's birth sex. The Aftermath is a space and time where women suffer for becoming "like men," and where femininity as a human characteristic is either erased, or offered only fleetingly, in nostalgic dreams of past lives and distant worlds of a previous time. Starbuck's character is therefore positioned in an undesirable futurity that is feminist in its outward appearance but sexist in its effects. In the next section, we expand on this idea by turning to the final episodes of the program, and we argue that the ending of *BSG* leaves little doubt about the future of women in the Aftermath.

Harbinger of Death: Starbuck and the Future of Woman

Post-apocalyptic science fiction stories seek to explore, question, and interrogate the cultural and social traumas and anxieties of modern societies. As a response to the anxieties brought about by gender nonconformity, and particularly those rooted in feminist social critiques, PASF offers a space within which our shared fears can be either put to rest or fully realized. Accordingly, one of the central questions of many PASF narratives, and of *BSG*, is whether these stories offer spaces for social and cultural transformation, or if they provide inherently conservative viewpoints.[13]

In its final season, *BSG* works toward a conclusion to the post-apocalyptic narrative that may have come as a disappointment to those viewers drawn to the disruptive representations of gender in the Aftermath. A revelation builds over the last few episode of the final season; it begins with the discovery that the Earth the humans are seeking has been destroyed in a nuclear holocaust. This "apocalypse within an apocalypse" storyline marks the beginning of the end of the Aftermath, and a move toward a final destination for the surviving characters of the show. A post-feminist reading of these final episodes reveals that gender plays a critical role in achieving this conclusion; it does so by settling gender back into a traditional pattern, first through the erasure of the masculine female character and second, with a return to what viewers recognize as pre-feminist ideals of the family and home.

A common challenge for post-feminist cultural texts is what to do with the female hero at the end of the show, and the solution is often her death. For Crosby, such deaths or killings represent not a feminist transcendence of a patriarchal community but rather, a way for the storywriters to restore social and moral order to a "normal" equilibrium.[14] Starbuck faces this fate not once but twice. In Season three, Starbuck crashes her Viper jet, resulting in what almost certainly seems to be her death ("Maelstrom", Season 3, episode 17). In the Season three finale, she returns (to the great surprise of viewers and the other actors in the show), as a celestial being who makes it her duty to find Earth and thus ensure the survival of humanity. It is a role that had been prophesied for her by a Hybrid (Cylon-human) oracle who foresaw her as a "harbinger of death"; after her "death," Starbuck is guided by visions and awareness of recurring patterns that allow her to see beyond the chaos and panic toward a final destination. Despite the important role she plays in finding a future for the remaining humans, Starbuck is ontologically set adrift, unclear what has happened to her and what or who she is. Seeing her own dead body amidst the wreckage of her Viper jet, she pleads for an answer: "If that's me lying there, then what am I? What am I?" ("Sometimes a Great Notion," Season 4, episode 13). Not only is Starbuck, like other post-feminist heroines,[15] killed off, she is brought back into the narrative in ways that underscore, in the first instance, her self-alienation and, in the second instance, her character's singular mission to help humanity survive (and thus resolve the overall plot of the show). To bring about the end of the Aftermath, Starbuck as we have come to know her must also end: our female hero and the Aftermath are indissolubly linked.

Even more significantly, once her mission is fulfilled and the humans and Cylons arrive at their final destination (New Earth), Starbuck mysteriously vanishes. This second death underscores the reality that there is no space for her character in the resettlement. Put another way, within the parameters of the post-apocalyptic narrative, Starbuck is positioned firmly in the Aftermath, and not the future, and the establishment of the new world order is contingent upon her absence. New Earth is a lush world of rich, green plains that are sparsely populated. It is an unspoiled, untainted paradise. It is represented as a site unburdened by the apocalypse and its aftermath. It holds out the promise of salvation for the human and Cylon species and it is founded on a simpler, more pre-technological way of life tied to the land. Rather than bring the dangers of their "modern" civilization with them onto the new planet, the settlers decide not build cities and to live a different way; they decide to "break the cycle . . . and leave it all behind and start over." The nostalgia for a pre-technological time is also at the same time a nostalgia for a moment when women and men assumed traditional roles in the family structure. Moreover, this familial structure seems to be a requirement for the survival of modern day humanity. Ultimately, the promise of a future for humanity is contained within a racially mixed nuclear family composed of Helo (a white human male), Athena (an Asian Cylon female), and their female Hybrid child, Hera. In playful optimistic banter, Helo declares himself a hunter, and Athena promises to teach her daughter how to farm and build a house. The future, it seems, begins with the nuclear family and all of its heterosexual, pre-feminist trappings. It is in this way that New Earth discloses the future of woman in this new civilization.

The fate of Starbuck's character is central to the fulfillment of the show's redemptive messaging. Her disappearance on New Earth settles the threat to the gendered order that was posed by her masculine, tough enactments of gender—it quells the panic induced by such gendered distortions. In effect, the erasure of the Starbuck character suggests to viewers that the masculine female hero resides only in a state of unnatural disorder, outside of which she ceases to exist. Starbuck is herself part of a cyclic return to normalcy: her pre-apocalyptic femininities, her tortured Aftermath masculinity, and her eventual death in a post-Aftermath setting, all lend credence to the importance of gender in telling the *BSG* post-apocalypse story. Rather than leave the fate of her character open and limitless, such an ending limits the transformative possibilities of her character's gender performance.

To be certain, gender is not the only allegory offered to viewers at the end of the series, as New Earth functions to remind us of the multiple sources of cultural anxieties faced by contemporary societies: moral nihilism, out of control urbanization, technology gone amok, and environmental degradation. At the same time, it is important to note how gender is used to deliver one of the last redemptive messages of the show. The final scene of the series is set

150,000 years after Galactica, in Times Square in New York City—the implication being that the *BSG* story is set not in the future, but in the past. The show therefore divulges a pattern of inevitability, guided by some divine force or intervention, where "all of this has happened and will happen again."[16] Here in modern day New York, we learn of the discovery of Mitochondrial Eve, the matrilineal ancestor to humanoids, whom we presume to be the child, Hera.[17] Walking through modern day Times Square, representational figures of Gaius Baltar (a human/god-like figure) and Six (a Cylon/angel-figure) have the following exchange:

> *Six*: Commercialism, decadence, technology run amok . . . remind you of anything?
> *Baltar*: Take your pick: Kobol; Earth—the real Earth, before this one; Caprica before The Fall.
> *Six*: "All of this has happened before . . ."
> *Baltar*: But the question remains: does all of this have to happen again?
> *Six*: This time, I bet "no."
> *Baltar*: You know, I've never known you to play the optimist. Why the change of heart?
> *Six*: Mathematics. Law of averages. Let a complex system repeat itself long enough, eventually something surprising might occur. That, too, is in God's plan.
> *Baltar*: You know, It doesn't like that name . . .
>   ("Daybreak Part III," Season 4, episode 22)

While references and allusions to God are made throughout the series, they play an especially important role in the show's last disclosure: all of this has happened before and the Capricans, and perhaps all humans—ourselves included, are pawns of divine providence. We learn that humanity is repeatedly led astray, and fumbling toward the apocalypse, through a temptation to "play god" by using technology to create life. We come to understand that the post-Aftermath settlement on New Earth, for all its promise, is only one stage in an eternal return. Fading away from Baltar and Six, the camera turns to a jumbotron, where a news broadcast on advancements in robotics is unfolding: in the first clip, an early generation, gender-neutral automaton is shown, and in the last, we see a more human-like, Japanese-looking, female robot, dressed in white, knee-high boots and a mini-skirt, blinking unknowingly into the camera. This image plays to an underlying current of fear that, ultimately, technological reproduction is a boundary that ought not to be transgressed by humans, lest we risk the collapse of civilization.

Though this ending reveals there is little escape, the message of salvation for the inhabitants of New Earth (and we the viewers) is made clear: it heralds a deep skepticism for technology, which goes in hand with a return to conventional, and more significantly, presumably "natural" gender roles and relations. The New Earth storyline, and the last scene of the show, together function to parcel out the most obviously transformative, progressive, and even feminist components of the program—life on the battleship—as temporary, liminal, and necessarily disavowed. In its final moment, *BSG* once again exhibits its post-feminist sensibility, returning to what television scholar Lynn Spigel describes as a post-feminist nostalgia for a pre-feminist future.[18]

Conclusion

In a blog "Why Feminists Love 'Battlestar Galactica,'" Hannah Moulton Belec notes that *BSG* offers a "gender-blind" space where women and men are treated equally and where, refreshingly, an "oppositional spectatorship" turns the male gaze back onto men.[19] Indeed, this explains in part why many feminists enjoyed the show: it depicts strong, powerful women who occupy nontraditional sites of power. In this chapter, we have used the post-apocalyptic frame to show how the representation of gender in *BSG* is limited in a number of ways. Our interest is in the way that *BSG* functions allegorically in relationship to cultural anxieties surrounding shifting practices of gender. It is clearly a televisual text that purposefully places a female character at the center of things. While others have analyzed the portrayal of gender in *BSG*, our chapter focuses on the importance of the wider post-apocalyptic narrative of the show which, we suggest, is central to any understanding of *BSG*'s representations of gender and gendered identity. Alongside other disruptive elements of civilization (e.g., terror, wars, Holocaust), shifting gender roles and gendered identities can be read as productive of cultural anxiety. They cast into doubt stable notions of gender assignment that map femininity/masculinity onto female/male bodies respectively—a point that is particularly clear in the figure of Starbuck in *BSG*.

As we have argued, the Aftermath in *BSG* establishes boundaries around gender. Rather than view gender as, in the words of Heffernan, a site that refuses resolution, the promise of *BSG*'s "gender-blindness" is trapped within the post-apocalyptic moment. Although Starbuck is portrayed as a strong, masculine woman, her potential to disrupt dominant cultural scripts of femininity is dependent upon and ultimately contained by the conventions of post-feminist storytelling. In the very moment that she (and other human women) attains many of the freedoms that have been most aggressively demanded by second-wave liberal feminist politics, a narrative of cyclical renewal and return to a pre-feminist, pre-technological era steps in to secure traditional terms of gender relations. The wider problem of the survival of the remaining settlers depends upon a disavowal of the gender parity we see on the battleship and the construction of a future that ultimately recommits itself to pre-feminist gender roles.

Notes

1. See James Berger cited in Teresa Heffernan, *Post-Apocalyptic Culture—Modernism, Postmodernism, and the Twentieth Century Novel* (Toronto: University of Toronto Press, 2008), 42.
2. Frederic Jameson cited in Eric Repphun, "'You Can't Hide from the Things that You've Done Anymore': *Battlestar Galactica* and the Clash of Civilizations Debate," *Westminster Communication and Culture* 4, no. 8 (2011): 119.
3. James Berger, *After the End—Representations of Post-Apocalypse* (Minneapolis: University of Minnesota Press, 1994).
4. Heffernan, *Post-Apocalyptic Culture*, 52.
5. See Judith Halberstam, *Female Masculinity* (Durham and London: Duke University Press, 1998).
6. See Sherrie Inness, *Action Chicks—New Images of Tough Women in Popular Culture* (New York: Palgrave Macmillan, 2004).
7. Ewan Kirkland, "Starbuck and the Gender Dynamics in Battlestar Galactica," in *Finding Battlestar Galactica—An Unauthorized Guide*, eds. Lynnette Porter, David Lavery, and Hillary Robson, 138 (Naperville, IL: Sourcebooks, 2008).
8. Ewan Kirkland, "A Dangerous Place for Women," in *Battlestar Galactica and Philosophy: Mission Accomplished or Mission Frakked Up?*, eds. Josef Steiff and Tristan Tamplin, 338 (Chicago and La Salle, IL: Open Court, 2008).
9. Kirkland, "A Dangerous Place," 346.
10. In the first instance, she sleeps with a renowned male scientist in order to gain access to a nuclear bomb. In the second, she ends the thirty-year armistice between the humans and Cylons by planting a kiss on a superior, white, male officer of the human fleet just as the bomb is detonated.
11. Sean Redmond in Glenda Shaw, "The Enduring Pathological Feminine Machine," *Intimate Machines* (blog), February 16, 2014, http://glendashaw-garlock.blogspot.ca/
12. See Angela McRobbie, "Post-Feminism and Popular Culture" *Feminist Media Studies* 4, no. 3 (2004): 255–264.
13. Heffernan, *Post-Apocalyptic Culture*, 22.
14. Sara Crosby "The Cruelest Season: Female Heroes Snapped into Sacrificial Heroines," in *Action Chicks*, Sherrie A. Inness (New York: Palgrave Macmillan, 2004), 162
15. In addition to Starbuck's disappearance, the president of the Twelve Colonies, Laura Roslin, also dies of cancer once she arrives on New Earth. In effect, the most visible displays of female power, liberation, and feminism are absent in this new civilization, thus paving the way for a more maternal, pre-feminist female figure (Athena) to emerge.

16. This is a common refrain used by various Hybrid Oracle characters that predict the future.
17. The two walk by a pedestrian (played by the producer of the show, Ronald D. Moore), who is reading a National Geographic entitled "Mankind's First Mother."
18. See Lynn Spigel, "Postfeminist Nostalgia for a Prefeminist Future," *Screen* 54, no. 2 (2013), 270–278.
19. Hannah Moulton Belec, "Why Feminists Love 'Battlestar Galactica,'" *aauw.com*, March 22, 2013, http://www.aauw.org/2013/03/22/feminists-love-battlestar-galactica/

CHAPTER 4

The Visibility and Invisibility of Class, Race, Gender, and Sexuality in *The Hunger Games*

Mary C. Burke and *Maura Kelly*

In the world of *The Hunger Games*, as depicted in Suzanne Collins's novels and their film adaptations, the citizens of the 12 districts of the country of Panem are controlled by their fear of the powerful central government, the Capitol.[1] People living in the districts furthest from the Capitol, particularly Districts 10, 11, and 12, primarily live in poverty, while those living closer to the Capitol and, especially, those living in the Capitol have access to resources and advanced technology. The book and film series focus on Katniss Everdine (played by Jennifer Lawrence), a teenage girl from District 12, who enters the arena of the Hunger Games as a tribute and, ultimately, becomes a leader in a class-based revolution against the Capitol. The society portrayed in *The Hunger Games* is best described as dystopian, but also includes elements of a post-apocalyptic narrative. We conceptualize the districts' uprising, subsequent war, and failed revolution, which included the partial annihilation of District 13,[2] as the apocalyptic event that disrupted the very structure of the society and resulted in the negotiation of a new social contract. Because 74 years pass between the end of the war and the beginning of the story, the story focuses less on the apocalyptic events than on the dystopian aftermath. However, *The Hunger Games* draws on several key post-apocalyptic narrative elements, including the emphasis on the struggle for survival after a major traumatic event, scarcity of resources, and lack of technology and infrastructure, particularly in the Districts.

In this chapter we examine *The Hunger Games*, focusing particularly on the first film in the series, to consider how class, racial/ethnic, gender, and sexual inequality are depicted in the film's narrative of the future. Specifically, we explore the ways that various axes of oppression are and are not named in the series. As we will demonstrate, there is a contrast between what *The Hunger Games* tells us about inequality and what it shows us. While the dominant narrative of *The Hunger Games* tells us that class and nation are the central axes of power and oppression, it shows us the persistent role of race, gender, and sexuality in organizing individuals' life chances.

Debates over the relative weight of various systems of power and oppression have been a common thread in academic and activist discourses over time. Feminist scholars have cautioned against the focus on class as the single overarching system of oppression, offering a corrective to Marxist approaches.[3] Further, contemporary feminist scholars have come to a consensus that inequality must be understood intersectionally, that is, in the context of various interacting systems of oppression.[4] As Audre Lorde wrote: "oppression and the intolerance of difference come in all shapes and sizes and colors and sexualities; . . . among those of us who share the goals of liberation and a workable future for our children, there can be no hierarchies of oppression."[5]

However, while intersectionality is an important emphasis in numerous contemporary academic and activist discourses, claims that racism, sexism, and heterosexism are things of the past are exceedingly common in contemporary culture. Thus, *The Hunger Games*' emphasis on class and the state and its simultaneous silence around race, gender, and sexuality makes it a fitting popular culture parallel to contemporary discourse, including social and political movement rhetoric, in the United States. Critiques of the state, government, and politics are incredibly salient on both the left and the right. And while there is considerable variation in terms of diagnosis and prognosis, there is also some definite overlap in terms of central issues, one of which is the relationship between economic and political institutions and actors, or more simply, money and politics. For example, Occupy, a movement with origins in leftist and anarchist politics, was able to draw widespread support in ways not common to radical politics in the United States via the populist appeal of some of its central rhetoric, which was directed at issues of class, the concentration of wealth, the disappearance of the middle class, and the role of "Wall Street," the "1%," and the federal government. By popularizing the slogan "We are the 99%," Occupy both centered class and created commonality across the population via shared economic and political disempowerment.

Although contemporary movements coalescing around class and the state have had some success in terms of widespread appeal, this is not true to the same extent with movements that more specifically address race and gender inequality. While the Occupy rhetoric was adopted (or perhaps co-opted) by more conservative populist and libertarian factions, the same cannot be said for Black Lives Matter, the movement that has emerged in response to widespread violence and discrimination against people of color by the police and the state more broadly, or for recent movements addressing sexual violence and administrative malfeasance on college campuses. While there is widespread disagreement about the ethics of economic inequality and about the nature of the problems with the state, the existence of class inequality and the existence of problems with the state are frequently taken as given. However, in the case of issues such as racism and sexual violence, there is still a great deal of denial about their very existence. These patterns of visibility and invisibility around various systems of inequality are clearly reflected in the future envisioned in *The Hunger Games*.

In assessing the emphasis on class oppression in *The Hunger Games*, we highlight a missed opportunity on the part of the author as well as the filmmakers to call attention to the intersection of inequalities that scholars argue is essential for beginning to understand oppression. The films seem to tell us, centrally via the silence around race, gender, and sexuality, that these are no longer relevant, while simultaneously showing us again and again that they are. The films portray a society that adopts a post-gender ideology as well as a colorblind or post-race ideology. However, we are also shown that race, gender, sexuality, and their intersections with class matter a great deal. In this sense, the future in imagined Panem is organized by systems of power and inequality that are not that drastically different from those in the present era. Likewise, this future is characterized by a strikingly familiar failure to think about race, gender, and sexuality as structures of inequality or to talk about these systems in tandem with critical interventions into economic inequality. The vision of the future in *The Hunger Games* is informed by the author and filmmakers' understanding of race, gender, and class in the contemporary United States. We see their limited ability to imagine a future world with different arrangements of power and privilege, perhaps not surprising given how race and gender inequalities are deeply entrenched in contemporary Western cultures.

Bread and Circuses: What *The Hunger Games* Tells Us about Inequality in the Future

The Hunger Games takes place in a post-apocalyptic dystopia hundreds of years in the future, in the fictional country of Panem, which is located within the geographic area of the contemporary United States. The Capitol, Panem's powerful central government that benefits from the poor outlying districts, has intentional similarities to the Roman Empire. The name Panem is taken from the phrase "panem et circenses," translated to "bread and circuses," which describes the practice of Roman politicians providing food and entertainment to distract and mollify the public. Indeed, the Hunger Games themselves serve this function, particularly for the citizens of the Capitol.

The names of some of the capitol dwellers, such as host and media personality Caesar Flickerman (played by Stanley Tucci) also allude to the Roman Empire. The Arena where the Hunger Games are fought has a parallel in the Roman Colosseum, where gladiators fought and killed both animals and other people for an audience. In *The Hunger Games*, this narrative has a postmodern twist as the Games are captured in the form of a reality show and televised to the country to encourage obedience to the Capitol.

Panem is defined by its extreme class inequality. In District 12, home of the story's heroine Katniss Everdeen, people live in deep poverty. At the start of the film, we see Katniss bathing in a wooden tub. Later, we hear a character comically quip that one major difference between the districts and the capitol is "the showers," noting that he now smells "like roses." While people in the outer districts do not have enough food to eat, people in the Capitol have plenty and Capitol partygoers drink emetics so that they can continue to eat. District 12 does not consistently have electricity, but the Capitol has hovercrafts and a train that travels 200 miles per hour.

We first see Katniss living in District 12 with her mother (played by Paula Malcomson) and sister Prim (Willow Shields), along with her closest friend Gale (Liam Hemsworth) and the other District 12 tribute, Peeta (Josh Hutcherson). After Katniss and Peeta are selected as tributes for the Hunger Games, they are transported by train to the Capitol. The poverty of District 12 is contrasted with the luxury of the train, which is beautifully furnished and has vast quantities of food and drink. Citizens of the Capitol are portrayed as extravagantly wealthy, with brightly colored avant-garde clothing, and colorful wigs and makeup, which is contrasted with the humble and muted attire worn by Katniss, Peeta, and the rest of the citizens of District 12.

Class status shapes individuals' chances in the Hunger Games themselves as well. Tributes from the wealthier districts, described as "career tributes," receive training from an early age and have a physical advantage in the arena, particularly compared to those coming from a life of poverty and malnourishment. While "career tributes" often volunteer to compete, the majority of tributes are selected by lottery. Here too, we see that class shapes individuals' chances, as those from poorer families can enter their children's names multiple times in exchange for basic rations. This means that the poorest children have a greater likelihood of being selected. Further, survival in the arena is also dependent on "sponsors" who will provide needed resources such as food and medicine. The career tributes are generally seen as "favorites" to win and are more likely to receive sponsorships. Indeed, Katniss, Peeta, and their coach Haymitch (played by Woody Harrelson) engage in some relatively complex strategizing to overcome this disadvantage and attract sponsors. Thus, the dominant narrative in the film is about class inequality and, ultimately, Katniss's and Peeta's resistance to the power of the Capitol. The story we are *told* is about class and state authority, and, yet, what we are *shown* is a society that is also organized around race, gender, and sexuality.

The In/visibility of Race, Gender, and Sexuality: What *The Hunger Games* Shows Us about Inequality in the Future

In a 2011 interview, just prior to the start of the filming of the first installment of the series, Suzanne Collins, author of the novels and coauthor of the screenplay, described how some of her characters, such as Katniss, were written to be racially ambiguous: "It is a time period where hundreds of years have passed from now. There's been a lot of ethnic mixing."[6] When asked specifically about the book's and film's depictions of the characters Thresh and Rue (played by Dayo Okeniyi and Amandla Stenberg, respectively), the tributes from District 11, Collins stated, "They're African American" and Gary Ross, the film's director and one of the coauthors of the screenplay, added "Thresh and Rue will be African-American. It's a multi-racial culture and the film will reflect that."

In contrast to Collins's and Ross's visions for a "multi-racial culture," the film presents a world that is racially segregated. Scenes of the Capitol show crowds that are predominantly white, with people of color occasionally included. People of color are generally shown singly, rather than in groups, signifying not only that they are a minority but also that racial/ethnic communities may not exist. In shots of District 12, such as the crowd scenes during the reaping ceremony, the population appears overwhelmingly white. *Catching Fire* (2013), the second film in the series, includes scenes from additional districts, and here too the populations are primarily white. While the Capitol and the other districts are predominately white, District 11 is portrayed as having a large African American population, making it the only location in Panem where white people are not the majority. In the first film, shots of District 11 portray a population that is at least half African American, and in the second film, shots of the same district portray a population that is almost entirely African American. Significantly, Districts 11 and 12 are portrayed as the poorest and least powerful. For District 12, this poverty is visually represented through a Depression-era aesthetic and through the construction of District 12 as a mining district, representing a historically poor and working-class white job in the United States. By contrast, District 11 is the agricultural district, and the films draw on the history of African Americans in agriculture, from the dependence of the earlier US agriculture on the system of slavery, to the exploitative sharecropping system, to more contemporary issues such as migrant farm work. Thus, audiences are presented visually with a world that is overwhelmingly white, with some explicit inclusion of African American actors and other individuals of color. While the filmmakers attempt to portray a post-race "multi-racial" society, ultimately, what they portray is not very different than the contemporary United States.

Similarly, when looking at the main characters, the film features an overwhelmingly white cast, while including people of color in several important roles.[7] Characters who hold varying positions of power or who act as representatives of the Capitol government are exclusively white. For example, President Snow (played by Donald Sutherland), the head of the nation, and almost all the Games-related workers, including the Head Gamemaker Seneca Crane (played by Wes Bentley), the District 12 escort, Effie Trinket (played by Elizabeth Banks), and the majority of judges and technicians featured in central scenes related to the Games are white, although people of color are occasionally included in minor roles, such as technicians who help to control the Games. Indeed, the only real exception to these trends is Cinna (played by Lenny Kravitz), Katniss's stylist.[8] Thus, we have a world where white people are both the numerical majority and where they hold the majority of power.

As noted above, race shapes where people live in Panem and their ability to access power as agents of the state. Further, race (alongside class) appears to shape people's chances of being included in the Games. While it was suggested, particularly in the first film, that District 11 was racially diverse, the two tributes in the first film, Thresh and Rue, as well as the two tributes from District 11 in the second film were African American. This actually suggests that the class structure in District 11 is distinctly racialized; that is, African Americans are more likely to be poor(er) and thus more likely to be chosen as tributes for the Games. Thus, *The Hunger Games* presents a world where race is never addressed, but where race clearly matters to the organization of everyday life. In this sense, *The Hunger Games* shows us a future shaped by colorblind ideology,[9] wherein racial inequality persists while both race and racism have ceased to be outwardly acknowledged. Of course, whereas *The Hunger Games* portrayal of an extremely class-divided society is clearly intentional, the same cannot be said for its portrayal of racial inequality. Class (and class-based political) inequality is the organizing narrative of the films; it is something that the film both shows and tells viewers about, whereas racial inequality can be seen but is never named in the films. Similar themes emerge in the films' portrayals of gender and sexuality as organizing systems.

Like race, hierarchies based on gender and sexuality are never explicitly referenced in *The Hunger Games* films. Instead we are ushered into a story that not only focuses on a relatively nuanced account of a strong, young woman, but that also has other strong women in supporting roles, and that to some extent upends prominent heteronormative tropes in film and literature. So, is the future one in which gender and sexuality are no longer central organizing systems? Hardly.

The opening scenes of the first film, which serve to introduce viewers to Katniss and her District 12 home, situate gender as an organizing feature of Panem. The scene opens on Katniss in the home, a private space historically gendered feminine; indeed she is in the home's innermost sanctum, an upstairs bedroom, comforting her younger sister, Prim. While in this space, Katniss is presented as gentle, loving, and nurturing, traits currently coded as feminine in US culture. After leaving her sister, she heads down the stairs and out of the house, and as she does so her demeanor changes, becoming visibly tougher. She puts on the leather jacket (that belonged to her father) and says to the cat (that she allowed her sister to keep though her plan was to kill it) when it hisses at her, "I'll still cook you." Katniss is leaving the house to hunt outside the boundaries of the district, an act that does not simply challenge norms of femininity but challenges the very laws enforced by the Capitol. The way that Katniss's character traverses gender and challenges both the rule of the Capitol and norms of femininity in these early scenes is representative of her character as a whole.

However, while Katniss repeatedly challenges normative notions of femininity, this is not the same thing as saying that gender is no longer an organizing system. In fact, what makes this early scene so strong is the way it is juxtaposed with highly gendered depictions of District 12 as a whole. Shots of Katniss running from her house, through fields, and into the woods outside the district are interspersed with very classically gendered scenes, including women and children in homes, women doing household work, little boys "playing," and men going to the mines.[10] Thus, from the initial scenes of the first film, the audience is introduced to a highly gender organized and segregated world. In District 12, women are shown at home taking care of children, while men are shown going to work. This gendered construction of public and private is made even more stark by Katniss's traversal of the two realms.

As with race, it is important to examine how Panem is populated and in what ways men and women are and are not featured. On the one hand, the films focus on a strong female protagonist and features women in a number of other central supporting roles, most notably Effie Trinket, Katniss's mother, Prim, and a number of the other female tributes, including Rue from the first film.[11] On the other hand, with a few exceptions such as Effie Trinket and some of the members of Katniss's prep team, women do not have a place in the Capitol government or among the workers responsible for orchestrating the Games.

In depicting gender presentation in the films, we see that clothing for most citizens of Panem is highly dichotomized by gender. While Katniss seems to prefer pants and boots and only wears more typically feminine clothing when dressed by others (e.g., her mother and her stylist, Cinna), and all the tributes are dressed in somewhat similar attire while in the arena, the majority of portrayals are heavily gendered. One interesting exception to this overall theme lies in the portrayal of Capitol citizens. While clothing is still relatively gender dimorphic in scenes set in the Capitol, we also see some (gender)queer presentations, particularly in shots of Capitol crowds. Here, gender nonnormativity is part of the broader emphasis on fashion, including extravagant costume and makeup, among inhabitants of the Capitol. These portrayals of gender nonnormative styles function primarily to add to the overall picture of the decadence, vanity, and privilege of the Capitol. Thus, while we may see (gender)queer styles in this future world, they are not adopted by any of the films' protagonists, and there is never any actual reference to the existence of genders or sexualities that are not heterosexual or cisgender.

Like class and race, gender and sexuality are important in organizing not only social life but also the Games themselves. Most obviously, the gender binary organizes the selection of tributes by requiring one male and one female tribute from each district. The very fact that one male and one female are selected in each district tells us that the gender binary is a central organizing system through which people in this future world are categorized. This is further demonstrated in the Third Quarter Quell, held for the 75th Anniversary Games, which is featured in the second film. For this competition, the age specifications are nixed because all tributes are selected from previous Games winners, but the gender specifications are maintained.

Male and female tributes are also presented in fairly gender normative ways, especially in the first film. Male tributes are primarily represented as physically strong and are generally larger in size, while female tributes are generally physically smaller and more often associated with other types of strength. Even when female tributes' strengths are portrayed as physical, the emphasis is on agility rather than brute strength (such as Katniss's skill with a bow). For example, tributes Rue and Foxface (played by Jacqueline Emerson) both survive for a time by, in essence, hiding, which they are able to do because of their intelligence and agility. Interestingly Peeta later also survives by hiding, but only after he is injured. In some ways, the depiction of gender in the Games seems to suggest that gender does not matter. For example, female tributes are shown as vicious killers and, as depicted in the second film, there are many examples of females who won their Games.

In the arena, male and female tributes are dressed identically. Yet we see from the start of the film and visually repeated throughout that the paired boy-girl tributes are central to the ceremony of the Games.

The manufactured romance between Katniss and Peeta is again and again responsible for their literal survival in the Games and in their fight against the Capitol. While Peeta is portrayed as actually being in love with Katniss, it is also clear that his on-air confession of this crush to Caesar Flickerman prior to entering the arena is a strategic move to endear the public to himself and especially Katniss.[12] Katniss is furious at Peeta for his confession, saying, "He made me look weak," to which Haymitch retorts, "He made you look desirable." This is significant because throughout the films Katniss is portrayed as being unappealing and unliked because of her toughness. It is of course typical of a Hollywood film that Jennifer Lawrence, an actress who was cast in part because she was "naturally pretty underneath her tomboyishness,"[13] could be constructed as needing help to make her "look desirable." However, the larger point is that in this future, women are still valued for their physical/aesthetic qualities and their appeal to men, and heternormativity structures ideas about gender, sexuality, and relationships. In the Games, they are able to gain gifts from sponsors who positively respond to their (pretend) love story. After Katniss and Peeta's act of defiance at the end of their first Games, they must make everyone believe that the act was done out of love, not resistance. Thus, it is continuously reinforced that only the creation of heterosexual romance can save their lives.

One of the most striking features of the first film is how it plays with heteronormative constructions of romance and sexuality. However, the powerful female protagonist who has no interest in romance beyond using it as a strategy in the Games is not sustained through the series. On the one hand, it is commendable that the film series does not immediately or only portray Katniss via romantic interests and attachments. On the other hand, that Katniss will develop romantic and sexual feelings for both young men in her life and that she will eventually choose one of them is nonetheless a foregone conclusion. In other words, that Katniss will develop romantic and sexual feelings, that these feelings will be heteroromantic/sexual, that they will be directed toward the two boys similar to her in age, race, and geographic origin, and that she may initially harbor feelings toward more than one of them, but that she must eventually choose one are completely in line with contemporary heteronormative ideology.[14] Thus, while the story line in some ways challenges heteronormativity by portraying it as manufactured, it ultimately reifies heteroromantic love as both natural and inevitable and magical and transformative.[15]

Conclusion

Race, gender, and sexuality are clearly organizing systems in the present-day United States, and they continue to be in the future world of Panem as envisioned by the creators of *The Hunger Games*. Indeed, in some ways, the future envisioned here differs primarily in that, while racism, sexism, and heterosexism are still very real, we are even less able and willing to address them. This contrasts with the critical account of economic and class-based political inequality that functions as a central narrative in the series. In a way the narrative of the films is telling us that the dystopian future is one in which class inequality has been taken to an extreme, an extreme that can only be addressed via revolution. Unfortunately, this somewhat radical message, certainly progressive for a mainstream, blockbuster young-adult series, is unable or unwilling to grapple with race, gender, and sexuality in an equally collective and systematic way. While the films contain interesting challenges to gender normativity and heteronormativity, as a whole, race, gender, and sexuality and challenges to inequalities based on these systems are portrayed in individual terms. This portrayal reflects the interrelated tendencies to center class in analyses of power and inequality, to fail to see race, gender, and sexuality as socially constructed and as institutional as well as individual, and to struggle to think intersectionally about various systems of oppression. While the depiction of a clear challenge to class inequality and (uneven) resistance to gender norms marks *The Hunger Games* as more political than standard Hollywood fare, we suggest that there is a missed opportunity to further delve into how multiple forms of oppression operate in this dystopian future society or to provide commentary critiquing intersecting systems of inequality in the contemporary United States.

Notes

1. *The Hunger Games* books, written by Suzanne Collins, include *The Hunger Games* (2008), *Catching Fire* (2009), and *Mockingjay* (2010). Lionsgate is responsible for the film adaptions, the first two of which were released in 2012 and 2013. In this chapter, we focus primarily on the first film adaption, *The Hunger Games* (2012), scripted by Suzanne Collins, Gary Ross, and Billy Ray and directed by Gary Ross. We also occasionally reference *Catching Fire* (2013), the second film in the series, which is based on a screenplay by Simon Beaufoy and Michael DeBruyn and directed by Francis Lawrence.
2. During the first uprisings, District 13 forced a stalemate by training their nuclear weapons on the Capitol. District 13 then agreed to essentially play dead in exchange for their independence. The Capitol bombed the surface and claimed that the entire district had been destroyed, though in reality the District inhabitants continued to live underground. However, the survival of District 13 was

hidden from the public and thus the inhabitants of the other districts believed that District 13 had been decimated and all its people killed. This manufactured annihilation served as an important tool in quelling rebellion in other districts.
3. Gayle Rubin, "The Traffic in Women: Notes on the Political Economy of Sex," in *Toward an Anthropology of Women*, ed. R. R. Reiter (New York: Monthly Review Press, 1975), 157–210. Rosemary Hennessy, *Materialist Feminist and the Politics of Discourse* (New York: Routledge, 1992).
4. Patricia Hill Collins, *Black Feminist Thought: Knowledge, Consciousness, and the Politics of Empowerment* (New York: Routledge, 2000). Kimberly Crenshaw, "Mapping the Margins: Intersectionality, Identity Politics, and Violence against Women of Color," *Stanford Law Review* 43 (1991): 1241–1299.
5. Audre Lorde, "There is No Hierarchy of Oppressions," *Bulletin: Homophobia and Education* 14 (1983): 9.
6. Karen Valby, "Team 'Hunger Games' Talks: Author Suzanne Collins and Director Gary Ross on Their Allegiance to Each Other, and Their Actors," *Entertainment Weekly*, April 7, 2011.
7. On the one hand, some fans objected to the casting of Jennifer Lawrence, a white woman, in the role of Katniss, who is described in the book as having "straight black hair" and "olive skin." This objection was fuelled further by the fact that the casting call specified "caucasian" actresses, meaning that women of color were not even considered for the role (John Jurgensen, "The Newcomers," *Wall Street Journal*, February 25, 2011). On the other hand, despite the book's explicit descriptions of nonwhite characters, there were fans who were vocal in their shock or objection to these characters being portrayed by people of color. These racist reactions in an unintentional way created the impression that casting in *The Hunger Games* was quite diverse. However, this overshadows several important issues in the overall racial and ethnic casting of the films.
8. While we do not discuss the third book or third and fourth installments of the film series in this chapter, the character of Boggs, who is second in command to District 13 president, is played by Mahershala Ali, an African American actor, in *Mockingjay, Part I* (2014).
9. Eduardo Bonilla-Silva, *Racism Without Racists: Color-Blind Racism and the Persistence of Racial Inequality in the United States* (Lanham, MD: Rowman and Littlefield, 2006).
10. Indeed, in these opening scenes, the one adult man not shown going to work or working in the mines is an old man featured sitting and eating outside of a home or some other building. He is elderly, so it is fitting that he is the one adult man not shown being "productive." In other words, only women, very young boys, and the elderly are not shown working in or going to the mines.
11. The second film included several other prominently featured women tributes and the third film features President Alma Coin (played by Julianne Moore), who is the female president of District 13. It is interesting though to note that the movies totally omit Katniss's one female friend from her home district, despite the fact that she is treated as an important albeit minor character in the books.

12. The interaction between Caesar and Peeta in this scene starts off somewhat flirtatiously with the two smelling one another, before Caesar quickly shifts the subject to ask Peeta if there is a "special girl." Thus, the implicit homoeroticism of their initial exchange is quickly rectified through the emphasis on Peeta's heterosexuality, a move that seems strikingly like the future-world equivalent of "no homo."
13. These are direct quotes from the casting guidelines used when looking for actresses to play the role of Katniss in the film, as cited in Jurgensen, "The Newcomers."
14. In contrast, Madge Undersee, the daughter of District 12's mayor, who is Katniss's only friend other than Gale, and the only other nonfamilial, age-similar character from the district that Katniss cares about, is never construed as a potential love interest. And while she is a relatively important supporting character in the books, responsible for instance for bestowing Katniss with the Mockingjay pin, she is completely omitted from the films.
15. Karin A. Martin and Emily Kazyak, "Hetero-Romantic Love and Heterosexiness in Children's G-Rated Films," *Gender & Society* 23 (2009): 315–336.

CHAPTER 5

Post-Apocalyptic Inequalities: Race, Class, Gender, and Sexualities in *Firefly*

J. Sumerau and *Sarah L. Jirek*

On September 20, 2002, many American television viewers tuned in to FOX Broadcasting Company and were greeted with the image of stars in a black sky. As the night sky shifted into images of a futuristic world, a calm voice explained:

> After the Earth was used up, we found a new solar system and hundreds of new Earths were terraformed and colonized. The central planets formed the Alliance and decided all the planets had to join under their rule. There was some disagreement on that point. After the war, many of the Independents who had fought and lost drifted to the edges of the system, far from Alliance control. Out here, people struggled to get by with the most basic technologies; a ship would bring you work, a gun would help you keep it. A captain's goal was simple: find a crew, find a job, keep flying.

With these words,[1] viewers were introduced to *Firefly*, a post-apocalyptic science fiction narrative exploring the adventures of nine people sharing a spaceship and their lives in a new world. Although the television show only lasted for one season, *Firefly* expanded into a media franchise including, but not limited to, a major motion picture (titled *Serenity*, 2005), comic books, novels, role-playing games, and a dedicated fan base referred to as "browncoats."[2]

Echoing recent trends and enduring patterns in the science fiction genre, *Firefly*[3] offers a speculative portrayal of human existence following the destruction of Earth, and, in so doing, reveals an attempt to imagine a social reality under different sociohistorical circumstances. Set on a variety of planets and moons in the year 2517, the series makes use of technological advances, social and natural environments, and mystical possibilities that lie beyond the realm of human experience and observation. Similarly, the events of the series rest at the end of an alternate timeline wherein humans render the earth uninhabitable, develop the technological ability to colonize and migrate to another solar system, and fight a massive war in the new solar system that results in the domination of all humankind by a central authority (named the Alliance) characterized by the integration of Chinese and American cultural traditions.

Despite the proliferation of similar narratives—including *I am Legend* (2007), *After Earth* (2013), *The Walking Dead* (2010), *The Hunger Games* (2012), *The Book of Eli* (2010), and *Battlestar Galactica* (2004–2009)—in recent years, the social implications of these narrative patterns have received little scholarly attention to date. This chapter examines some ways in which this post-apocalyptic narrative reproduces existing societal patterns of inequality. Specifically, we examine how *Firefly*, despite being a futuristic vision of a post-apocalyptic world, reproduced contemporary societal notions of race, class, gender, and sexualities that facilitate the ongoing subordination of racial and sexual minorities, women, and lower-class (especially rural) people. Although the ability to create a new world could have provided an opportunity to present a more progressive future, our analyses reveal that *Firefly* replicates and reinforces social inequalities by transplanting existing stereotypes, hierarchical social relations, and notions of imperialism into their post-apocalyptic environment.

Importantly, social scientists have long conceptualized media representations as "enabling conditions" for the reproduction of social inequalities.[4] Rather than explicitly causing phenomena, behavior, or patterns within society, media depictions reflect existing patterns of inequality in the environments wherein they are created. As a result, the production, content, and consumption of media may be used to justify and encourage racist, sexist, classist, and heterosexist understandings of the way the world is or should be.[5] Critically evaluating the content and implications of media thus offers an important avenue for making sense of existing social inequalities, as well as potential mechanisms for progressive social change.

To this end, research convincingly demonstrates that a wide variety of media offerings often reproduce societal patterns of inequality. In her examination of daytime talk shows, for example, Collins[6] found that such shows reproduced the devaluation of lower-class people and racial minorities by depicting them as irresponsible parents, unfaithful and promiscuous romantic partners, and morally deficient beings. Similarly, Ezzell[7] found that mainstream pornography, "men's" magazines, and popular video games often valorized sexual violence against women and notions of manhood predicated upon asserting control over women. Further, researchers have found that even seemingly progressive depictions of minority groups may reproduce systems of inequality by, for example, presenting racial minorities as magical beings devoted to helping white people reach their potential,[8] feminizing gay male characters,[9] or encouraging girls to focus upon the needs of others and downplay their own goals.[10] Whereas these studies do not explicitly focus upon post-apocalyptic media, they do suggest that there may be much to learn by examining the ways in which these depictions subvert and/or reproduce societal patterns of inequality. Building upon these insights, we examine the representation of race, class, gender, and sexualities in *Firefly*.

Racial Representations in *Firefly*

Superficial readings of *Firefly* could give viewers the impression of a racially progressive enterprise. By offering a series containing three people of color in primary roles and many examples of people of color in background settings, for example, the series offers more racial diversity in terms of casting than is common in mainstream media. In a similar fashion, the presentation of an interracial marital relationship within the main cast demonstrates recognition of the diversity of racial relationships in contemporary mainstream society. Whereas these representations are promising at the beginning of the series, a closer reading of the overall depiction of racial and ethnic relations reveals a tendency to rely upon and reproduce "controlling images"[11] that have long been used to facilitate and justify the subordination of people of color.

A notable example of such controlling images may be found in the portrayal of women of color as either overly masculine or highly sexualized. Zoe, a multiracial woman who serves as the first mate on the ship, for example, is typically depicted as a hypermasculine fighting machine (e.g., see her portrayal in the television show's opening credits) who often dominates her white male husband (e.g., see her argument with her husband concerning future offspring in episode 13) and is not even allowed an emotional reaction other than traditionally masculine reactions including anger, recklessness, and violence at the sight of her husband's death (see *Serenity*). In a similar fashion, the other woman of color in the main cast (named Inara and portrayed by a Brazilian American actress) plays the role of a "companion" (similar to a modern-day, high-end escort) wherein she is almost always dressed in a sexual manner, repeatedly referred to as a "whore" by the ship's captain, and often the site of white men's violence. Rather than fully formed characters capable of a broad spectrum of emotions and self-presentations, these characters are limited to longstanding racialized constructions of the "exotic lover" and the "overly masculine warrior woman."[12] Following Collins,[13] these controlling images reproduce racial themes that justify the subordination (e.g., use for battle or sex) of racial minorities while bolstering existing sexual (e.g., moral sexual subjects do not sell access to their bodies) and gendered (e.g., women of color are not sexually passive and devoid of masculinity like white females) stratification systems.

Another example of these controlling images may be seen in depictions of the other racial minority in the main cast. Shepherd Book, an African American male, is constructed as a Holy Man with a complicated past who often provides spiritual and practical guidance to white crew members, rarely partakes in the battles, and is one of only two main characters to die (the other is the white male married to Zoe). While the portrayal of a spiritual man of color might seem unworthy of notice in isolation, Shepherd Book fits perfectly into a common media trope that researchers refer to as the "magical negro" (MN).[14] Especially popular in American media since the 1990s—see, for example, films like *Bruce Almighty* (2003), *The Green Mile* (1999), *The Legend of Bagger Vance* (2000), and *The Matrix* (1999)—the MN is usually a male person of color that exists within storylines for the sole purpose of helping white characters reach their true potential or navigate through times of personal turmoil.[15] Rather than providing an advancement in the social construction of racial minorities, such characters ultimately reproduce the subordination of racial minorities to the desires and dreams of white others, and provide white audience members with a "more comfortable" form of racial exploitation. Further, these depictions typically rely on the presentation of "good" or "moral" men of color as devoid of sexual and masculine development (Shepherd Book has no sexual plotline and stands in contrast to the more assertive white male characters), which reproduces sexual and gender hierarchies embedded within contemporary society.[16]

Importantly, Shepherd Book stands in stark contrast to the other two men of color that hold prominent speaking roles. Both of these characters (see episode 14 and *Serenity*) are presented as villains, and they reproduce widespread images of black masculinity predicated upon physical prowess and violence.[17] Not surprisingly, the white male captain of the ship ultimately defeats them both, albeit, in the case of the first character's defeat, with the assistance of a white female character. Further, the distinction between these two villains and the three people of color in the main cast also reproduces longstanding patterns of "colorism"[18] in American society, wherein lighter-skinned racial minorities like the three main characters are treated more favorably than darker-skinned racial minorities like the two villains. More than mere villains in a story, these characters echo the racial and color hierarchies within contemporary American society. Further, the presentation of black male villains echoes longstanding American fears about the potential power and aggressiveness of men of color, and supports the oft-repeated theme regarding the ultimate victory of white masculinity.[19] Similar to the other controlling images noted above, the portrait of the villains ultimately serves to reinforce the combination of racial hierarchies and existing patterns of gender inequality.

Social Class Representations in *Firefly*

Similar to the depiction of race in *Firefly*, the series' treatment of social and economic classes could initially be interpreted as somewhat progressive. For example, the villains tend to be either rich people benefiting from colonization or violent adversaries devoted to the pursuit of money. Considering that American media typically celebrate people that get rich via exploitation (e.g., the founding fathers of the United States) or through methods that have little to do with merit (e.g., many depictions of US presidents and leaders of industry), the portrait of all wealthy people as villains stands in stark contrast to existing norms, which may echo growing criticism of the concentration of wealth within 1% of the American population.[20] On the other hand, *Firefly* echoes longstanding American appreciation for stories of self-made "men" who pull themselves up by their own bootstraps in the face of incredibly difficult odds. Specifically, the series focuses on the exploits of a group of heroes that, for the most part, would be considered "working class" in terms of cultural presentations, monetary possessions, and personal backgrounds. While the challenge against the power of rich people is once again promising on the surface, even if nestled within comfortable storylines about plucky heroes from the bottom strata fighting against corruption, the overall class representations offered in the series ultimately reproduce and implicitly justify existing economic inequalities.

Although the show's creators could have taken the opportunity to design an equitable economic structure created via peaceful means for their futuristic world, this is not the path they took. Instead, the series takes place within an Empire established through violent means and the colonization of other lands, worlds, and peoples. In fact, the form of imperialism represented in the show mimics our own world history by hoarding technological, monetary, and military resources within the central locations of the Alliance, while leaving the outer rims of the empire to make do with outdated and limited technology, weaponry, and economic resources. As scholars of socioeconomic status have long shown, such depictions, regardless of the creators' intentions, suggest that economic inequalities are natural, expected, and necessary parts of social life.[21] Further, such depictions reinforce the normalcy of violence, imperialism, and colonization by suggesting that these atrocities would likely occur at any time and within any environment.²² Rather than using artistic speculation to present the possibility of a more economically egalitarian world, *Firefly* thus asks viewers to accept economic inequalities as natural and inevitable manifestations of human experience.

Alongside the normalization of economic disparities and imperial governing structures, the series often reproduces existing economic class tensions by relying upon stereotypical depictions of upper and lower classes. In its representation of people on the outer planets, for example, the series draws upon cultural notions of "backward rednecks," rural hostility and violence, and "quaint" small town traditions to define rural, lower-class people as utterly distinct from decent, economically prosperous folk (see, for example, episodes 1, 2, 6, and 7). Similarly, the series paints urban life as riddled with riches, style, and corruption wherein upper-class people automatically seek to abuse and oppress others (see, for example, episodes 2, 3, and 4, and *Serenity*). For example, the character of Simon, a white doctor raised in an upper-class home, often draws distinctions between the "rough" behaviors (e.g., drinking alcohol, engaging in lewd behavior, and using foul language) of the rest of the crew and the more "gentle" behaviors (e.g., engaging in conversation, valuing education, and having faith in people) of the people where he grew up. Echoing contemporary cultural distinctions between rich and poor, these representations thus reinforce and justify capitalistic beliefs concerning the inherent "difference" between economic classes of people.²³

Finally, *Firefly* reproduces economic stratification by mirroring patterns of historical imperialism in their depiction of the Reevers. Although the Reevers are portrayed throughout the television series as violent savages that kill and eat other people, the companion film reveals that they became this way because of experiments conducted by the Alliance on the outer planets. Seeking to find a way to better control the working people of the empire, the Alliance tested chemicals that were supposed to reduce aggression in humans, but in so doing they killed the vast majority of test subjects and produced the hyperaggressive Reevers. Similar to depictions of Native Americans, the Reevers are basically deemed "savages" due to their response to the practices of their white overlords (i.e., experiments by the Alliance in the Reevers case and mass extermination policies and relocation efforts in the Native American case).²⁴ Further, the use of Reevers for medical experimentation echoes the experimental starvation, testing, and imprisonment of Native Americans (justified as a way to create a more docile and obedient Native population)²⁵ and experimental sterilization and drug-testing programs on African Americans (justified as a way to better control African American sexualities).²⁶ As such, the economic structure—as well as the imperial constructions of disadvantaged people—of *Firefly* recreates the sexual, economic, and racial violence of our present in the construction of a potential future. In so doing, *Firefly* ultimately tells viewers that the structural violence that established contemporary capitalism, the separation of our world into industrial and nonindustrial sectors, and international patterns of racial disparities are common and predictable outcomes of world-building, and that they are likely to occur in all times and places.

In fact, *Firefly* does not use the Reevers to address similar issues in our world. Instead, the Reevers are depicted as unsalvageable others, sacrificed to the Alliance forces so that the main characters can escape from attacks, and not even mentioned in the closing lines of the story (see *Serenity*). Further, the story ends with the Alliance still in power, and without any further attempts by the main characters to spread awareness about the cruel and tragic backstory of the Reevers. The atrocities of the past—much as they are in contemporary American history textbooks[27]—are only mentioned to further the storyline of the main (mostly white) characters who demonstrate shock and disgust at what happened to the Reevers without actually accomplishing any meaningful change or dissemination of this information after the fact (see *Serenity*). As such, the violent exploitation of the Reevers and the role of this mistreatment and oppression in the economic might of the Alliance are offered to the viewers without critique or resolution. While these elements could have been used to shed light on the exploitation at the foundation of our own economic system, *Firefly* instead uses them only for dramatic effect, and, in so doing, implicitly justifies and normalizes such devastating societal patterns, both in *Firefly* and in our world.

Gender Representations in *Firefly*

In terms of gender, *Firefly* mirrors the patriarchal organization of contemporary American society. Following Johnson,[28] a society is patriarchal to the extent that it is male-dominated, male-identified, and male-centered. Although all men will not have power over all women in such an arrangement, men typically dominate positions of power and authority, the valuable resources and attributes of society tend to be associated with men and masculinity, and the cultural focus tends to be on men and what men do.[29] *Firefly* reflects each of these patriarchal patterns while promoting a version of manhood characterized by men's control over the environment and others.

Firefly can be defined as male-dominated throughout its entirety. Despite the numerous female characters, men hold all of the prominent positions within the storyline, including the leaders of the Alliance, the captain and pilot of the ship, the only doctors and religious leaders ever mentioned, and the vast majority of military roles. Similarly, most of the camera time is taken

78 • J. Sumerau and Sarah L. Jirek

up by the endeavors of the ship's captain, and when the occasional dispute breaks out within the group, his word is the final authority that others must follow. As such, the futuristic universe presented in *Firefly* could be considered a patriarchy.[30]

Patriarchal arrangements also tend to be male-identified (i.e., arrangements where men and what men do are identified as the primary sources of value) and *Firefly* is no exception. During numerous sequences, for example, characters emphasize the importance of being tough, strong, and cool under pressure, which are qualities historically associated with masculinities and male bodies within the context of the American popular imagination.[31] Further, the series regularly defines men as powerful beings and equates power with men's control over the ships and planets, which are typically referred to by feminine pronouns. In fact, the impetus to demonstrate manhood by controlling feminine "things" is explicit at times. In episode 7, for example, a rich white male explains that his son is "not a real man" yet because he has not "had" a woman. Similarly, in episode 13, the primary villain of the episode marshals a fighting force while demonstrating what "a woman really is to a man" by having a female prostitute perform fellatio on him in front of the crowd. In these and other examples, *Firefly* consistently identifies power with men and men's bodies, and demonstrates this identification through men's control over feminine others.[32]

While *Firefly* explores the experiences of female characters at times, the overall focus of the series remains male-centered or fixed upon the endeavors of men. Throughout the entire storyline, men outnumber women in every scene except for episode 13, where the majority of the action takes place in a brothel. Similarly, there are entire episodes where the show primarily focuses upon specific male characters. In episode 10, for example, the plot revolves around two men (the ship's captain and pilot) fighting over a woman (the pilot's wife and the ship's first mate, Zoe), and in episode 14, the plot focuses upon a bounty hunter's search for River (a female crew member), which primarily involves him having an extended conversation with the ship's male doctor. Importantly, there were no complementary episodes where women were the primary focus of the plot or where women consumed most of the episode fighting about or searching for male characters. Episode 14 actually comes the closest, but since the entire story revolves around the attempts of one man (the bounty hunter) to wrestle control of River from another man (the ship's doctor), the episode ultimately reaffirms men's control of women. In fact, the greatest proportion of screen time for women involved them serving the needs of men (e.g., Zoe in relation to the ship's captain or the ship's companion with her clients), seeking the attention of men (e.g., the mechanic's crush on the doctor), or running away from men that wanted to harm them (e.g., River seeking to escape the Alliance). As a result, *Firefly* presented a world for men where women typically played supporting roles.

This observation is especially striking since the show's creator (Joss Whedon) is often celebrated for creating shows with "strong" female characters. While many have debated this point, *Firefly* regularly demonstrates that some depictions of "strong" female characters may ultimately serve to reproduce patriarchal patterns. For example, *Firefly* offers "strong" female main characters like Zoe, a multiracial woman whose strength lies in military combat, but who serves at the pleasure of a male captain and exists within a limited depiction of black womanhood; Inara, a woman of color whose strength lies in the ability to sexually control men, but who also relies upon men for her value and protection; and Kaylee, a white woman whose strength lies in the ability to control the ship, but who spends most of her screen time chasing the affection of a man. In fact, episode 14 walks a similar tightrope wherein River demonstrates strength by outsmarting the bounty hunter, but does not actually handle his dismissal. Rather than leading him out of the ship and then pushing him into space herself, she leads him to the ship's captain who then dispatches him. Considering that either character could have pushed an unsuspecting person off of the ship, it is striking that the strong female character instead relies upon the strength of a male to accomplish this simple task. It becomes less notable, however, when viewed through the overall patriarchal depiction of gender throughout the rest of the series.

Sexual Representations in *Firefly*

Alongside the elevation of men, patriarchal patterns of organization typically rely upon the devaluation of women and sexual minorities. Specifically, they are built upon foundational sexual beliefs that define women as objects for the pleasure and desire of males, and reserve masculine status, and the privileged social position that comes with it, for males capable of demonstrating heterosexual prowess.[33] In *Firefly*, this process is accomplished through the construction of female sexualities and the devaluation of sexual minorities. In so doing, *Firefly* reproduces sexual stereotypes that distinguish between overly sexual and asexual femininity, and that posit sexual minorities as separate from normative social relations.[34]

Echoing longstanding racial and sexual distinctions between pure, asexual femininity and sexually aggressive, promiscuous females,[35] *Firefly* presents the sexual habits of female main characters as either sexualized or desexualized. In the case of the white female crew members, the series presented innocent, shy, and timid women who either did not show any interest in sex (River) or demonstrated interest without the ability to acquire sex (Kaylee), and, in so doing, essentially desexualized these characters. In contrast, the series portrayed the women of color in the main cast in a highly sexualized fashion, wherein one of them made her living from sex (Inara) and the other spent more time on screen having sex than any other character (Zoe). This twin process of sexualizing some women (especially women of color) and desexualizing others (especially white women) is part of a historical pattern wherein sexually aggressive women have been defeminized, attacked, and chastised while sexually passive women have been cherished, protected, and sought after to provide sexual services to dominant men.[36] Further, these depictions reinforce controlling images[37] of white women as pure beings in need of protection, and women of color as overly sexual beings that must be controlled.

The series also depicted sexual minorities in overly sexual ways in the few instances where the topic arose. In the case of the ship's companion (Inara), the series contained one episode (episode 10) where she provided services for a female client. During this episode, however, Inara's business is portrayed quite differently. Whereas Inara generally meets her clients away from crew members, the female client is escorted past the crew, who, in turn, react in shocked and sexually suggestive ways. Similarly, whereas Inara is generally only shown with her clients for a moment or two before and after their "business," this episode shows her working on the female client by giving her a massage and shows the two of them kissing. Although her experiences with male clients are primarily private, this plays up the sexual content of her experience with another woman for the benefit of both the rest of the crew and the (presumably) male audience.[38] *Firefly* thus reproduces social patterns wherein female sexual minorities are utilized to please male audiences.[39]

Alongside the aforementioned examples, women are often sexualized throughout the background of the overall story. In episode 13, for example, viewers are shown a visit to a brothel where Jayne (a white male crew member who often serves as the "muscle" of the group) and the ship's captain take advantage of the "services" offered. Importantly, the reactions of these two men mirror societal standards for masculine sexuality by having Jayne (the brutish, aggressive male character) jump at the chance for service and Mal (the masculine leader of the group) initially refuse service before giving in to his seemingly natural urges. In so doing, this depiction reinforces societal beliefs about the inherent and inevitable sexual desire of males, while also differentiating between the ways in which two stereotypes of men (e.g., powerfully aggressive workers versus more restrained and rational leaders) respond to such urges. In another storyline (see episodes 6 and 11), a former companion (a white female named Saffron) continuously uses her sexuality to manipulate, rob, and take advantage of men. In so doing, the storyline reflects long-standing societal notions that women's sexuality is not simply a matter of desire, but rather something women use to control and take advantage of men.[40]

Considering that there is no mention of Saffron actually wanting sex, this depiction defines her sexual prowess—rather than an aspect of her self or urges—as merely an instrumental weapon that may be used against the (supposedly) natural sexual desires of men.[41]

These patterns find their culmination in the limited depiction of sexual minorities aside from the aforementioned example of Inara. In fact, the only other explicit mention of sexual minorities' existence in the *Firefly* universe occurs in episode 13 when the proprietor of the brothel offers her "boys" to the ship's captain. With the classic uneasiness typically associated with homo- and biphobia, as well as heterosexual masculinity,[42] the captain quickly and emphatically informs her that he is not interested. The only other mentions of sexual minority experience occur within the context of homo- and biphobic jokes made by the primary male characters. In these scenes, as well as the scenes noted above, *Firefly* presents a futuristic world where heterosexuality remains dominant, homo- and bisexualities remain unnerving and worthy of ridicule, same-sex activity between females is sensationalized for the male gaze, and women's sexualities are still limited to a no-win decision between asexual purity and promiscuous disgrace. Despite the passage of over 500 years, it would thus appear that little progress has occurred in the realm of sexual relations.

Conclusion

In conclusion, *Firefly* presents a futuristic, post-apocalyptic world wherein humans have migrated away from our current environment and built a brand-new civilization far from Earth. Rather than take the opportunity to construct a fresh new world with more progressive social and political structures, relationships, and norms, however, the series reflects and reproduces many of the problems contained within our current social arrangements. As a result, the future presented throughout the series bears greater resemblance to our current social problems than to an actual exercise in creativity. Specifically, *Firefly*, despite a few superficial suggestions of potential progress, reproduces racial, classed, gendered, and sexual stereotypes that facilitate the ongoing subordination of racial and sexual minorities, women, and lower-class people.

The case of *Firefly* reveals the importance of attending to the ways in which post-apocalyptic media may reinforce, justify, and reproduce existing social inequalities. Rather than simply creating a universe out of thin air, the people producing media draw upon the cultural beliefs, values, and ideals of their own experience, and, in so doing, may, regardless of their intentions, reproduce harmful patterns of action, ideas, and discourses within their works. These practices may in turn naturalize and normalize socially constructed patterns of oppression and privilege including, but not limited to, racism, classism, sexism, heterosexism, and imperialism. Alternately, the people who produce media could be encouraged to use these opportunities to educate media consumers regarding existing and historical patterns of inequality, and to create representations of more progressive and equitable possibilities. Although media producers are in no way obligated and may have to risk financial resources to do so, such actions could bolster efforts toward social change instead of facilitating the ongoing subordination of minority communities. Since we all possess the power to decide what types of media we support, the responsibility falls upon each of us to make media consumption choices that encourage positive social change.

Notes

1. It is important to note that subsequent iterations of the *Firefly* storyline have changed parts of this monologue and backstory. Further, readers should be aware that FOX aired the original episodes out of order, and, as a result, this "beginning" actually takes place at the beginning of episode 2 of the series.
2. "Browncoats" was a nickname given to soldiers on the Independents' side against the Alliance in the Unification War, which was subsequently adopted by the series' fan base in much of the media accumulated since the beginning of the series.
3. Throughout this chapter, we use the phrase "*Firefly*" to refer to the television series and the companion film, *Serenity*. While there are many other components within the overall franchise, we limited our analyses to these cultural artifacts.
4. See, for example, Denis McQuail, *McQuail's Mass Communication Theory*, Sixth edition (Thousand Oaks, CA: Sage, 2010); Michael Schwalbe, *The Sociologically Examined Life: Pieces of the Conversation* (New York: McGraw-Hill, 2007); Michael Schwalbe, Sandra Godwin, Daphne Holden, Douglas Schrock, Shealy Thompson, and Michelle Wolkomir, "Generic Processes in the Reproduction of Inequality: An Interactionist Analysis," *Social Forces* 79 (2000): 419–452.
5. See also Patricia Hill Collins, *Black Sexual Politics: African-Americans, Gender, and the New Racism* (New York: Routledge, 2005); Laura Grindstaff and Joseph Turow, "Video Cultures: Television Sociology in the 'New TV' Age," *Annual Review of Sociology* 32 (2006): 103–125; Robert Jensen, *Getting Off: Pornography and the End of Masculinity* (Cambridge, MA: South End Press, 2007).
6. Collins, *Black Sexual Politics*.
7. Matthew B. Ezzell, "Pornography, Lad Mags, Video Games, and Boys: Reviving the Canary in the Cultural Coal Mine," in *The Sexualization of Childhood*, edited by S. Oflman, 7–32 (Westport: Praeger, 2009).
8. Matthew Hughey, "Cinethetic Racism: White Redemption and Black Stereotypes in 'Magical Negro' Films," *Social Problems* 56 (2009): 543–577.
9. Thomas J. Linneman, "How Do You Solve a Problem Like Will Truman? The Feminization of Gay Masculinities on *Will & Grace*," *Men and Masculinities* 10 (2008): 583–603.

10. Kathleen E. Denny, "Gender in Context, Content, and Approach: Comparing Gender Messages in Girl Scout and Boy Scout Handbooks," *Gender & Society* 25 (2011): 27–47.
11. Collins, *Black Sexual Politics*.
12. Ibid. Also see Miguel Picker and Chyng Sun, *Latinos Beyond the Reel: Challenging a Media Stereotype* (Northampton, MA: Media Education Foundation, 2012) for usage of this image especially in relation to Hispanic women.
13. Collins, *Black Sexual Politics*.
14. Hughey, "Cinethetic Racism."
15. Ibid.
16. See Douglas Schrock and Michael Schwalbe, "Men, Masculinity, and Manhood Acts," *Annual Review of Sociology* 35 (2009): 277–295.
17. Ibid.
18. Collins, *Black Sexual Politics*.
19. Ibid.
20. James W. Loewen, *Lies My Teacher Told Me: Everything Your American History Textbook Got Wrong*, Revised edition (New York: Touchstone Publishing, 2007).
21. Schwalbe, *The Sociologically Examined Life*.
22. Schwalbe et al., "Generic Processes in the Reproduction of Inequality."
23. Candace West and Sarah Fenstermaker, "Doing Difference," *Gender & Society* 9 (1995): 8–37.
24. Loewen, *Lies My Teacher Told Me*.
25. Andrea Smith, *Conquest: Sexual Violence and American Indian Genocide* (New York: South End Press, 2005).
26. Collins, *Black Sexual Politics*.
27. Loewen, *Lies My Teacher Told Me*.
28. Allan G. Johnson, *The Gender Knot: Unraveling Our Patriarchal Legacy* (Philadelphia, PA: Temple University Press, 2005).
29. Schrock and Schwalbe, "Men, Masculinity, and Manhood Acts."
30. Johnson, *The Gender Knot*.
31. Michael Kimmel, *Guyland: The Perilous World Where Boys Become Men* (New York: Harper, 2008).
32. Ibid.
33. Ibid.
34. Michael Warner, *The Trouble with Normal: Sex, Politics, and the Ethics of Queer Life* (New York: Free Press, 1999).
35. Collins, *Black Sexual Politics*.
36. Ibid.; Ezzell, "Pornography, Lad Mags, Video Games, and Boys"; Johnson, *The Gender Knot*.
37. Collins, *Black Sexual Politics*.
38. Ezzell, "Pornography, Lad Mags, Video Games, and Boys."
39. Warner, *The Trouble with Normal*.
40. Kimmel, *Guyland*.
41. Warner, *The Trouble with Normal*.
42. Ibid.

Part II

The Future in Flux

CHAPTER 6

Queer Resistance in an Imperfect Allegory: The Politics of Sexuality in *True Blood*

Stacy Missari

Introduction

The following is from a public service announcement brought to you by the American Vampire League:

> Don't let anyone tell you that discrimination no longer exists in this country, because it does. Our darkest moments as a nation have been when good people turn a blind eye to oppression, intolerance, and injustice. Our greatest triumphs have stemmed from an unwillingness to accept these conditions. When our citizens have stood up and said, "No not in my country, not in my name." Stand up. Let yourself be heard. Vampires were people too. Support the Vampire Rights Amendment.

The social and political struggle for and against vampire assimilation serves as the backdrop for the television series *True Blood*, which ran for eight seasons on HBO, from 2008 to 2014.[1] In contrast to the world-destroying events that characterize most post-apocalyptic speculative fiction, *True Blood*'s Great Revelation offers a subtler representation of the difficulties of figuring out a new social order after a major world changing event. In addition to the interpersonal struggles associated with vampire assimilation, the Great Revelation opened up the opportunity for the show to critique a wide range of traditional institutions such as religion, citizenship, family, and sexuality throughout the series run.

True Blood initially gained notoriety for its portrayal of vampires as the presumed stand-in for the LGBTQ community. However, as the show was renewed season after season, the writers were able to further develop the personalities and backstories of its large cast of main characters. Although the political allegory served as the backdrop for the show, its unique contribution lies in its representation of a wide range of sexual, familial, and platonic relationships not typically seen on television. The apocalypse of the Great Revelation has created a permanent space for impermanence—sexuality is more fluid (and all of us, humans in the show and humans watching the show, are forced over and over to confront that); the lines between good and evil are a bit more blurred, and even previously held static notions of personhood are now permanently altered, as vampires demand human rights on the formal policy level and look for love on the personal level.

This chapter will argue that in contrast to much of the post-apocalyptic television and movies which do not capitalize on the opportunity to reimagine traditional societal arrangements after they are destroyed, (see Sumerau and Jirek, Chapter Five, and Gurr, Chapter Two), *True Blood* succeeds as a meditation on the impending future, including sustained challenges to heteronormativity, rather than on a retreat to the past.

A Subtler Apocalypse

True Blood is loosely based on *The Southern Vampire Mysteries* book series by Charlaine Harris, and its central characters—Sookie Stackhouse, a 25-year-old telepathic waitress, and 173-year-old vampire Bill Compton—live in the fictional Bon Temps, Louisiana. The show begins in real time in 2008, two years after its apocalyptic moment—The Great Revelation—when vampires, headed by the American Vampire League, decided to "come out of the coffin." "Mainstreaming" (as it is called in the show), was aided by the creation and distribution of synthetic blood called "Tru Blood," which ostensibly quelled the vampire thirst for real blood and allowed humans to coexist with vampires without fear of being eaten. As an apocalyptic event, the Great Revelation is different than the typical apocalypse we are used to seeing in science fiction. Rather than an event that destroyed Earth, either through nuclear war, alien invasion or a natural disaster, the Great Revelation was a man-made (well, vampire-made) apocalypse which had a slow-moving ripple effect across the United States. Coming out of the coffin not only raised questions about how vampires and humans would live side by side on the individual level, but how this new social group would fit into existing institutions. Although vampires are seemingly identical to humans in all but a few traits, coming out challenged almost everything that humans believed about society and raised a host of fundamental questions. How would this new group of people be classified? Would they have the same rights as humans?

Would they be able to marry humans? Would they be able to own property? Would they be able to vote? Although they were not faced with rebuilding their social world from scratch, the residents of Bon Temps were arguably faced with a more complicated task: to establish a new social order while the old systems were still intact.

Queer Representations and Resistance

Early on in the show, the rules of sexuality, and who could have sex with whom, are challenged by the advent of the Great Revelation. Bon Temps is the stereotypical Deep South town—swampy, sweaty, and conservative, with a constant simmer of racism and homophobia under the surface. The main characters consist of waitresses, cooks, the local sheriff and police, and construction workers. The setting hardly seems ripe for one of the most nuanced portrayals of queer sexuality on television.

Scholars have argued that despite the subversive potential of science fiction, its representation of queer characters in television and film has been "ambivalent" at best.[2] And although the genre has expanded on the monster/victim binary, the storylines of queer characters in contemporary science fiction and fantasy still primarily serve to shore up the normalness of heteronormativity for the audience. For example, at first glance it seems that *True Blood*'s Lafayette Reynolds is just another stereotypical flamboyant black gay man. Lafayette wears makeup and jewelry and is known for his sassy quips and his frequent use of the word "hooker." However, as the series progressed, the audience got to see many different sides to Lafayette. For example, in a scene at Merlotte's Bar and Grill, Lafayette's burger gets sent back because, as the customer Royce Williams says, he "didn't order a burger with AIDS." Lafayette walks up to the table to confront him when Royce says: "I'm an American and I got a say in who makes my food." To which Lafayette replies, "Oh baby, it's too late for that. Faggots been breeding your cows, raising your chickens, even brewing your beer long before I walked my sexy ass up in this motherfucker. Everything on your goddamn table got AIDS." When Royce says that he still doesn't want to eat the "AIDS burger," Lafayette licks the bun, smashes it in his face, and then handily punches him and the two other men at the table out.

Although Lafayette claims to be a person of "poor moral character" and is seen engaging in unseemly activities such as selling drugs, prostitution, and getting into fights, he is also portrayed in equal measure protecting his family and friends, standing up to homophobia, and being a loving and loyal boyfriend. In his analysis of *Torchwood* and *True Blood*, Frederik Dhaenens argues that characters like Lafayette are unique examples of queer resistance to heteronormativity, homophobia, heterosexism, and racism in fantasy and science fiction. I would go further to argue that *True Blood* as a series is a representation of queer resistance.[3] Although there has been debate in scholarly and popular media regarding the "transgressive potential" of *True Blood*, the diversity and complexity of representations of queer characters is an important contribution to increasing the visibility of queer characters in television and film.[4] By showing queer characters as simultaneously heroic, selfish, sexual, violent, and vulnerable, *True Blood* helps us move away from the static representations of gay characters that have dominated media.

In addition to the sheer number of queer characters that make *True Blood* unique, the show consistently presents story lines that normalize gay, lesbian, and bisexual desire and eroticism.[5] Being on a cable network like HBO obviously aids in this respect, but unlike other cable dramas that show explicit sex, *True Blood* does not shy away from showing all types of relationships, sexual identities, and sexual practices. Even if it just takes place in a dream sequence between two heterosexual characters, *True Blood* challenges the notion that "normal" relationships consist of one man and one woman who only engage in missionary sex. And unlike many television shows which may feature one "type" of queer person that fills a certain stereotype, the queer characters in *True Blood* come from all different walks of life. They are powerful vampire kings and queens like Russell Edgington and Sophie-Anne Leclerq. They are closeted political and religious figureheads like Nan Flanagan and Steve Newlin. They are working-class African Americans like cousins Tara Thornton and Lafayette Reynolds.

True Blood also disrupts traditional representations of female heterosexuality and desire. In early seasons of the show, the primary vehicle for this was human/vampire sexual relationships, since being bitten or drinking even a drop of vampire blood ("V") would produce a euphoric sexual experience. Drinking V was illegal in Bon Temps, so humans would indulge in places like the vampire bar Fangtasia, a sort of stand-in for the underground gay bar, where vampires can feed on humans out in the open. Sookie's relationships with vampires Bill and Eric Northman and werewolf Alcide are also a site where traditional notions of female heterosexuality are challenged. Sookie's sexual encounters with vampires has a BDSM-tinged quality to them and throughout the series, we see how Sookie has desires not just for her "one true love" but for different types of men, including the fairy-vampire hybrid Macklyn Warlow.

True Blood also challenges the notion of a static sexual identity and heterosexuality as natural, universal, and fixed at birth.[6] This is true for both vampires and humans in the show. For example, Tara Thornton, Sookie's best friend, has relationships strictly with men until season 4 when she moves to New Orleans and begins dating Naomi, a fellow boxer. Tara also begins a relationship with her vampire maker, Pam Swynford De Beaufort, before meeting the true death. Pam identifies as a lesbian on the show, but through flashbacks we see that she had a sexual relationship with Eric Northman after she was first turned into a vampire by him in the early 1900s. Another example of the rejection of heteronormativity is James Kent, who is introduced in season 6 as the love interest of Jessica Hamby after they meet in a vampire concentration camp. James later falls for Lafayette, and begins a relationship with him in season 7. None of these changes are cause for major discussion between characters in the show and what is considered "modern sexuality" is constantly shifting and being redefined.

Politics in Bon Temps

True Blood is primarily known as a supernatural soap opera in which the drama centers on the sexual and romantic relationships of its characters. The show has also had a notable political undercurrent throughout its entire run that has been the source of many debates and think-pieces from television critics and academics alike. Starting from the show's opening credits, the audience is bombarded with stylized images of religion, racism, sexuality, death, and politics. Most notably is the image of a church billboard reading "God Hates Fangs," a play on the anti-gay Westboro Baptist Church's famous picket slogan "God Hates Fags." Early in the show's run, the central plot revolved around the tension between those who accepted vampires and even engaged in sexual and romantic relationships with vampires—derogatorily called "fangbangers"—and those who rejected the mainstreaming of vampires.

True Blood also features many characters that are stand-ins for actual players in the same-sex marriage debate. The series run coincided with a period of rapid change within the real same-sex marriage movement in the United States. When the show premiered in September 2008, gay marriage was legal in two states and the Defense of Marriage Act (DOMA) still outlawed gay marriage at the federal level. By the time the series wrapped up in 2014, DOMA had been ruled unconstitutional by the Supreme Court and gay marriage had been legalized in 35 states. Although *True Blood* creator Alan Ball has publicly denied that the vampires in the show are a direct metaphor for the LGBT community, it is hard to ignore all of the obvious references. For example, the American Vampire League (AVL) is similar to LGBTQ advocacy organizations like the Human Rights Campaign (HRC) and the Gay and Lesbian Alliance Against Defamation (GLAAD) in its structure and political messaging. Leaders of the AVL, like Nan Flanagan, are seen appearing on political talk shows debating conservative politicians about the Vampire Rights Amendment (VRA)—a Civil Rights Act/anti-DOMA-type of legislation. In their political statements, the AVL's party line is similar to mainstream marriage equality discourse. For example, in an interview Nan Flanagan says: "It's important to remember that we're not asking for any special privileges. We simply want to be treated like any other member of society. It comes down to equality, a concept I think all Americans can understand and are willing to fight for." In another interview, Nan debates David Finch, a conservative Louisiana congressman about the political maneuvering surrounding the VRA. In response to Finch's claim that Americans are not behind the VRA, Nan cites specific statistics: "We are two states shy of the three-quarter majority needed to change the US constitution" and "marriage between a human and a vampire is now legal in six states."

Continuing the thick political allegory, *True Blood* also features the viewpoints of anti-vampire groups and politicians, who adopt the language of the conservative right. For example, the anti-vampire church/activist group the Fellowship of the Sun released the following PSA:

> I don't want them living in my neighborhood. As soon as one moves in, the property values go down all over the place. I just don't feel safe at night anymore. I don't want them anywhere near my kids. Children see this lifestyle and maybe they want to imitate it. They're just so unnatural. Should we just let them go into whatever they want? Absolutely not. They make me scared. Say no to the Vampire Rights Amendment.

The appeal to keeping children safe and protecting families from a certain "lifestyle" is similar to the political discourse of anti-gay groups such as the National Organization for Marriage and Focus on the Family. The appropriation of this political rhetoric from the left and right is not only featured in episodes of the show, but also in an extensive selection of web-based extras featuring PSAs, ads, mock White House conferences, and other media produced by the show and fans, with very little distinction between the two.

Later seasons of the show introduce political and religious figures who arguably represent the schisms within the gay marriage movement. One of these characters is the nearly 3,000-year-old Russell Edgington, vampire King of Mississippi, who was introduced in season 3. Edgington is a foil to vampires like Nan Flanagan who are trying to push the equal rights message that "vampires were people too." He represents a more radical viewpoint, questioning why vampires would want access to the same capitalist, patriarchal structures that endorse such ills as "global warming, perpetual war, toxic waste, child labor, torture, and genocide." In one of the most shocking moments of the series, Russell rips the spine out of a news anchor on live TV and offers a diatribe against mainstreaming:

In the end, we are nothing like you. We are immortal . . . And that is the truth the AVL wishes to conceal from you because, let's face it, eating people is a tough sell these days. So they put on their friendly faces to pass their beloved VRA. But make no mistake, mine is the true face of vampires. Why would we seek equal rights? You are not our equals. We will eat you, after we eat your children.

Albeit extremely outrageous, Russell's perspective could arguably be a representation of radical queer groups such as Against Equality, who argue that the social, economic, and legal privileges conferred only via marriage should be available to all people regardless of gender, sexuality, race, or economic status. Advocating for access to the institution of marriage as it is currently constructed, these groups argue, only reaffirms the conservative perspective that family is defined through monogamous legal commitment between two adults.[7]

In later seasons, the show includes references to other injustices such as hate crimes, the Holocaust, terrorism, natural disasters, and the AIDS crisis. In a direct reference to the Civil Rights movement, Nicole Wright, an activist who traveled to Bon Temp to advocate for the rights of supernaturals, urges Sam Merlotte to come out as a shifter. She uses the story of her white grandmother and black grandfather who were Freedom Riders in the 1960s to urge Sam to "stand up and be counted, because then you'll inspire other supernaturals to do the same." In the final season, Sookie and others visit a deserted town where they come across a mass grave and a Hurricane Katrina–like message spray-painted on the road: "FEMA HELP US."

During this point in the series run, the show's central drama moves away from the same-sex marriage allegory to a HIV/AIDS–like outbreak of Hepatitis V, a virus that weakens vampires, causing great pain as it spreads through their bodies, ending in death. The disease spreads rapidly throughout the vampire community, and has no known cause or cure. Vampires infected with Hep V, called H-Vamps, are driven to mania and violence in their search for food, and have decimated surrounding towns. The residents of Bon Temps decide to pair each human with an uninfected vampire for protection against gangs of H-Vamps. The response to the Hep V outbreak mirrors the panic and uncertainty of the early HIV/AIDS epidemic in the United States, when infected gay men were feared and ostracized, even by others in the gay community. In both cases it is clear that the disease marks its host, whether vampire or homosexual human, as a threat to everyone.

In the midst of the outbreak, Bill realizes he has become infected with Hep V and quickly meets with a lawyer to change his will so his estate can be passed down to his progeny, Jessica Hamby. The attorney informs him that because Congress did not pass the Vampire Rights Amendment, Jessica will not be recognized as family and the estate will be auctioned off after Bill dies. He is offered the option of adopting Jessica if he can pay the $10 million fee to be bumped to the beginning of the line, since so many other infected vampires are signed up to do the same. Bill's right to leave his estate to Jessica, whom he considers family, echoes the stories of many gay and lesbian couples who were denied access to shared property, even if they were legally married in another state or country. Bill's case, and many other real cases like it, critique the notion of family as defined by the State to the exclusion of others forms of family, as represented by vampires and their progeny in *True Blood*.

In the final episode of the series, the H-Vamps have been defeated and an antidote for Hep V has been discovered from the blood of televangelist Sarah Newlin. In an infomercial at the end of the episode, we see that Pam and Eric have gained control of the antidote and start selling it, calling it "New Blood." In the end, the antidote is doled out not as a cure, but as a way for Hep V–positive vampires to live a normal life with the disease. The conclusion of the Hep V crisis, which coincides with the end of the series, seems to be a subtle nod to modern HIV/AIDS drugs that allow for the possibility of living with HIV/AIDS rather than an immediate death sentence as it was in the beginning of the epidemic.

Critical Reaction and Public Action

Throughout the series, critics have been mixed about the utility of *True Blood* as a positive representation of the LGBTQ community and the same-sex marriage movement.

The show has been called everything from "a muddled analogy"[8] to "an advertisement for social conservatism."[9] One of the most significant critiques of the show is that vampires, who are claiming they deserve equal rights, are shown perpetrating extreme acts of violence against humans, vampires, and other supernaturals. There are many scenes in which vampires are shown torturing and brutally killing humans for apparently no reason other than for revenge or sport. When the Hep V epidemic takes over Bon Temps, H-Vamps become rabid and take humans as prisoners for their blood. As Louis Peitzman argues, "[i]n this case, the so-called bigots are right. Their discrimination of vampires is reasonable, because all of their fears about vampires are true."[10] Despite their best attempts at mainstreaming, vampires will never fully assimilate into human society, since at their core they have a violent bloodlust and superhuman strength that could be ignited if an alternative source of blood was ever to cease production.

Even Alan Ball, the show's creator, has tried to dissuade the audience from interpreting the show as an overt political statement. In a press conference in

2009, Ball argued that it is "lazy" to see the vampires as a representation of the LGBTQ community because if you do, he said, "then the show could be seen to be very homophobic because vampires are dangerous: They kill, they're amoral."[11] Ball also acknowledges and then dismisses the central criticism of the show saying: "I just hope people can remember that, because it's a show about vampires, it's not meant to be taken that seriously. It's supposed to be fun."[12]

Other critics argue that the show does not just confuse the gay rights metaphor, but is causing actual harm to the LGBTQ community. Lauren Gutterman, coordinator of OutHistory.org, argues that the representations of hypersexual and violent vampires on *True Blood* may in fact perpetuate the negative stereotype of predatory sexuality historically associated with gay men if vampires are to be seen as a stand-in for this group.[13]

Whatever the show-runners and writers of *True Blood* did or did not intend to represent, many of the cast and crew have been visible in the gay rights movement. Anna Paquin, who plays Sookie Stackhouse, has arguably been the most outspoken cast member due in part to her position as lead in the show and her clout as a celebrated actress and celebrity (she won the Academy Award for Best Supporting Actress in 1994). In 2010 Paquin came out as bisexual in a video for the Give a Damn Campaign, created by Cyndi Lauper's True Colors Fund to increase support for LGBT equality. Paquin has subsequently spoken out about bisexual invisibility following her marriage to costar Stephen Moyer, who plays Bill Compton on the show. In the summer of 2014, during the promotional tour for the final season of *True Blood*, Paquin fielded questions from Larry King about her sexuality. King asked Paquin if she is now a "non-practicing bisexual" after marrying a man and becoming a mother. Paquin responded, "Well, I don't think it's a past-tense thing . . . if you were to break up with [somebody] or if they were to die, it doesn't prevent your sexuality from existing. It doesn't really work like that."[14] Paquin reiterated this sentiment, tweeting: "Proud to be a happily married bisexual mother. Marriage is about love not gender."[15] Evan Rachel Wood, who played vampire Queen of Louisiana Sophie-Ann Leclerq, also came out as bisexual in 2011, and has spoken out about bisexual invisibility.[16]

Other cast members have also commented on the political nature of the show. In an interview with the *Advocate* in 2012, Stephen Moyer was asked to comment on some critics' assessment that *True Blood* is "too gay." He responded:

> Is there such a thing as too gay? We live in a very different world than we grew up in, so if people can't embrace that aspect of our show, then that's a shame. I certainly don't think it's specifically gay, but our show ticks a lot of boxes for

a lot of people. We have an incredibly broad audience, one of the widest demographics in terms of sexuality and age groups, so obviously we're doing something right.[17]

Kristin Bauer van Straten, who played Pam, was also quoted in the *Advocate* about the show's function:

> How do you get people to see another viewpoint that they are closed to? Art is a wonderful way to do that. . . . I'm sure there's a lot of people who are watching *True Blood* who are not pro–gay rights, but maybe that opened the door. Maybe it got them to think a little bit.[18]

However problematic *True Blood*'s political discourse is, the show has been consistently praised for its diversity of queer main characters that represent different genders, races, ethnicities, and socioeconomic statuses. Critic J. Bryan Lowder called *True Blood* "one of the most dependably and grippingly queer shows on television"[19] and GLAAD's 2010–2011 "Where We Are on TV" report named the show "the most inclusive program" on cable television.[20] In its 2011–2012 report, GLAAD president Mike Thompson praised *True Blood* not just for its inclusiveness, but also because stories about gay and lesbian characters are woven "into the fabric of the show."[21] Additionally, HBO was given an "Excellent" grade in GLAAD's 2014 Network Responsibility Index, which is "awarded based on the quality, diversity, and relative quantity of LGBT representations in cable and network original programming."[22]

Conclusion

As this chapter shows, the HBO series *True Blood* has been adept at using the "politics of carnival, transgression, and parody" to critique what is consider "normal" at the individual and institutional level, especially when it comes to sexual practices and sexual identity.[23] The supernaturals and humans of Bon Temp exist in a world where traditional, heteronormative desires and relationships coexist with so-called "deviant" categories of gender and sexual identity. As Kristin Bauer van Straten states, one of the main criticisms of the show is actually its strength: "The characters are many shades of good to evil . . . Nobody is really black or white . . . Everyone has one redeeming quality, much like the real world. Life is not so simple and clear."[24]

As Bauer van Straten argues, *True Blood*'s strength as a queer text comes from its nuanced portrayal of its characters, which is more true to how people are in the real world. The damsel in distress may decide on multiple princes, the flamboyant queen can also kick your ass, and the vampire who rips out your spine is just grieving the loss of his boyfriend. It is true there are problematic aspects of *True Blood*'s central allegory of vampires as a direct stand-in for the LGBT community. However, I would argue that this focus obscures the ways in which the show succeeds as a transgressive and innovative representation of queer resistance using the post-apocalyptic vampire narrative.

Notes

1. *True Blood*, Various directors (2008–2014, Home Box Office).
2. Frederik Dhaenens, "The Fantastic Queer: Reading Gay Representations in *Torchwood* and *True Blood* as Articulations of Queer Resistance," *Critical Studies in Media Communication* 30 (2013): 102–116.
3. Although Dhaenens (ibid.) is the first to explore queer resistance in *True Blood*, his analysis only covers seasons 1 and 2.
4. Ibid.; J. M. Tyree, "True Blood and Let the Right One In," *Film Quarterly* 63 (2009): 31–37; Sabrina Boyer, "'Thou Shalt Not Crave Thy Neighbor': True Blood, Abjection, and Otherness," *Studies in Popular Culture* 33 (2002): 21–41.
5. Teresa de Lauretis, "Queer Theory: Lesbian and Gay Sexualities: An Introduction." *Differences: A Journal of Feminist Cultural Studies* 3 (1991): 296–313; Judith Butler, *Gender Trouble: Feminism and the Subversion of Identity* (New York: Routledge, 1990).
6. Ibid.; Michael J. Ryan, "Queer Theory," in *Modern Sociological Theory*, ed. George Ritzer, 507–514 (Boston: McGraw-Hill, 2008); Arlene Stein and Ken Plummer, "'I Can't Even Think Straight:' 'Queer' Theory and the Missing Sexual Revolution in Sociology," *Sociological Theory* 12 (1994): 178–187.
7. Ryan Conrad, ed., *Against Equality: Queer Critiques of Gay Marriage* (Lewiston, ME: Against Equality Publishing Collective, 2010).
8. Louis Peitzman, "Why the Civil Rights Allegory on True Blood is So Misguided." *Buzzfeed*, Last modified June 2013, http://www.buzzfeed.com/louispeitzman/why-the-civil-rights-allegory-on-true-blood-is-so-misguided
9. Annalee Newitz, "Let's Face It: True Blood Hates Gay People," *io9*, Last modified November 2008, http://io9.com/5071755/lets-face-it-true-blood-hates-gay-people
10. Peitzman, "Why the Civil Rights Allegory on True Blood is So Misguided."
11. Maxine Shen, "Flesh & 'Blood,'" *New York Post*, Last modified June 2009, http://nypost.com/2009/06/23/flesh-blood/
12. Ibid.
13. Ibid.
14. Eliel Cruz, "Larry King is Confused by Anna Paquin's 'Non-Practicing' Bisexuality: In a Recent Interview, the *True Blood* Star Talked Fangs, Blood, and Her Sexuality." *Advocate*, Last modified July 2014, http://www.advocate.com/bisexuality/2014/07/31/larry-king-confused-anna-paquins-non-practicing-bisexuality

15. *Twitter.com*, Last modified June 2014, https://twitter.com/AnnaPaquin/status/475840799775547392
16. Trish Bendix, "Evan Rachel Wood on Her Queer Roles, Educating Others about Bisexuality and Her Preference for Suits." *After Ellen*, Last modified February 2013, http://www.afterellen.com/tv/105500-evan-rachel-wood-on-her-queer-roles-educating-others-about-bisexuality-and-her-preference-for-suits/2
17. Brandon Voss, "Stephen Moyer: Bleeding Heart: True Blood's Stephen Moyer would Love to Consummate His Onscreen Bromance with Alex Skarsgård, but He Doesn't Really Need to See Costar Joe Manganiello Strip in Magic Mike," *Advocate*, Last modified July 2012, http://www.advocate.com/print-issue/current-issue/2012/07/12/stephen-moyer-asks-there-such-thing-too-gay
18. Daniel Reynolds, "The Supernatural Civil Rights Movement of True Blood: Actress Kristin Bauer van Straten and Media Authorities from GLAAD and Outfest Reflect on the LGBT Legacy of True Blood," *Advocate*, Last modified June 2014, http://www.advocate.com/arts-entertainment/television/2014/06/20/supernatural-civil-rights-movement-true-blood?page=full
19. J. Bryan Lowder, "True Blood's Queer Legacy," *Slate*, Last modified June 2014, http://www.slate.com/blogs/outward/2014/06/25/true_blood_reviewed_why_hbo_s_vampire_show_is_a_queer_masterpiece.html
20. The Gay & Lesbian Alliance Against Defamation (GLAAD). *Where We Are on TV, 2010–2011* (2011).
21. Ibid.
22. GLAAD, *Network Responsibility Index, 2014* (2014).
23. Stein and Plummer, "I Can't Even Think Straight," 178–187.
24. Reynolds, "The Supernatural Civil Rights Movement of True Blood," 2014.

CHAPTER 7

Woman as Evolution: The Feminist Promise of the *Resident Evil* Film Series

Andrea Harris

Global warming? Alien invasion? Nuclear war? Machine overlords? Global plague? Pandemic virus? Contemporary post-apocalyptic films and television programs provide us with multiple potential world endings, and, as if the world ending wasn't bad enough, our neighbors in the after-world seem likely to be the flesh-eating undead. Largely silent at the end of the twentieth century, zombie hordes can once again be heard moaning in movie theaters and living rooms. Perhaps the clearest evidence of a zombie revival is the record-breaking 17.3 million viewers who tuned in to watch the season 5 premiere of *The Walking Dead* on cable in October 2014. Today's zombie flicks are the descendants of George Romero's *Night of the Living Dead*—"the Patient Zero of zombie movies and the patron saint of every horror film made after 1968."[1]

Like their ancestors, contemporary zombie tales reveal much about the culture in which they are made and consumed.

The revival of the zombie has been traced to a shift in popular culture coinciding with the September 11, 2001, attacks on the United States: "zombie films came to reflect the worst-case fears of an apprehensive media culture, entertaining the same anxieties about world events, in this case, a fear of terrorism and epidemic in the zombie form."[2] Similarly, Kyle Bishop argues that "a post-9/11 audience cannot help but perceive the characteristics of zombie cinema through the filter of terrorist threats and apocalyptic reality."[3] We recognize, even as we fear, the world in the contemporary zombie movie: in its bleak images of destruction, violence, and human decay, we cannot help but see terrorist attacks and health epidemics.

The current zombie revival is not contained to cinema, however. Zombies first appeared in video games as early as 1993, when first-person shooters took on zombie marines in *Doom*. The first video game to draw directly from Romero's movies was Capcom's *Biohazard* (since renamed *Resident Evil*) in 1996. *Biohazard* is considered part of the survival horror game genre—a genre that "'remakes' the previous conventions of horror, suspense and action that were once only familiar in film."[4] The *Resident Evil* franchise now includes more than a dozen games, five films (with a sixth planned for release in 2016), a plethora of merchandise, multiple websites, a series of graphic novels (endorsed but not owned by Capcom), and even a theme park in Japan. The base storyline of the film and video game series is that the multinational Umbrella Corporation has created a global apocalypse through its secret research into military weaponry and biological engineering. Umbrella's experimental T-Virus has been released into the public, resulting in zombie-like creatures and other, even more dangerous, monsters. Although both the general public and cinema critics tend to have a negative perception of game-to-film adaptations,[5] the commercial success of the *Resident Evil* film adaptations has prompted analysis of the series within both the gaming and the film industries. One component of the film series' success is attributable to *Resident Evil* gamers who have recognized that the films are "in keeping with the evolutionary spirit of the game."[6]

In this analysis, I will be focusing upon the film series specifically. In the games, the character of Alice is only one choice for the first-person gamer role, but in the films, Alice, played by Milla Jovovich, is the protagonist—*the* hero who drives the action. In the films, Alice originally works for Umbrella Corporation as a security operative, but, after deciding to help political activists expose the corporation's secret research, she is forcibly infected with the T-Virus by Umbrella researchers who deem her to be corporation property. When Alice's body unpredictably bonds with the T-Virus, she becomes in essence a biological weapon. However, Alice never behaves as Umbrella's property, let alone their weapon, and instead uses her new powers to save what is left of humanity and take down the corporation. According to Richard J. Hand, part of the series' appeal is that "at its heart *Resident Evil* exploits a sense of conspiracy and cynicism about global capitalism."[7] This placement of the multinational corporation in the role of the evil force against which humanity must defend itself [8] coincides nicely with feminist critiques of capitalism's prioritization of profits over people.[9] However, my particular feminist analysis was prompted by the recognition of the ways in which the character of Alice undoes what Laura Mulvey has termed the "active/passive heterosexual division of labor" in film narrative.[10] Alice, as the protagonist of the action film series, is the character with whom the targeted male audience is meant to identify. Unlike the typical female character in mainstream films, Alice's presence does not "work against the development of the story line" or "freeze the flow of action in moments of erotic contemplation."[11] This positioning of Alice as the action hero indicates possibilities for women's empowerment.

Feminist media analyses focusing on "empowerment" do not share a common understanding of women's empowerment. How one understands female empowerment tends to be linked to how one understands feminism. Third-wave feminists Jennifer Baumgardner and Amy Richards reassure young women that "feminism isn't about what choice you make but the freedom to make that choice."[12] Within this context, any choice, so long as it's freely made, can be viewed as empowering for the individual woman and for women as a whole; the individual woman's freedom to choose is understood as a collective good—the goal—of contemporary feminist struggle. Within post-feminist thought, individual lives are viewed apart from societal institutions and the distribution of power, and it is assumed that society already provides equal freedom of choice to men and women. Thus, there is no longer any need for the collective political action of feminism.[13] From a post-feminist perspective, what matters is individual empowerment, as defined by whatever choice the already "free" woman makes.[14] By way of contrast to both post-feminism and third-wave feminism, second-wave feminism rejects the post-feminist idea that women's freedom has been achieved *and* insists that equality for women includes more than individual freedom. Within second-wave feminism, empowerment cannot be assessed apart from the collective and complete liberation of all women from continuing patriarchal oppression.[15] In this essay, I will be taking a second-wave feminist perspective on female empowerment. In my analysis of the *Resident Evil* film series, women's empowerment is understood as the potential for resisting and rejecting the dynamics of oppression which seek to deny, limit, or control woman's access to both individual and group power. My assessment of empowerment considers possibilities for dismantling the hierarchy upon which patriarchal oppression is based. Within this system, man's place at the top of the social hierarchy is justified through essentialism—the idea that man is both inherently different from *and* superior to woman. Woman is defined only in relation to man, as what man is not, and she becomes "the Other."[16] The *Resident Evil* film series opens up new possibilities for women's empowerment by disrupting the naturalization of woman as the inferior Other to man.

Finding potential for women's empowerment in film designed to appeal to young, heterosexual male gamers requires what is termed an oppositional reading. In reception theory, "the social meaning of film—the uses made of a film by its audience—is produced through the encounters between texts and audiences in contexts."[17] Drawing from Stuart Hall's encoding-decoding paradigm, cultural studies identifies three types of readings—preferred, negotiated, and oppositional.[18] An oppositional reading places the text in an alternative frame of reference.[19] As a viewer participating in the construction of the text's meaning within a specific time and place, I can interpret *Resident Evil* within the context of feminism and its concerns with women's empowerment. According to bell hooks in *The Oppositional Gaze: Black Female Spectators*, "Even in the worst circumstances of domination, the ability to manipulate one's gaze in the face of structures of domination that would contain it opens up the possibility of agency."[20] Even when watching a fashion model-turned-actress kill zombies for the enjoyment of the male gamer, an oppositional gaze can reveal possibilities for women's empowerment. Admittedly, though, this oppositional reading is further complicated by the linking of women's empowerment with the violence perpetrated by Alice throughout the films. When female characters are violent, they are often interpreted to be adopting the destructive masculine behaviors against which feminism has been historically aligned.[21] In addition, since audiences tend to identify with the film's protagonist, there is some concern that increases in actual female violence may be linked to the prevalence of representations of women perpetrating violence.[22] However, it is also commonly acknowledged that "fantasizing that one could be effectual and powerful as an action hero may provide temporary escape from existing feelings of powerlessness."[23] This "escape" from powerlessness is significant because a premise of my analysis is that women must be able to *imagine* themselves with power—must no longer accept women's state of disempowerment as either natural or inevitable—in order to experience empowerment.

According to Monique Wittig in "The Straight Mind": "Although it is has been accepted in recent years that there is no such thing as nature, that everything is culture, there remains within that culture a core of nature which resists examination, a relationship excluded from the social in the analysis . . . I will call it the obligatory social relationship between 'man' and 'woman.'"[24] My argument is that the feminist promise of *Resident Evil* lies in its undoing of the naturalization of that "obligatory social relationship between 'man' and 'woman.'" First, the film series resists key elements of femininity ideology which typically function to confine female action heroes and render them harmless. Although the level of this resistance varies according to specific films, scenes, and characters, overall, the female characters within the series and, in particular, Alice, resist those aspects of traditional femininity which typically function in media to reinforce notions of male superiority. A second way in which the film series disrupts patriarchal ideology is by severing gender from sex and thus revealing the gender dichotomy to be a constructed falsehood.

Throughout the series, human survival trumps gender performance: strong characters within the films possess similar traits and behave in similar ways, regardless of sex. Gender is revealed to be "performative"—created through specific acts, as contrasted to being innately sexed.[25] The third, and perhaps most controversial, way in which the series disrupts patriarchal essentialism is through the imagined reconstruction of the hierarchy upon which patriarchal power rests. The films present the possibility that woman may have the biological potential to be more than man, more than human. This possibility for a reversal of position in the sex binary is empowering for women because it undoes the naturalization of male superiority and power.[26]

The film series' resistance to key elements of femininity ideology is one space for women's empowerment, one way in which *Resident Evil* disrupts acceptance of male superiority. Specifically, the series resists the corollary ideas that what is most important *about* a woman is her physical appearance and that what is most important *to* a woman is heterosexual male desire. As Lisa B. Rundle notes, "It's no accident that studios insist that strong women must remain feminine. They know what they're selling and who they're selling it to. As long as the Alpha female is still 'female' (read: counts sex appeal among her most powerful weapons), she remains safely an object of entertainment."[27] An appropriately feminized hero who knows her value to be skin deep and wants nothing more than to please men is, of course, no threat to male audiences. Arguably, the very selection of model Milla Jovovich to play the role of Alice was a calculated move to satisfy the most important criterion for the contemporary female action hero—that she be beautiful.[28] However, I would like to adopt Rikke Schubart's characterization of the female action hero as "a contested site, a paradoxical and ambivalent creature open to feminist as well as postfeminist interpretations, a figure of oppression as well as liberation."[29] While I recognize *Resident Evil's* potential to affirm the idea that women must be young, thin, beautiful, and white if we are to be of value, I also contend that Alice's character breaks free from traditional femininity and the expectations for female heroes in significant ways for audience members seeking women's empowerment.

David Roger Coon observes, "The trend in action heroines has been toward women who can perform not only the violence and physical stunts associated with traditional masculinity but also the beauty and sexuality associated with traditional femininity."[30] The female hero's performance of feminine beauty and sexuality disarms the threat of her performance of masculinity. Thus, a female action hero who does not perform feminine beauty retains her threat. Although the *Resident Evil* films do not conceal Milla Jovovich's beauty, to the extent that beauty is *constructed* as part of the "performance" and "masquerade" of femininity, Jovovich's portrayal of Alice resists the femininity ideology.[31] Throughout much of the series, Jovovich has a deliberately unmade-up look appropriate for the films' apocalyptic settings; we recognize her as beautiful but do not associate that beauty with a desire upon her part to appear beautiful, to perform femininity for us. The usual trappings of femininity are not visibly present in Alice's appearance. Her hair is short with little discernible styling. She is unconcerned with clothing and accessories beyond their functionality for survival. Alice wears what is readily available and what most suits her role in the apocalyptic environment. For example, at the beginning of the second film, *Resident Evil: Apocalypse*, we watch Alice quickly put together an outfit at an abandoned surplus shop. She stops for the guns, and picks up a wardrobe while she's there. When the world has become a virtual desert in the third film of the series, *Resident Evil: Extinction*, Alice's outfit is reminiscent of gunslingers in the American West; she is fully protected from the harsh sun, and we see little of her skin. Although the gun holsters strapped to her legs do somewhat suggest the garter belt of feminine lingerie, when the holsters are revealed from under her coat, it is because she needs access to her weapons, and the camera does not linger. When taken together, Alice's lack of concern with make-up, hair styling, and fashionable clothing suggests a woman who has much more important things to do than to consider, let alone construct, the way she looks. Alice seems to operate outside Laura Mulvey's theory in which woman connotes "to-be-looked-at-ness" in film.[32]

In Mulvey's theory, "the split between spectacle and narrative supports the man's role as the active one of forwarding the story, making things happen."[33] However, in the *Resident Evil* film series, it is predominantly Alice (and sometimes other strong female characters) who drives the action in the film. Alice's actions in the film, like her appearance, are designed to reflect the apocalyptic atmosphere. Just as there is no time or reason for performing femininity through appearance modifications, so also is there no time or apparent desire for performing femininity through heterosexual scripts designed to elicit male desire. In fact, in the first film, Alice explicitly rejects a common heterosexual fairy-tale script by refusing to go along with her male lover's promise to make all her "dreams come true." His plan consists of stealing and then selling Umbrella's dangerous biological research. We last see her lover when Alice embeds a fire axe in his zombied head and then tosses her Umbrella-branded wedding ring next to his lifeless hand, on which a ring is still worn. The ring and marriage were a part of their cover as Umbrella Security; however, the relationship was real, and the symbolism of the ring's abandonment is clear. With that toss, Alice is discarding all attachment to the male-ruled Umbrella Corporation and the feminine role of acquiescence to patriarchal authority.

The specific treatment of Alice's body throughout the film series also suggests resistance to the idea that male sexual desire must be of paramount importance to women. Alice is conspicuously missing the most popular "female sign"—large breasts.[34] No attempt is made to make Jovovich's small breasts look any bigger than they are, and the camera does not linger voyeuristically on her chest, or any other part of her body. In fact, the fourth film, *Resident Evil: Afterlife*, seems to mock the traditionally voyeuristic gaze of the camera and the male viewers by showing Alice entering a shower room, only to pull a weapon on a male voyeur before she has removed a single item of clothing. Even when Jovovich *is* nude in the films, her body is not displayed for heterosexual male arousal. The first time we see her nude she is wrapped in a torn shower curtain and lying on the floor where she has fallen, unconscious. We again see her nude when she awakens on an examination table in the abandoned Raccoon City Hospital, where she has been left by Umbrella. We also see her nude and suspended in a clear container when Umbrella tries to clone her. In each of these cases, Jovovich's nude body—knocked unconscious, attacked by electrodes, and harvested for its precious materials—serves to emphasize the dehumanizing horrors of the Umbrella Corporation rather than to titillate the male audience. Alice seems most feminine in these moments: her thin, seemingly frail body suggests the vulnerability for abuse which we associate with the female body. This apparent vulnerability creates a startling juxtaposition to Alice's heroic physical feats in the film, and feminist viewers are reminded of descriptions of femininity "as a mask, strategically concealing the strength that is on the inside."[35] As we wait expectantly for Alice to reveal her true strength, we are comforted by the knowledge that, even when she is at her most vulnerable, Alice's body is not displayed as the object of male desire: she has successfully resisted the ideology of femininity.

Resistance to femininity ideology is limited in its potential for women's empowerment, however, because as long as the patriarchal gender dichotomy remains undisturbed, a woman who does not enact femininity will be perceived as enacting masculinity. In order to further disrupt patriarchal essentialism, conformity to traditional notions of gender must be questioned, and, in fact, the *Resident Evil* film series posits adherence to traditional gender norms as laughable at best and fatal at worst. For instance, in one of the earlier scenes of the second film, a woman fleeing from zombies is caught and bitten when the heel of her shoe causes her to stumble. In the world of *Resident Evil*, gender markers such as high-heeled shoes can literally result in the loss of one's humanity. The character of L. J., one of the few surviving humans in Raccoon City, provides us with a second warning against the performance of gender. While staring at topless zombie prostitutes, L. J. wrecks his vehicle and is forced to flee the hordes of zombies on foot. Such traditionally masculine behavior as staring at female breasts simply has no place in the apocalypse. In a final example of a gender warning from the second film, the character of Nicholai, a member of Umbrella's STARS (Special Tactics and Rescue Squad) unit who has proven to be quite adept at survival, is unceremoniously killed when his attention is deflected by the sight of attractive police officer Jill Valentine. He introduces himself, and then, the second a gallant "At your service" leaves his lips, he is attacked by infected dogs and mauled to death. Chivalry will get you dead in *Resident Evil*. By prompting us to question conformity to rigid notions of gender, such examples function to destabilize the patriarchal gender dichotomy.

If the gender dichotomy is to be broken apart, rather than simply shaken, masculinity's superior position in the dichotomy must be denaturalized. Sharon Willis argues that "the spectacle of women acting like men works to disrupt the apparent naturalness of certain postures when performed by a male body."[36] According to Willis' argument, female heroes who perform masculinity can trouble notions of innate male superiority by revealing masculinity to be a construction. In *Resident Evil*, this troubling of patriarchal essentialism can be seen in Rain, the Umbrella soldier played by Michelle Rodriguez in the first film. The first words we hear Rain utter after she is revealed to be a woman are "Blow me." Later in the film, after Rain has been bitten several times by infected Umbrella employees and has joined with Alice to try to find a way out of the underground Umbrella installation in which they are trapped, she remarks, "When I get out of here, I think I'm going to get laid." Lines like these, when delivered by a woman, reveal masculinity to be a performance, perhaps even a ridiculous performance. According to Gamman, such "mockery" creates "fissure in the representation of power itself" by disrupting male dominance.[37] When masculinity becomes the butt of the joke, the power of the fathers is weakened. Rain's death at the end of the film, just before she and a few others make it to safety aboveground, can be interpreted as further weakening patriarchal power by alluding to the impotence of masculinity in the new world.

The impotence of masculinity in the post-apocalyptic world is perhaps most effectively demonstrated in a scene in the third film, *Resident Evil: Extinction*. In the first part of this film, Alice is traveling the countryside alone in search of survivors to help and bad things to kill. Somewhat frightened by the magnitude of her new powers, she has decided to remain aloof from the caravan in which she has several friends. Alice responds to what sounds like a radio distress call only to find herself trapped by what appears to be a family of ruthless survivors. She is held down by several of the family members as one of the men spreads her legs and prepares to rape her by unzipping his pants. Alice calmly says "I wouldn't do that" and then kills the would-be rapist with a swift kick. Within the context of the series' mockery of gender and the understanding of the raped body as a marker of femininity, Alice's comment can be read as a prohibition against the attempt to reinscribe gender onto her body. Furthermore, to the extent that rape is recognized as an assertion of masculine power, the scene can also be read as a symbol of masculinity's fall from the position of power within the gender dichotomy.

The attempted rape scene reminds us of both the rejection of the gender dichotomy and the continuing perception of Alice as gendered according to her female body. It is her female body that positions her as a potential victim of rape for the men. The unraveling of the naturalization of male superiority requires not only that we reject the old gender dichotomy but also that we open our minds to a potential reconstruction of the biological hierarchy upon which patriarchal power rests. Through Alice, a new notion of biological essentialism is presented—the possibility that woman, by virtue of her DNA, may in fact be superior to man. Such a possibility is empowering not as a reality—which would only serve to reverse the order of an oppressive hierarchy—but as a *possibility* because such a possibility denaturalizes the notion of male superiority. In other words, it allows female spectators to see themselves and to see men in a different position in relation to one another. When Alice in injected with the T-Virus, her body bonds with the virus, and she receives superhuman powers without losing the positive aspects of her humanity. Significantly, she is the only one directly injected with the virus (and not given the antidote) who does not become a "monster": she is the only person directly injected who remains physically recognizable as a human being and retains the ability to make independent, ethical decisions apart from the instinct for violence and the corporation's directives. In two of the films, Umbrella executives attempt to recreate themselves as Alice by injecting themselves with the virus. In both cases, the results are disastrous. Upon injection, the men become physically altered so as to be read as non-human and, unwilling or unable to control their insatiably violent lust for complete power, they meet their deaths at the hands of Alice. Whereas Alice laments what she perceives to be her loss of full humanity due to her body's bonding with the T-Virus, the Umbrella executives can only obsess at how to reassert their supremacy in the new world order. In the third film, *Resident Evil: Extinction*, Umbrella's head of research, Dr. Isaacs, quickly loses all humanity when exposed to a new strain of the virus. As he faces off against Alice, he tells her confidently, "I am the future." Alice replies, "No. You're just another asshole." In *Resident Evil: Afterlife*, Umbrella's chairman of the board, Albert Wesker, injects Alice with a serum to neutralize the virus in her body and then tells her, "I'm what you used to be. Only better." By the end of the film, however, he admits to Alice that he cannot control the virus and announces his plan to ingest her—the only one who has bonded with the virus—in an attempt to regain power. The actions of the men suggest they are terrified of losing their place at the top of the hierarchy. Through her biological superiority—her ability to successfully bond with the virus—Alice has dealt a fatal blow to the patriarchal authority of the Umbrella Corporation. When she escapes and successfully resists the corporation's control, they desperately attempt to replicate her, but, by the end of the third movie, even the Alice replicas are working with the original Alice to destroy the Umbrella Corporation.

In this world of the zombie apocalypse, the controls of patriarchy—femininity ideology, the gender dichotomy, male biological supremacy, and even male control over reproduction—have been broken. Feminism has often called for a dismantling of patriarchy, and, as luck would have it, the zombie apocalypse creates the ideal situation for just such a dismantling. The breakdown of social order and societal infrastructure is a key ingredient of apocalyptic horror,[38] but, in *Resident Evil*, the collapse of the social order brings hope along with horror. Within the images of the zombie apocalypse, Alice represents our hope, the realization of the feminist promise that we will one day be seen in the fullness of our human potential; however, the hope of Alice is not limited to the post-apocalyptic world. Alice is a cyborg, what Donna Haraway defines as a "hybrid of machine and organism, a creature of social reality as well as a creature of fiction."[39] Turned into a biological weapon by the Umbrella Corporation, she remains human, but also becomes something more. Haraway argues that "Cyborg imagery can suggest a way out of the maze of dualisms in which we have explained our bodies and our tools to ourselves."[40] Although made by man, Alice surpasses and destroys her maker. She can be read as a symbol of technology's threat to humanity, but, from a perspective of cyberfeminism, she can also be read as a symbol of the hope technology offers humanity. "The main trouble with cyborgs, of course, is that they are the illegitimate offspring of militarism and patriarchal capitalism, not to mention state socialism. But illegitimate offspring are often exceedingly unfaithful to their origins. Their fathers, after all, are inessential."[41] Alice invites us to walk through the glass with her as she shatters the patriarchal illusion.

Ultimately, the new world order being suggested by *Resident Evil* is not female supremacy, but rather a fuller existence, free from gender restraints and hierarchical prisons. At the end of the second movie, Major Cain, an Umbrella leader, excitedly pits Matt Addison, the political activist who has been turned by the Nemesis Project into an unthinking, unfeeling killing machine, against Alice to see which of the corporation's pet projects is "superior." Although Alice initially refuses to fight, she relents when human lives are at stake. Just as she is about to kill the monster, though, she looks into its eyes and recognizes Matt Addison. When she refuses to kill, Major Cain tries to convince her by declaring her to be unlike the monster but rather "magnificent. Not a mutation. Evolution." He then laments, "All that strength but no will to use it." Alice, the more human of the experiments, is also the superior one, the next step in our species' evolution. Throughout the series, Alice will reject the superiority afforded by her powers and will continue to fight for the survival of humanity. She has surpassed her maker's primitive patriarchalism and enslavement to power. As a new species, as a cyborg, she has fulfilled Haraway's hope that "we can learn from our fusions with animals and machines how not to be Man."[42] Within my oppositional feminist reading, the *Resident Evil* film series becomes, like Haraway's "Cyborg Manifesto," a "political myth"[43]—a reshaping of reality through a reimagining of what could be. Through Alice, women can imagine ourselves as no longer defined in relation to man or assumed to be man's inferior; we can imagine ourselves as more than mere man. And with that reimagining of ourselves lies the power to recreate our world. "We require regeneration, not rebirth, and the possibilities for our reconstitution include the utopian dream of hope for a monstrous world without gender."[44] *Resident Evil* offers us a vision of the regeneration we require—our regeneration as cyborgs, freed from essentialism.

Notes

1. Richard Harland Smith, "The Battle Inside: Infection and the Modern Horror Film," *Cineaste* 35, no. 1 (2009): 42.
2. Nicole Birch-Bailey, "Terror in Horror Genres: The Global Media and the Millennial Zombie," *Journal of Popular Culture* 45, no. 6 (2012): 1137.
3. Kyle Bishop, "Dead Man Still Walking: Explaining the Zombie Renaissance," *Journal of Popular Film and Television* 37, no. 1 (2009): 24.
4. Scott Lucas, "Horror Video Game Remakes and the Question of Medium: Remaking *Doom, Silent Hill,* and *Resident Evil,*" in *Fear, Cultural Anxiety and Transformation: Horror, Science Fiction, and Fantasy Films Remade*, eds. Scott A Lukas and John Marmysz, 234 (Lanham: Rowman, 2009).
5. Ibid., 237.
6. Richard Hand, "Survival Horror and the Resident Evil Franchise," in *Horror Film: Creating and Marketing Fear*, ed. Steffen Hantke, 132 (Jackson: University Press of Mississippi, 2004).
7. Ibid., 130.
8. Lucas, "Horror Video Game Remakes," 235.
9. Audre Lorde, "Age, Race, Class, and Sex: Women Redefining Difference," in *Sister Outsider: Essays and Speeches*, ed. Audre Lorde, 114–115 (Freedom, CA: Crossing, 1984).

10. Laura Mulvey, "Visual Pleasure and Narrative Cinema," in *Feminist Theory: A Reader*, eds. Wendy K. Kolmar and Frances Bartkowski, 257 (New York: McGraw-Hill, 2013).
11. Ibid., 256.
12. Jennifer Baumgardner and Amy Richards, "The Number One Question about Feminism," *Feminist Studies* 29, no. 2 (2003): 450.
13. Elana Levine, "Remaking *Charlie's Angels*: The Construction of Post-Feminist Hegemony," *Feminist Media Studies* 8, no. 4 (2008): 376.
14. Rikke Schubart, "Introduction: Female Heroes in an Age of Ambivalence," in *Super Bitches and Action Babes: The Female Hero in Popular Cinema, 1970–2006*, 16 (Jefferson, NC: McFarland, 2007).
15. Ibid., 17.
16. Simone de Beauvoir, "From *The Second Sex*," in *Feminist Theory: A Reader*, eds. Wendy K. Kolmar and Frances Bartkowski, 163 (New York: McGraw-Hill, 2013).
17. Bernie Cook, "'Something's Crossed Over in Me': New Ways of Seeing *Thelma & Louise*," in *Thelma & Louise Live!: The Cultural Afterlife of an American Film*, ed. Bernie Cook, 9 (Austin: University of Texas Press, 2007).
18. Barna William Donovan, "The History of a Modern Crisis," in *Blood, Guns, and Testosterone: Action Films, Audiences, and a Thirst for Violence*, ed. Barna William Donovan, 15 (Lanham, MD: Scarecrow, 2010).
19. Brenda Cooper, "The Relevancy and Gender Identity in Spectators' Interpretations of Thelma and Louise," *Critical Studies in Mass Communication* 16, no. 1 (1999): 22.
20. bell hooks, "The Oppositional Gaze: Black Female Spectators," in *Black Looks: Race and Representation*, ed. bell hooks, 116 (Boston: South End, 1992).
21. Lisa Coulthard, "Killing Bill: Rethinking Feminism and Film Violence," in *Interrogating Postfeminism: Gender and the Politics of Culture*, eds. Yvonne Tasker and Diane Negra, 154–155 (Durham: Duke University Press, 2007).
22. Dara Greenwood, "Are Female Action Heroes Risky Role Models?: Character Identification, Idealization, and Viewer Aggression," *Sex Roles* 57 (2007): 725.
23. Ibid., 730.
24. Monique Wittig, "The Straight Mind," *Feminist Theory: A Reader*, eds. Wendy K. Kolmar and Frances Bartkowski, 294 (New York: McGraw-Hill, 2013).
25. Judith Butler, "From *Gender Trouble: Feminism and the Subversion of Identity*," *Feminist Theory: A Reader*, eds. Wendy K. Kolmar and Frances Bartkowski, 443 (New York: McGraw-Hill, 2013).
26. Cooper, "The Relevancy and Gender Identity," 31.
27. Lisa Rundle, "Fearlessness: The Final Feminist Frontier," *Herizons* 17, no. 2 (2003): 31.
28. Schubart, "Introduction: Female Heroes," 5.
29. Ibid., 7.
30. David Roger Coon, "Two Steps Forward, One Step Back: The Selling of *Charlie's Angels* and *Alias*," *Journal of Popular Film and Television* 33, no. 1 (2005): 2.
31. Veronica Hollinger, "(Re)reading Queerly: Science Fiction, Feminism and the Defamiliarization of Gender," in *Future Females, The Next Generation: New*

       Voices and Velocities in Feminist Science Fiction Criticism, ed. Marleen S. Barr, 202 (Lanham: Rowman, 2000).
32. Mulvey, "Visual Pleasure and Narrative Cinema," 256.
33. Ibid., 257.
34. Rikke Schubart, "High Trash Heroines: Lara, Beatrix, and Three Angels," in *Super Bitches and Action Babes: The Female Hero in Popular Cinema, 1970–2006*, ed. Rikke Schubart, 299 (Jefferson, NC: McFarland, 2007).
35. Coon, "Two Steps Forward, One Step Back," 5.
36. Sharon Willis, "Combative Femininity: *Thelma & Louise* and *Terminator 2*," in *High Contrast: Race and Gender in Contemporary Hollywood Film*, ed. Sharon Willis, 108 (Durham: Duke University Press, 1997).
37. Cooper, "The Relevancy and Gender Identity," 28.
38. Bishop, "Dead Man Still Walking," 18, 22.
39. Donna Harraway, "A Cyborg Manifesto: Science, Technology, and Socialist-Feminism in the Late Twentieth Century," in *Feminist Theory: A Reader*, eds. Wendy K. Kolmar and Frances Bartkowski, 344 (New York: McGraw-Hill, 2013).
40. Ibid., 354.
41. Ibid., 345.
42. Ibid., 351.
43. Ibid., 344.
44. Ibid., 354.

CHAPTER 8

Cops and Zombies: Hierarchy and Social Location in *The Walking Dead*

Melissa F. Lavin and *Brian M. Lowe*

Cinematic narratives must be understood as products of the social, cultural, political, and economic expressions of the society in which they are created. Apocalyptic cinema in the United States is in part inspired by geopolitical and environmental preoccupations, such as an endless "War on Terror," threats of nuclear annihilation, increasing prevalence of "natural" disasters, and growing awareness of climate change and the threat it poses to human life. These social problems could threaten the very existence of the human species. In addition to fears on a broad scale, apocalyptic story lines are also inspired by domestic, cultural fears such as those inspired by social change, which is often met with reticence and suspicion. Twenty-first-century social change includes, as examples, gay and lesbian marriage, and legalization of previously demonized drugs. Progressive developments are thrust against traditional attitudes regarding family and social life, and therefore rattle the status quo.

As society changes, different apocalyptic narratives have arisen and dissipated. Because the events of 9/11 catapulted the United States into continual war with the Middle East, that period is particularly salient in initiating an increase in post-apocalyptic pop cinema, including AMC's *The Walking Dead* (2010–present). The post-9/11 era has seen the rise of different cultural and legal forms for the twenty-first century, and these shifts have played out through an increased fascination with end-of-world stories. Since 2001, the US government has waged perpetual war on "terrorists" and other abstracted foreign enemies, while ordinary people have submitted to ubiquitous surveillance regimes (such as mandatory immigration checks or drug stops), and have endured relentless economic distress in their everyday lives. Directors, producers, screen writers, and actors have shaped cinematic stories to reflect these social problems. Such artists, perhaps unwittingly, build the divisions and inequalities that exist among social groups into their story lines.

In particular, the appeal of *The Walking Dead* continues to grow. This is due in part to the fact that the show uses a classic American monster, as well as depicts post-apocalyptic themes that resonate with modern anxieties shared by the viewing audience. Zombies (known as "walkers" on the show) are fundamentally irrational and predatory, just like the "terrorist threats" that have intermittently dominated news cycles since September 11, 2001. As the walkers close in on the survivors of the viral apocalypse that produced them, surviving humans must combat the mindless (yet formidable) threat the walkers pose. The human characters continually lose members of their group, and they prevail over the walkers only from moment to moment. Once zombie threats are stabilized, new disasters, like dangerous people and plagues, terrorize survivors of the zombie apocalypse. Viewing audiences relate to these continuous and varied threats because twenty-first-century politics and culture indicate that threats to American safety and sovereignty are numerous and unpredictable. Moreover, the show depicts societal collapse. This resonates with conservative anxieties about twenty-first-century social change, which includes but is not limited to changing attitudes and evolving laws regarding marriage and drugs.

In this chapter, we address the ways in which *The Walking Dead* deals with post-apocalyptic themes, including the ways *The Walking Dead*'s directors and producers (re)create hierarchical social organization on the show, and the relationship of the group configuration to reigning political ideologies. The chapter also addresses how *The Walking Dead* reproduces, resists, and extends constructions of race, class, gender, sexuality, and age present in everyday life, particularly norms regarding leadership, division of labor, and the nature of policing and surveillance among survivors. We argue these matters are shaped by issues of inequality and social location.

The Walking Dead television series first aired in October 2010, and has completed four seasons. (AMC has renewed it for a sixth season.) The fourth season attracted considerable viewer attention, its popularity evident in part by *The Talking Dead*.[1] *The Walking Dead* continues to be the number one show on television among 18–49-year-old viewers, and remains the highest-rated series in the history of cable television. The first eight episodes of its fourth season delivered an average of 13 million viewers and 8.4 million adults between 18 and 49. The popularity of *The Walking Dead* has propelled it into ranges of viewership seldom experienced by cable television dramas. The sheer popularity of the series suggests that viewing audiences relate to it, and this alone makes it worth investigating the social themes that predominate in the show.

The Walking Dead

The premise of *The Walking Dead* is macabre and intriguing. The show is littered with the structures and equipment of contemporary society, but the institutions themselves have been eviscerated by the rise of walkers, which are corpses that reanimate to feast on the blood and flesh of living creatures. The cause of walkers is unknown, but people assume they arise as a result of a deadly and mysterious virus. In the pilot episode ("Days Gone By"), Sheriff Deputy Rick Grimes, protagonist of the show, is shot during a roadside altercation, and awakens weeks later completely alone in a hospital. A chained door with the handwritten message "Don't open, dead inside," is his first introduction to the radically altered world, along with a filthy hand struggling to escape from behind a barrier. Rick continues walking through the hospital, encountering evidence of violence and chaos. Unable to find any medical personnel, he flees to his home, only to discover that his wife Lori and son Carl have fled this unexplained catastrophe. Subsequently, Rick stumbles upon a character named Morgan, and he and his young son briefly capture, release, and educate Rick about the essential nature of the walkers (their attraction to sound and motion, how their bites infect, and how to destroy them with blows to the head). Together, they travel to Rick's police station, finding it abandoned. All the major governmental institutions—law enforcement, military, medical, civil authority, etc.—have either fled or been destroyed.

The Evolution of the Show: Season One

Season one follows Rick in his journey to Atlanta to successfully reunite with his family, and to join a larger group of survivors on the edge of Atlanta. The group sustains itself largely by looting the city for supplies while attempting to avoid the mass of walkers that now roam the streets. After debating the merits of fleeing to Fort Dixon (and risking the hazards of the interstate), the group finally arrives at the Center for Disease Control (CDC) in the hope of finding a sanctuary from walkers, and in search of a medical solution to the crisis. After the sealed metal doors are opened to allow the group inside (they narrowly escape a group of advancing walkers in the process), they discover the CDC is now inhabited by a lone scientist named Edwin Jenner, who remained behind while other staff fled to save their families and themselves. Through Jenner, the survivors learn the pandemic is global, and he informs them that no nation-state, military team, or scientific body has been able to develop a cure or vaccine. They learn that the infected die of fever, and only the brainstem reanimates after death, thereby extinguishing the memories and personality of the (former) person. The last scenes in the season see the

CDC go up in flames, as Jenner detonates the building in a fatalistic gesture. The survivors barely escape the building in time, fleeing seconds before it explodes. Season one establishes that the institutional order of the United States has been destroyed, leaving behind some valuable resources (weapons, medicine, vehicles), but none of the personnel who made these institutions function. By the end of season one, Rick and other survivors have lost hope in the existence of a sanctuary.

Season Two

Season two begins with renewed hope in the form of the bucolic farm of Hershel Greene. Greene is a veterinarian who resides with his daughters Maggie and Beth, and some family friends who survived the apocalypse. Hershel is willing to share his medical knowledge and skills, and allows the survivors on the farm temporarily. As members of the group make "runs" to scavenge supplies and search for a missing person, the magnitude of the apocalypse becomes more apparent, as even rural Georgia cannot escape its ravages. A violent confrontation between Rick, Hershel, Glenn, and two survivors from an unknown (and possibly larger) group, yields rumors of a refuge deep in Nebraska. Peaceful coresidence on Hershel's farm does not last and tensions threaten to fracture the group, especially when the new arrivals learn that the Greenes have been harboring family-members-turned-walkers in their barn. The season culminates in the violent destruction of these walkers, followed by a brawl between Rick and Shane (Rick's former friend and nemesis) that results in Shane's death and an attack from a herd of walkers on the farm. The farm is overrun and burned, with the surviving Greenes and the traveling group fleeing for their lives.

Season Three

Season three is characterized by efforts to provide security. The season opens several months after the destruction of the farm. The discovery of a prison becomes a beacon of hope for the group, as Rick (now the group leader), declares that its walls and fences may offer protection from walkers, and that it may contain medicine and supplies. After staging an attack on walkers roaming the prison, the group establishes a foothold and begins the dangerous, but potentially fruitful, project of "clearing" the prison of them. Meanwhile, Andrea (one of the main characters in seasons one to three) and Michonne (introduced in the last episode of season two) witness a helicopter crash and, after traveling to the site, are captured and taken to "Woodbury." Woodbury appears to be a small, secured replicate of pre-apocalyptic civil society, and includes a medical facility, a school, a library, and residential accommodations. Woodbury is led by the charismatic "Governor" who invites Andrea and Michonne to join their community. Michonne is suspicious of the Governor, and discovers that Woodbury is ultimately controlled by him and his armed minions. While feigning benevolence, the Governor is a despot, fixated on maintaining autocratic power. The remainder of season three features a build-up toward a violent conflict between Woodbury inhabitants and the prison faction. The Governor informs the people of Woodbury that they must confront the prison occupants because of the threat they pose. Meanwhile, the survivors in the prison deliberate whether they should flee in order to avoid battle, or remain and fight. The climatic final episode features the citizens of Woodbury leading an attack on the prison. In response, the prison survivors stage an ambush that ultimately defeats the Woodbury forces. After defeat, Woodbury survivors refuse to mount another attack on the prison, and the Governor, in a rage, slaughters them. The season concludes with some Woodbury survivors coming to reside in the battle-damaged prison. While there is the hope of a life inside the prison that is safer than the outside, there is little hope of establishing ties with another community or entity to generate security and stability.

Season Four

Thematically, the collapse of makeshift sanctuary dominates season four. The first half of the season portrays the prison, the subject of the battle between the Governor and his followers, and the survivors of the Greene farm. In the first half of season four, the prison transforms from a sanctuary into a biological hot zone. The prison's inhabitants struggle to treat a lethal flu-like disease. While they are dealing with this, the previously defeated Governor (despite a narrative arc of transformation), persuades another camp of survivors to take the prison. Upon the destruction of the prison (and the slaying of Hershel Greene), the characters scatter, and the subsequent episodes in season four feature smaller groups of survivors. The season ends with many of our main characters reunited at the mysterious "Terminus," a dubiously proclaimed "haven," where they are captured.

Hierarchical Social Organization

Hierarchical social organization drives and organizes everyday American life. As a capitalist society, the United States creates and maintains unequal categories and differentially situated people. In other words, people or groups experience inequality based on their social roles, and women, marginal men, and children are more often auxiliary to decision-making since they have less social power. These social forms present in US society also feature in *The Walking Dead*, and we see them reproduced in the stratification of the survivor group. Just like in real life, characters from the post-apocalyptic society of *The Walking Dead* have different levels of power, status, and responsibility, and groups organize by reproducing these inequalities and differences. These inequalities are especially reproduced in early seasons of the disaster, before desperation reaches its apex.

Hierarchy construction on *The Walking Dead* is reflected in the organization of group leadership, as survivors dole out responsibilities along lines of race, gender, or age. The first two seasons of *The Walking Dead* feature overt, continual struggles over group leadership, but struggles are confined primarily to two men vying for such leadership. These two characters, Rick and Shane, rise to candidacy because they embody hegemonic masculinity, which is an ideal-type masculinity that includes being strong, male, heterosexual, and white.[2] Rick and Shane also wielded authority in law enforcement before the collapse of society. These traits render them "credible" leaders. Notions of gender category, and (allegedly) associated attributes, inform leadership opportunities on the show, as other strong leaders (Andrea, Dale, and Glenn) are rendered second-tier contenders because they are not hegemonic white men; they are female, older, and racialized, respectively. In short, in *The Walking Dead's* rendition of Armageddon society, we see that US norms and values are reflected in stories of end-days. The story is created through a reliance on social stereotypes, as character assignments on *The Walking Dead* are often based on (imaginary) dispositional traits assigned according to demographic category. We argue later that, as we get further into the post-apocalypse, these traditional assignments break down and social actors are afforded more role flexibility.

The political, social, cultural, and economic arrangements that organize American life are those that support our brand of capitalist patriarchy. The capitalist patriarchy of the pre-apocalypse is redeployed among survivors when the zombie apocalypse descends on Georgia, the United States, and the entire globe, and thus hegemonic values from the pre-apocalyptic reality are transmitted to representations of the post-apocalyptic world. Theoretically, in a noncapitalist society, creators of Armageddon cinema would create egalitarian dynamics among characters that reflect a democratic social organization and accompanying value system. Anti-authoritarian group construction among survivors would look anti-hierarchical; an anarchistic or libertarian communist configuration would not be compelled to construct role hierarchies on the basis of race, gender, class, sexuality, or age. Rather, the construction of the group would be horizontal (sideways, collective) rather than vertical (top-down, authoritarian), and role responsibilities and role relationships would be more fluid. Roles would be defined and designated on basis of achievement, skill, or talent, and not on categories such as race, class, gender, or age.

Intersections

In creating scripts about the post-apocalypse, writers, directors, and producers frequently re-create the normative social organization of the society out of which the story comes. Much like white supremacist, capitalist patriarchy is normalized in everyday society, and success attributed to merit rather than structural advantages, role placement of characters in *The Walking Dead* is not based on talent or virtue, but rather, assigned on the basis of race, class, gender, and sexuality; thus *The Walking Dead* reproduces and extends constructions of race, class, gender, and sexuality in everyday life. However, these features break down as the series proceeds. As our characters spend more time dislocated in the post-apocalyptic, their desperation and disconnection from previous society increases. This allows greater flexibility of social roles, and in particular, the relationship between social location—a person's complicated and nuanced demographic category, which shapes their interactions and opportunities—and power.

Stringent adherence to norms of American cultural life is more prominent in early seasons, and dissipates as the catastrophe deepens. In season one, Rick and Shane "naturally" emerge as two men who vie for the number one position in group leadership based on their hegemonically masculine characteristics. They compete for power, control, and even (hetero) sexual conquest, as both men fight for access to Rick's wife, Lori. The choice to feature conflict and competition among these two men, against a wide variety of total character choices, suggests a depiction that reproduces authoritarian power in mainstream society; the characters' social characteristics conform to the ideal type. They are young enough to be physically agile, but old enough to be wise. They are handsome, heterosexual, male, and white. Daryl also shows potential for "ideal-type leadership," but his class position as "poor, white trash" gives him less occupational status than former professional cops and middle-class men. As the show advances, stringent adherence to norms of stratification relaxes and we see a proliferation of characters of color; the emergence of women and marginal men in combat roles; and the diminishing of traditional forms of authority. This signifies that once structured society becomes more distant in our collective memory, we have more freedom from the constraining categories (i.e. masculine, feminine, young, old) that bound us during civilization.

Early seasons had few characters of color, and online criticism in the form of comical memes depicted the African American character (T Dog) as undeveloped, for example not given lines because of his race: he was given assignments appropriate to lower-order masculinity. In early seasons, marginalized men are not given authority, but rather, are utilized as mute and peripheral brute force, like T Dog. Similarly, non-hegemonic men are given a greater role in strategy or planning, as is seen with Glenn, an Asian man in his twenties who is stereotypically depicted as smart and boyish. Older men, like Dale or Hershel, mind the RV, engage in more stationary activity, or do weapons work that is less vigorous. Dale and Hershel act as advisors and sage moral compasses. The creation of these characters exploits stereotypes regarding race and age. Gender roles are also less mobile in early seasons. Women in early seasons are directly held out of leadership and combat positions (and even chastise each other) when they stray from caring for the children, cooking, and washing clothes.

In advancing seasons, we see more characters of color, and we see them move to the center of the narrative arc as developed characters. Seasons three and four also see a proliferation of women in combat, like Andrea or Michonne, as well as women transitioning from meek and hyper-feminized to formidable fighters, like Carol and Maggie. We also see marginal men in combat emerge to a greater extent, as Glenn transitions from "clever pizza guy" to warrior. Lastly, there is less reliance on one or two leaders, and more reliance on physical prowess and skill. Blue-collar masculinity is respected and emphasized, as Daryl's (another of the core characters) tracking and hunting skills become central to survival. Daryl's "redneck" expertise is provided a context in which to advance and lead, whereas pre-apocalyptic civilization limited someone in his class position.

Norms of social location play out in division of labor mandates also. In particular, division of labor amongst the show's characters is gendered. How characters divide labor is pertinent for understanding surveillance and social control on the show. While men are held responsible for protection, surveillance, physical power, and decision-making, women in *The Walking Dead* are held accountable for the safety and care of children. Even as Shane and Rick vie for fatherly control of Carl, male parenting takes the form of mentoring Carl—not as a child, but as a future male defender of the group. When tough and outspoken Andrea, a civil attorney in the pre-apocalypse, chooses to arm herself, learn how to kill walkers, and protect perimeters of the camp from potential predators, she is literally disarmed by the men, including Dale and Rick, who try to regulate her access to firearms. In multiple scenes in the show, Andrea is compelled to ask permission to have her gun, and is forced to plead her case. Since social rules are even more stringently enforced among like group members (i.e. men enforce masculinity on other men,[3] and women enforce gender norms on other women), it is no surprise that Lori, Carol, and other women characters deride Andrea for making more work for the rest of them because she is pursuing gender inappropriate activities. In subsequent seasons, we see more powerful women characters, including Andrea, finally achieving their (chosen) combat role. Maggie (Glenn's girlfriend, Hershel's daughter), a traditionally feminine character, becomes formidable in hand-to-hand combat, as does Michonne, the mysterious black woman who first appears at the end of season two.

While hierarchies stretch, they don't disappear. Rick is still in some ways "de facto" leader. He has unilateral executive power to cast Carol from the group for making an (albeit rash and foolish) executive decision to kill two inhabitants of the prison who come down with the flu. The show at times doles out gendered penalties, even as role flexibility becomes more available. For example, Lori (the unpopular character that Rick and Shane fight for) dies in childbirth, Andrea is killed off after becoming sexually involved with a villain (the Governor), and Carol is unilaterally banished by the hegemonic male leader. Killing women off in childbirth and after ill-advised sexual involvement, or expelling a major female character for atrocities no worse than those the hegemonic leader committed, all suggests that women characters are at times extinguished or villainized in feminized ways. *The Walking Dead* faithfully kills off little girls as well, as all four female children depicted in the show thus far (all between the ages of roughly 8 to 12) succumb to zombies. This is an entire season after Rick "steps down" from his official leadership position, which had shifted from informal to official, from democratic to dictatorial, before it was relinquished altogether.

Even after Rick is no longer leader, he remains an informal authority of the group. His hegemonic social location affords him power that he uses to order Carol to leave the prison. Carol's executive action and violent behavior symbolize a threat to male authority, and Rick penalizes Carol's unpredictability, and independent decision-making. Because of Rick's demographic hegemony, this decision (thus far) goes unreversed, if not unquestioned, by other prison inhabitants.

The Walking Dead also reproduces heterosexual privilege found in American life. As society continues to break down, race, class, and gender forms begin to evolve. Yet even as evolutions progress with the seasons of the show, there is also a traditionalism that pervades; for example, we see no advancements regarding heterosexism and hetero-normativity; they remaining unflinching throughout. Rigid hetero-normativity and latent homophobia are manifest in the creation of exclusively heterosexual characters and couplings. Queer, hetero-flexible, and homosexual identities and relationships are utterly absent in *The Walking Dead* in the first four seasons. Despite civil rights gains for GLBTQIA people in the last decade, mainstream television does not reflect this social progress, but instead, reproduces twentieth-century forms of hetero-normativity. This suggests that, despite some overt depictions of GLBTQIA on television (for example, *Will and Grace* and *Modern Family*), incidental depictions of diverse sexual forms (like featuring gay couples as normative) still lag in popular television despite changing norms and laws. Fluidity of role, power, and behavior has increased in general as the show progresses, so assorted sexual identities may also proliferate as we move further into the post-apocalypse. As of halfway through season five, we have not seen any gay, lesbian, bisexual, or transgender characters.

In short, we see social forms both reproduced and ruptured in the character building of *The Walking Dead*. At times, we see men who are racialized or classed gain power, as Daryl and Glenn vie for central leadership roles in the later seasons. While we see an increasing variety of capable women as the show advances, we also see them penalized for their leadership. Depictions of sexuality remain consistently regressive in all seasons of the show, with the creators only now discussing the introduction of a single gay character sometime in season five or six.

Giddens argues that one of the defining characteristics of modern societies is the identification of, and efforts to reduce, sources of risk. He contends that modern societies developed through innovation in virtually all spheres of social life, such as entering uncharted geographic areas or developing new technologies, and that modern societies have always been interested in identifying and ameliorating risk. However, as Giddens notes, such efforts are unending, as new risks are identified, and efforts to curb them meet with limited success.[4] Moreover, while we seek to engage the losing battle of purging risk and uncertainty, these same forces frighten and excite us. One of the sites in which this ambivalence plays out is in popular cinema.

The Walking Dead is a powerful (inter)national force in twenty-first-century entertainment. It resonates with viewers in part because it resonates with the terrifying call of our futures. Apocalypse scenarios carry particular weight, in addition to the thrill of fantasizing about the chaos of end days. Armageddon depictions represent fears and concerns (war, natural disasters, political unrest, economic collapse, etc.) about an evolving world. As a fantasy creature, zombies symbolize our uncertainties, but also provide a safe distance from our myriad fears by displaying impossible characteristics.

The Walking Dead features survivors that must develop strategies that will, at minimum, allow them to survive and meet the demands of this new world. Balkin describes this process as simultaneously produced by and productive of social life.[5] In season one, Glenn demonstrates his capacity to safely move through a zombie-infested Atlanta based, in part, on his experience as a pizza-delivery person. Daryl utilizes skills acquired in an abusive and dysfunctional childhood in rural Georgia to become a central provider and protector of the group, effectively transformed from social junk[6] in the previous capitalist society. Other survivors, such as Andrea, find that skills as a civil rights attorney must be transmuted and augmented, and new skills learned. The massive physical destruction that is a constant backdrop to *The Walking Dead* mirrors the destruction and re-creation of identity that the characters endure in the zombie apocalypse. However, even as identities are refashioned in the face of the ever-deepening apocalypse, in many cases, the show depicts social roles that are merely a reinstallation of canonized forms found in the pre-apocalypse.

The Walking Dead reproduces constructions of race, class, gender, and age present in everyday life: in particular, norms of leadership and authority, division of labor mandates, and power differentials. This is accomplished through assigning characters' traits on the basis of demographic categories. These forms break down or extend as the show moves further into the post-civilization. To encourage American audiences to connect emotionally to such shows and characters, major elements of the normative social order are reproduced (i.e. we assign people to well-worn constructions of race, class, gender, age, and sexuality), but at times they are extended, supplanted, or resisted. Traditional social forms endure early in our visions of a post-society, but the traditionalism diminishes as the show moves forward.

This demonstrates the entrenchment of traditional social forms both in the creative class itself (writers, artists, directors, producers, etc.), and in the collective imagination. When writers and producers create fantasy, horror, or science fiction, they are arguably less tightly bound by real-life conventions than the writers of realistic fiction are. If creative minds can conjure monsters, goblins, or zombies, surely they could devise a social order in which someone other than a white male cop serves as leader of a group, or an order in which same-sex or non-monogamous couples exist. We see some rupturing of conventions as the show advances, including women as powerful fighters, and the centralizing of interracial relationships, but the show often reimagines the social order to reflect stratification and inequality in society. Given the overwhelming popularity of the show, the American public appears to be both comfortable with traditional social roles, and open to moving away from such roles in a dramatically different world, like that of *The Walking Dead*. This collective ambivalence to social forms and social change suggests that the series reflects broader cultural efforts to make sense of mixed messages of crisis about US domination and safety in a rapidly changing post-9/11 world.

Notes

1. *The Talking Dead* is a show that airs immediately after a new episode of *The Walking Dead*, and features actors and producers from the show, along with other well-known fans. The mid-season finale of *The Talking Dead* delivered a record 6 million viewers, including 3.8 million adults 18–49 years old.
2. R. W. Connell, *Masculinities*, 2nd ed. (Berkeley: University of California Press, 2005).
3. C. J. Pascoe Dude, *You're a Fag*, 2nd ed. (Berkeley: University of California Press, 2011).
4. Anthony Giddens, *The Constitution of Society: Outline of the Theory of Structuration* (Berkeley: University of California Press, 1984).
5. J. M. Balkin, *Cultural Software: A Theory of Ideology* (New Haven: Yale University Press, 2003).
6. Steven Spitzer, "Towards a Marxist Theory of Deviance," *Social Problems* 22 (5) (1975): 638–651.

CHAPTER 9

"We Don't Do History": Constructing Masculinity in a World of Blood

Amanda Hobson

"Welcome to Stake Land, kid": Mister's words here signal Martin's induction into a vampire hunter apprenticeship in Jim Mickle's 2010 movie *Stake Land*.[1] This role as apprentice also indicates a shift from childhood to young adulthood for Martin, and demonstrates a bond between Mister (played by Nick Damici) as stand-in father figure and Martin (Connor Paolo) as filial learner. In this taut film written by Mickle and Damici, the undead stalk the night with fangs bared, while what is left of humanity huddles in gated communities with armed guards. As in most apocalypse tropes, it is not just the monsters at the gate that are terrifying: other human beings, more specifically here men, are frequently far more dangerous than the vampires. In *Stake Land*, cultural stereotypes of masculinity replicate and reinforce gendered norms about male violence and emotional distance.

This chapter examines the construction of masculinity and the restoration of a masculinity that relies upon a conservative and essentialist concept of gender. In *Stake Land*, the prevalent masculinity grows from a revitalization of religious zealotry and a perceived necessity for violence in a world overrun with vicious human and vampire predators. *Stake Land* highlights constructions of masculinity that mainly reify hegemonic ideals, although it does briefly show the potential for a masculinity that can question these predominant notions. Masculinities scholar R. W. Connell articulates hegemonic masculinity as "the configuration of gender practice which embodies the currently accepted answer to the problem of the legitimacy of patriarchy, which guarantees (or is taken to guarantee) the dominant position of men and the subordination of women"[2] (see also in this volume Barbara Gurr, Chapter

Two; Melissa F. Lavin and Brian M. Lowe, Chapter Eight; and Brent Strang, Chapter Ten). The hegemonic construction of masculinity operates under a hierarchical notion of gender. In the film, men dominate the narrative, driving the plot, and essentially rule the Stake Land. Women serve as catalysts for Mister and Martin's actions throughout the film and are peripheral characters in light of the main triangle of characters, Mister, Martin, and Jebedia Loven. This reliance on predominant ideas of gender norms—men as actors and women as acted upon or through—reveals that though a great deal has changed for humanity in the post-apocalyptic world, gender roles sustain.

Stake Land opens with Mister, a vampire slayer, rescuing teenaged Martin from the vampire who killed his mother, father, and infant sibling. Mister trains Martin to eliminate vampires as they travel north to New Eden, a zone rumored to be free of vampires, and an ordered and protected haven for humans. Mister and Martin slay vampires along their road trip, sometimes saving others in the process. But they also make enemies when they encounter the Brotherhood, an extremist and violent religious cult. Over the course of the film, they pick up three additional travelers: Sister (Kelly McGillis), a nun whom they rescue; Belle (Danielle Harris), a pregnant young singer; and Willie (Sean Nelson), a black Iraq war veteran. Willie's presence is minimal, but it is palpable, as he is one of only three people of color in the film. Though they interact with a few outposts of humanity, Mister and Martin spend most of the film alone together. The climax centers upon Mister and Martin's battle with the Brotherhood's leader Jebedia Loven (Michael Cerveris), as the most dangerous and ultimately most unique thing in this world—a thinking vampire. The vampire Loven kills Sister, Willie, and Belle, torturing Belle to draw Mister and Martin to him. Mister and Loven fight, and Loven nearly defeats Mister, who is gravely injured before Mister and Martin destroy Loven. *Stake Land* ends quietly with Martin and Mister finding a young woman, Peggy, alone in her family's restaurant. Mister leaves Martin to return to vampire hunting, while Martin and Peggy continue to travel to New Eden.

Examining the niche of the vampire trope within post-apocalyptic narratives reveals the constructions of gender and the portrayal of violence embedded in conservative notions of normative gender structures. Like broader post-apocalyptic films and television as well as examples of apocalyptic vampire tales from literature, female characters within vampire post-apocalypse films, such as *Stake Land*, are lacking. When women are present, they are most frequently cast in the role of victim to be rescued and of the violated woman. The hero's role is to protect the beleaguered women. Additionally, the heroes of vampire apocalypse films demonstrate an image of masculinity built upon isolation, both physical and emotional. The landscapes are bleak and desolate, and social instability and physical insecurity caused by vampire and human attacks is a constant force that drives individual choices. Male characters in these narratives embody the tenet that "only the strong survive," and centralize the Wild West and military mantra of "sleeping with one eye open." These depictions of masculinity rely heavily on extreme violence not only for survival but also for entertainment in the cases of the treacherous villains, as if violence can stave off the ennui and instability of their lives.

Hierarchical constructs of gender thus remain and are distilled through vampire apocalypse fictions. The underlying concept is a tendency toward social Darwinism's "survival of the fittest," which is most predominant in vampire apocalypse fictions but also underpins a great deal of all vampire fiction. *Stake Land* demonstrates a particularly conservative vision of gender generally and masculinity specifically as it relies heavily on the idea that gendered norms must remain embedded in biological determinism. As Mary Wilson Carpenter writes, "In these patriarchal apocalyptics, 'Apocalypse' not only valorizes male divinity but is secured through the subordination or incorporation of the feminine, demonstrating a vested interest in maintaining the gender status quo."[3] As Carpenter articulates, many visions of the apocalypse reinforce gendered norms and stereotypes, which *Stake Land* demonstrates through the representations of Mister and Loven.

The Intersection of Religion and Masculinity

The specter of religion, from the Catholic Church to insane cults, haunts vampire apocalypse films. In *Stake Land*, the main foes of Martin, Mister, and their band of survivors are not the vampires, but a Christian-based religious cult, the Christian Army of Aryans, also known as the Brotherhood. It is an all-male organization that keeps women captive to fulfill domestic and sexual duties through a slavery system. The Brotherhood controls a vast amount of territory and wantonly rapes, pillages, plunders, and kills. It uses fear and violence to police the borders of its territory and consistently expand its area of control.

The Brotherhood sees vampires as a portent from God, harkening back to medieval notions of the vampire.[4] The leader of the Brotherhood, Jebedia Loven, says to Mister, "You kill them that come back. Them that serve us. Them that God brought down to do His work. Leaving us to purify the blood of our fathers. And when that day comes, He will bring them back, and peace and purity will reign on the earth forever. Amen." For Loven and his followers, God set the plague of vampires upon the earth to cleanse it of the impure, and the vampires are holy workers of sorts. For Mister and Martin, religion has nothing to do with this plague beyond its use by madmen and egomaniacs to influence others, and as an excuse for violence and control.

It is through the character of Sister that there is a glimpse of religious faith as a solace. Introduced in a torn nun's habit and wearing a thick silver cross, she does not falter in her belief in God in the face of either personal violence at the hands of the Brotherhood or the mindless pursuit of the vampires. When cornered by the vampires set upon her by Loven, she simply prays for forgiveness from God and takes her own life. While her faith is consistent, it is Mister and Martin's belief that religion is a tool of misdirection and self-deception that the film consistently reinforces. Martin, in his ever-present voiceover narration, relays, "In desperate times, false gods abound. People put their faith in the loudest preacher and hope they're right. But sometimes they're wrong, dead wrong." People distort religion, and therefore, it is a useless pursuit. Fear, in a world gone wrong, drives people to dangerous beliefs. Faith in God or humanity is misplaced, and only faith in oneself seems to ensure survival. For Mister and Martin, following a religious tradition is a mistake, as faith is easily manipulated. At moments throughout the film, Mister's reactions indicate a lack of belief in God or a belief that God has abandoned humanity. Moreover, Martin's voiceover implies that it is religion, or more specifically religious zealotry, not faith or a belief in a deity, that has diminished humanity.

Religion, in the form of Loven's fanatic cult, serves as a conservative force that seeks to amplify societal norms and structures surrounding gender and other social issues. Based in his reading of biblical scripture, Loven and his followers envision gender as a biological function grounded in reproduction and hierarchical ordering of male domination, and therefore, masculinity relies on physical power and desire is enacted through violence. The religion of the Brotherhood reinforces patriarchal power.

This religious patriarchy is reproduced through Loven's indoctrination of the young men he recruits through various methods, including violence and destruction of pre-existing family structures. Loven tells Martin, "We'll get you some religion, and bring you to God and the right way." For Loven, this means teaching Martin not only about their vision of religion but also their moral code, which includes torture, rape, and murder. His conservative and fanatical rhetoric comprises his leadership style. He believes that his right to speak and to take what he wants is divine, given to him by God, as is his position as leader of the Brotherhood and, therefore, of the world. That leadership position and his role as a messenger of God shape his masculinity. He views himself as a God-given leader in this post-apocalyptic world, and his hegemonic masculinity underscores his power to lead through violence and terror. Loven's role, as he sees it, is to enforce his belief system and his vision of order upon those around him. He has the power of life and death over not only his followers but also anyone who happens into his territory. Though he does not verbally articulate a specific idea of masculinity or gender roles, his actions and religious philosophy are clear, and embrace the patriarchal order.

Similarly, Mister does not articulate any particular concept of religion or gender roles, but he also has a philosophy, which is about rejecting a need for history. Mister's comment, "We don't do history. It doesn't do anyone any good," sets forth an ideology that the past, whether from before the vampire pandemic or after, has no role in a society in which humanity has come undone. His rejection of history and memory allow Mister to function as a warrior. Mister does not fight for the memory of dead loved ones or for the life that he lost: he fights only for survival. Forgetting the past creates an emotional distance for Mister from others. This distance allows Mister to slay vampires, and to function in the mad world of these bloodsuckers and cults.

Stake Land portrays forgetting the past as necessary for emotional survival and leadership. Mister sees history and remembrance as weaknesses or as vulnerabilities that can be exploited. The personal past serves only as a reminder of what is gone, and for Mister, those reminders are useless. Even the use of a person's name is a connection to the past that Mister rejects. The viewer knows Mister by no other name than Mister, which is what Martin calls him in his narration, and no character, including Mister himself, offers another name for him. By refusing a name, he further distances himself from his past. Memories of the past serve no purpose in a fight for survival in Mister's philosophy, and thus he rejects the connections that a name can allow.

In contrast, the women in *Stake Land*, Sister and Belle, use reminders of the past to signify hope for the unknown future. Mister's rejection of history and memory is consistently juxtaposed with the women's feminine-coded celebrations of the past. The film codes them as feminine by linking ideas of memory and history with the feminine stereotypes of emotionality and irrationality, demonstrated by Sister and Belle's collection of trinkets from the past and their desire to talk about their emotions, about other people and events, and about their hopes and dreams for the future. Mister's refutation of history opposes this feminization of remembrance and emotion. Because he lives only in the moment without regard to the past, it serves as an allowance for the violence that he must commit.

Linking Violence and Hegemonic Masculinity

A key element to post-apocalypse tales, including vampire apocalypses, centers upon violence; human beings are ultimately portrayed in these vampire apocalypse narratives as violent and self-serving as a whole. Mister and Martin must use violence to combat the violence of other humans and to survive in the face of the monstrous; there is seemingly no other way to survive in the apocalypse but through violence. There is, however, a distinction—a hierarchy or justification system of violence—between necessary and sanctioned violence, and unnecessary and unsanctioned violence. Mister justifies his use of violence as needed within the context of the vampire apocalypse in order to survive and to protect others. He relies on violence to combat the violence of the world of vampires. In this manner, *Stake Land* replicates stereotypes about hegemonic masculinity, in which men are inherently violent and must be able to react to situations with violence. Two options exist for men under the hegemonic construction of masculinity: they can be violent for self-gain and/or entertainment, or they can utilize violence in protection of others. Nuances to these rules of violence include acts of mercy, compassion, and tenderness that show the difference between pugnacious cruelty and necessary violence, but the use and acceptability of violence, especially sexualized violence toward both women and men, demonstrates the film's essential linking of violence with masculinity.

Sexualized violence is a regular tool of those whom the narrative codes as evil or villainous. Connell writes, "Many members of the privileged group use violence to sustain their dominance . . . Most men do not attack or harass women; but those who do are unlikely to think themselves deviant. On the contrary they usually feel they are entirely justified, that they are exercising a right. They are authorized by an ideology of supremacy."[5] Sexual violence is a key apparatus for the enforcement of patriarchal constructs of gender, in which male domination and superiority are maintained. While not all men use sexual violence as an instrument of oppression and domination, the threat of force and violence underscores the vulnerability of women to the vampires as well as human men.

In *Stake Land*, this sexualized violence, or the threat of sexual violence, is prominent throughout the film. In a telling early scene, Mister and Martin come upon Sister as she is escaping two members of the Brotherhood who have raped her. One of the men is still pulling up his pants as he chases her, which indicates that she escapes recent, imminent, and potentially continuing sexual violence. To Martin, this act is horrific on multiple levels: because of the sexualized violence against women as a whole, but also because she is an older woman and a nun, one who is visibly coded as such. Mister kills both men. He calms Sister and helps her into the backseat of the car. When questioned by Sister about his killing of the men, Mister replies, "In my book, rapists got no place to live." His code is one that states that sexualized violence is off-limits; even though he lives by violence and has no compunction about killing, rape is untenable. This demonstrates the manner in which the good guys and the bad guys are constructed; how and why they use violence indicates one's place within the schema of hero and villain. This moment demonstrates the dual uses of violence in proving manhood within hegemonic masculinity's stereotypes and constructions. Mister and Martin's masculinity is built upon an ethic of respect for other people who meet their criteria of humanity, and those criteria rest upon how those others interact with and demonstrate respect for other people. Those whom Mister views as less than human though, he punishes violently. In the case of the two who rape Sister, Mister is quick but brutal in his punishment, rupturing one of the men's trachea with a single blow to his throat and impaling the other with a stake through his back. His punishment of the men demonstrates his strength and ultimately his power over other men, but unlike Loven, he does not torture. Mister uses violence to protect and to punish, and as his apprentice, Martin embraces Mister's view of violence.

While Mister and Martin use violence for self-protection and to aid others, Loven and his followers utilize violence to profit and entertain themselves. The Brotherhood, on Loven's orders, terrorizes anyone who enters its proclaimed territory. Its members shoot some immediately, steal from others, and take intruders back to their camp as forced labor, mainly women for forced sexual interactions. They mislead and capture Mister initially because they want to kill him as a trophy because Mister has gained a reputation for his vampire hunting. Pursuing others, especially another hunter, is entertainment for the Brotherhood in much the same ways it utilizes rape, as a way to stave off boredom by terrorizing women. Its exercises of violence underscore the Brotherhood's vision that masculinity imbues men with power over others through physical and moral superiority. Loven, as the leader of the Brotherhood and the identified villain, acts as a distorted mirror to Mister throughout *Stake Land*.

Mirroring Hegemonic Masculinity

Stake Land is demonstrative of a set of vampire apocalypse films that include Francis Lawrence's *I Am Legend* (2007), David Slade's *30 Days of Night* (2007), and Scott Stewart's *Priest* (2011). In these vampire apocalypse films, a male protagonist puts himself at great risk, even to the point of self-sacrifice, in order to save others against a male nemesis that is portrayed as a mirror and a distortion of the hero. Various interactions between the hero and the villain explore and construct concepts of masculinity in these films. Through this mirroring, hegemonic masculinity splits into two visions: one in which a character's use of culturally predominant stereotypes of masculinity protect and help other people, and one in which a character's use of those same stereotypes harm others. The former is associated with the hero, and the latter with the villain.

The core story arc of *Stake Land* centers upon this mirroring and distorting of the masculinity of the hero, Mister, and his nemesis, Loven, as is the case also in *I Am Legend*, *30 Days of Night*, and *Priest*. The hero is flawed in some way, but he is essentially trying to do the right thing for humanity and his group of survivors, while his nemesis, whether human or monster, desires self-aggrandizement and the annihilation of humans as a whole, or at least those who do not belong to his own group. Susanne Kord and Elizabeth Krimmer argue that, "Contemporary masculinity is defined by its ability to navigate between the threat of betrayal and the challenge of trust, between the splendor of heroic individualism and the need for cooperation and community, between killing and caring."[6] As Kord and Krimmer point out, contemporary masculinity hinges on a balancing act of survival and ethics. Mister and Loven must traverse a world that that has the potential to physically destroy them, and also strip away their humanity and their moral code. Ultimately, Mister overcomes his mirrored nemesis. Loven loses his human life as he has already lost his humanity, and Mister maintains his moral code but sacrifices his relationship with Martin in order to give his adopted son a chance at a perceived better life. Mister's willingness to risk death and to go into exile offers a view of self-sacrificing masculinity that is at odds with the villainous self-centeredness of his nemesis, Loven, who wants only his own continuation.

Mister and Loven both seek survival for themselves and outwardly appear to uphold the concept of normative masculinity in which men hold the ultimate authority, use their physical strength to overcome adversity, and seek vengeance when wronged. While Mister and Loven both rely on violence and their power to lead, Mister's masculinity may be slightly more complex than Loven's: he is taciturn but paternally caring, although he appears to be a hardened Wild West-type gunslinger with no soft feelings at all; he upholds aspects of socially constructed versions of hegemonic masculinity, but he also undoes this image as a hardened man lacking softness and emotional connections; his staid compassion shows through small gestures. For example, after Mister kills a nun-turned-vampire in front of Sister, who knew the woman, he buries the dead nun, which is not his normal practice. Mister buries her for Sister's benefit because of her visible devastation at the nun's state and her death. Martin says, "Mister dug a grave. I think he felt bad for the sister. He did pull the fangs out, but he waited until she went to pick the flowers." Mister cannot pass up the opportunity to collect his trophy from his vampire kill, as the fangs grant him cultural capital in the gated communities. His collection of fangs gains respect for him as a vampire slayer, but he demonstrates a concern for Sister's sensibilities and emotions. Sister has an emotional connection to the other nun that Mister respects through his actions.

Martin indicates that both Mister's burial of the nun and his decision to remove the nun's fangs when Sister is not present reveal Mister's pity for the dead nun and his kindness for Sister, because neither are typical of Mister's treatment of the vampires or of the living. Though there is no direct address of Mister's motivations outside of Martin's above narration, this moment is the only on-screen burial of the dead—either vampire or human—in the film. The burial act is indicative of Mister's compassion for Sister as well as his asking for her forgiveness for his brutality when staking the nun-turned-vampire.

In his role as Mister's fun-house style mirror reflection, Loven's masculinity signals hegemonic masculinity. His constant stream of dialogue reveals his egomania and his mental instability. Aside from the narration by Martin, Loven likely speaks the most words in the film. His reliance upon sexualized violence underscores his hyper-masculinity because it is made possible by his position within the Brotherhood but also as a man who asserts his will through his physical strength. Loven is unstable, but his instability grows from his inability to embrace a different vision of masculinity—one that incorporates an ethic of care or disavows violence for entertainment. Thus he becomes a psychotic despot, bent on destroying humans in order to implement what he sees as God's plan to rid the world of the unrighteous. Here lies *Stake Land*'s most straightforward critique of hegemonic masculinity: Loven strongly signals that it is not the vampires, but rather other humans, specifically other men, who are the most frightening in this world gone awry.

Ironically, when he becomes a vampire, Loven seems poised to become one more feminized male in a long line of feminized monsters. Barbara Creed writes, "Whenever male bodies are represented as monstrous in the horror film they assume characteristics usually associated with the female body: they experience a blood cycle, change shape, bleed, give birth, become penetrable, are castrated."[7] Creed argues that vampires are the ultimate feminized male monster, as they replicate images of the *vagina dentata* and have blood cycles akin to menstruation. Jebedia Loven, though, is not the feminized male vampire of earlier psychoanalytic theories, such as Creed describes. He does not bleed or give birth, nor is he castrated: he becomes torturer and destroyer extraordinaire. Loven's vampire is a new type of vampire in the Stake Land: "a thinker"—one who plans and stalks. In this way, he reinforces the vision of hegemonic masculinity that relies on intellect, rationality, and cunning. His egomania, his faith, and yes, his hegemonic rendering of masculinity, all lead to his belief that he is now a god that walks the earth. When confronting Mister for their final battle, Loven says, "I am a vengeful god. Eye for eye, tooth for tooth, son for son . . . I am your god now." For Loven, he is the ultimate masculine authority in his role as vampire and vengeful god.

In the end, the film returns to Mister and Martin's complications of masculinity. In the final battle with Loven, Martin's rush to save Belle results in Loven knocking him unconscious. When Mister enters, Loven overpowers him and crucifies him by pinning him to the wall with Mister's own stakes. Using a broken beam, Martin stakes Loven through the back but is not able to drive enough force to penetrate the heart. Mister kicks Loven back driving the stake through Loven's heart. Both Martin and Mister fail to kill Loven individually; it is Mister and Martin combined that triumph, and they defeat Loven only through their combined forces. Through their cooperation and trust of each other, Mister and Martin overcome Loven. Their cooperative and familial relationship complicates the vision of masculinity demonstrated through the early part of the film. This moment empowers multiple masculinities, in which various ideas of gendered norms can intersect and thrive. Mister does not have to defeat Loven single-handedly in order to maintain his manhood. He can accept help from his surrogate son to defeat his foe and also, afterward, to care for his battered body.

Masculinity and the Post-Apocalyptic Context

The moment of the apocalypse seems as if it should offer a place in which stereotypes, roles, and norms of gender could be reimagined. Yet as evidenced in *Stake Land*, the world after the apocalypse most frequently reverts to patterns of oppression and, in fact, reinforces gendered norms. Wheeler Winston Dixon states, "Equality will at last be achieved in the final seconds before Armageddon, when countries, boundaries, and political systems instantaneously evaporate, making a mockery of all our efforts at self-preservation."[8] It is in the moment of the impending end of the world that humanity can come to understand the pointlessness of oppression and structures of normative constructions of gender, race, and sexuality. In post-apocalypse narratives such as *Stake Land*, the need to rebuild society often replicates that which has come before without questioning previous norms and oppressions. As I have argued, *Stake Land*, in fact, reproduces pre-apocalypse ideas about masculinity, and maintains a certain patriarchal and structural dominance of men over women.

Yet at the same time, some individuals potentially move away from these oppressive structures. Martin, for example, begins to complicate hegemonic masculinity. His induction and transition to adulthood comes at the point in which he makes difficult decisions and struggles to overcome the enemy through intelligence, teamwork, and compassion. Hope emboldens Martin's masculinity. He does not have to live as a taciturn hermit in order to demonstrate his masculinity, as the ending of the movie allows him to accept a partnership with a young woman, Peggy. For a time, Mister, too, lives in relationship with others, and while this causes pain in the form of loss, he also survives because of his connection to Martin.

Martin incorporates aspects of stereotypes and norms of masculinity as well as femininity. Through his apprenticeship with Mister, Martin learns to embrace the life of violence and fighting that men, particularly, must engage in the world of the vampire hoards. But he also embraces the act of remembrance, through storytelling. *Stake Land* codes storytelling and remembrance of the past as feminine values, and therefore, Martin's honoring of the past and present interrupt a notion of hegemonic masculinity for him. Though he does not reveal a great deal about his own history from before the vampires, he chronicles his travels with Mister and his journey into adulthood. His oral history and his desire to know about those around him demonstrate a break from Mister's philosophy. Martin shows emotions, such as fear and hope, even while acknowledging the necessity of violence in the world filled with blood-craving monsters. In part, Martin's identity blends visions of masculinity and femininity, which allows for the slippage in gendered stereotypes and norms. Through blending his identity, Martin will thrive in his hybrid role, as the film ends with a literal sign of hope: a town limits sign with New Eden inscribed upon it.

Conclusion

The rising of the vampire from the graves of our imagination shows the way in which the vampire tale is able to articulate and shape our understandings of social norms, fears, and ideals. The vampire has long stood as a marker for the cultural outsider: the Other against which we articulate ourselves. In the world of *Stake Land*, vampires represent the basest and most degraded portion of humanity. They look like us, but they are driven only by their hungers and appetites. The vampires are merely predators who cannot control their need to feed, which makes them a terrifying adversary. The true enemy of this film, though, is the human being who is remorseless, and rejects both compassion and restraint. The hybrid, the thinking vampire Loven, incorporates the worst of both the human enemy and the vampire predator.

Post-apocalyptic vampire narratives act as a lens for examining the production of violence as well as exploring the deconstruction and replication of gendered norms within contemporary American popular culture. They allow for an examination of cultural norms through a medium that can be fantastical and in which anything can happen. They are, therefore, a place to analyze, critique, and reinforce the current visions of a hegemonic masculinity; they are also a safe space for articulating an idea of multiple, competing, and cooperating masculinities that allow room for the negotiation of a fluid and destabilizing image of genders. The post-apocalyptic context of *Stake Land* should offer a space to re-create and re-envision masculinity, but unfortunately, *Stake Land* mainly works to reinforce stereotypes of hegemonic masculinity. In many ways, the vampire apocalypse reestablishes conservative articulations of masculinity that reinforce stereotypes of emotional distance and violence. Through engaging with cultural institutions such as religion, and examinations of social mores and norms, *Stake Land*, as a genre-mixing horror, science fiction, and action film, offers a reading of contemporary American culture that questions but ultimately reaffirms many norms of hegemonic masculinity, though it does offer a glimmer of hope for a new vision of gendered norms.

Notes

1. I will likely spoil major plot pieces via my analysis of *Stake Land* and likely other films as well, so readers beware.
2. R. W. Connell, *Masculinities*, 2nd ed. (Berkeley: University of California Press, 2005), 77.
3. Mary Wilson Carpenter, "Representing Apocalypse: Sexual Politics and the Violence of Revelation," *Postmodern Apocalypse: Theory and Cultural Practice at the End*, ed. Richard Dellamora, 107–135 (Philadelphia: University of Pennsylvania Press, 1995), 120.
4. The medieval Catholic Church sent priests out to investigate vampire outbreaks throughout Christendom because these outbreaks indicated a signal from God, as chronicled for instance by Dom Augustin Calmet's *Traité sur les Apparitions des Esprits et sur les Vampires* written in 1746. This work is known today as *The Phantom World: Or, The Philosophy of Spirits, Apparitions* based on Henry Christmas' 1850 translation and edition.
5. Connell, *Masculinities*, 83.
6. Susanne Kord and Elisabeth Krimmer, *Contemporary Hollywood Masculinities: Gender, Genre, and Politics* (New York: Palgrave Macmillan, 2011), 5.
7. Barbara Creed, "Dark Desires: Male Masochism in the Horror Film," in *Screening the Male: Exploring Masculinities in Hollywood Cinema*, eds. Steven Cohan and Ina Rae Hark, 118–133 (London: Routledge, 1993), 118.
8. Wheeler Winston Dixon, *Visions of the Apocalypse: Spectacles of Destruction in American Cinema* (London: Wallflower Press, 2003), 2.

CHAPTER 10

The Apocalypse Is No-Thing To Wish For: Revisioning Traumatic Masculinities in John Hillcoat's *The Road*

Brent Strang

There is a curious irony in the young adult male habit of indulging in survival fantasies while sitting idly on the couch. Digitally interfacing with fingers and thumbs, sheltered by modernity's creature comforts—their bodies could not be further removed from the strife-torn apocalyptic landscapes depicted onscreen. The myth of regeneration through violence surely animates this brand of entertainment, but perhaps there is another psychodynamic at work that rivets viewers and gamers to specifically apocalyptic and dystopic virtual worlds. Trauma-studies scholar E. Ann Kaplan's forthcoming work on "trauma future-tense cinema" explores what's culturally productive in this genre of violent, seemingly gratuitous, spectacle.[1] Though I take her point that the traumatic function of these films rouses audience awareness of the politics of our contemporary moment, cultural studies of popular phenomena must also consider how genre conventions perpetuate a discourse that underwrites and often undermines political statement.

Genres speak to mass audiences, and the genres under examination in this essay are embedded with masculinist assumptions. I consider here how the Post-Apocalyptic, Survival, War, Western and Zombie genres comprise a wider generic field—a trans-generic cluster of shared tropes and conventions that spans film, television, video games, comic books, advertisements, etc. When analyzed through Dominick LaCapra's model of "trauma, absence, and loss," this generic field shows a problematic tendency to stage perceived crises in masculinity in narrative terms as "paradise lost." The assumption here is that historical events have eroded away an "essential" core of masculinity and the male hero must endure apocalyptic extremes in order to regain it. Although John Hillcoat's 2009 film *The Road*, based on Cormac McCarthy's titular novel, partakes in many of the tropes and iconography of the aforementioned genres, it distinguishes itself through its formal style and structure. In its mise-en-scène and strategic use of flashbacks and plot sequencing, the film creates an aesthetics of trauma that runs against the generic grain. It empathically unsettles viewers with a temporality of hopelessness and presentness so that they might glimpse an alternate, more ethical, representation of masculinity.

For some 20 years now, there has been a marked increase in apocalyptic and dsytopic narratives in film, television, video games and other media. Kaplan understands this phenomenon as a cultural practice of vicarious trauma. She wonders if this proliferation might have a healing function, or if it merely fuels an ever-circulating feedback loop of anxiety. Trauma future-tense cinema refers to a cycle of films that include *Children of Men* (2006), *28 Days* (2000), *The Day after Tomorrow* (2004), *The Book of Eli* (2010), *The Road* and others that are set in the near-future. Unlike other "futurist technological" sci-fi such as *The Matrix* (1999–2003) or *The Terminator* series (1984–2009), trauma future-tense films depict worlds that are "already seemingly possible given scientific projections (of, for example, the devastating impact of climate change)."[2] "These films are not allegories," Kaplan stipulates, "they insist on the probability of the worlds shown or . . . the possibility of these worlds already being here."[3] Images of civilization's degeneration are inferred as the logical outcome of current socio-economic, political and environmental conditions. To the degree that these films construct an aesthetics of trauma in similar ways, Kaplan argues trauma future-tense cinema can be productive by helping to "demonstrate how we will get to any future we think of from where we are now."[4] For example, *Children of Men* warns of our present susceptibility to totalitarian control; it critiques late capitalism and the attendant issues of immigration, security and climate change.

Although Kaplan counts *The Road* as an instance of trauma future-tense, the film deviates from her model in an important manner. The setting is some 15–20 years in the future, after an unnamed catastrophe has devastated the planet to the point where no animals, plants or insects remain. All vestiges of civilization have collapsed, leaving a few bands of roving cannibals and scrounging nomads to endure the impossible landscape. The unnamed protagonists, Man and Boy (his son), uphold their moral imperative against eating human flesh as they slowly waste away from hunger. Foraging for whatever scraps have been overlooked by the thousands of dying scavengers who've passed before them, their sole aim is to survive the trek southward to the warmth of the ocean coastline. The world represented is imaginable given scientific projections of ecological disaster, but since there is no account for the recent apocalypse, we cannot infer how or even if humanity is to blame. Not knowing whether the cause was nuclear war, a meteorite, a super volcano or something else prevents any political critique of humanity's responsibility for the demise of civilization. What then ensues is a morality tale about cultivating compassion and ethical masculinity on a frontier rendered grey by the absence of Gaia's regenerative power as well as horrifying by the omnipresence of zombie-like cannibals.

Despite the lack of socio-political and economic commentary, *The Road* still functions as a form of cultural criticism. Thematically and aesthetically it plants its roots in the soil of the Western, War, Zombie and Survivor genres. Yet in staging trauma as something that needs to be worked through as opposed to conquered, it subverts the myth of masculine regeneration that has become so prevalent in the generic field. The hugely popular *Survivor* television series (2000–) has spawned a spate of others including *Survivors* (2008, 2010), *Survivorman* (2004–) and *Man vs. Wild* (2006–2011). Survivor plots and tropes also crop up in the contemporary zombie craze, in films like *I am Legend* (2011), the *Living Dead* remakes (1978–2009), the *28 Days* series (2000, 2002) and *The Walking Dead* comic book, video game and television series (2010–). So, too, do we see survivor themes in Western and War films like *The Proposition* (2005), *The Three Burials of Melquiades Estrada* (2005), *Rescue Dawn* (2006) and the war-zombie hybrids *World War Z* (2013) and *Zombie Wars* (2007). In video games ranging from *Resident Evil* to the *Fallout* series, post-apocalyptic/survivor scenarios are too many to count. In any case, the central trope in these video games, comics, films and television shows is the need to persevere with scarce resources in harsh and hostile environs.

We may read this fetishization of survival practice as a way of allaying anxieties about over-dependence on creature comforts. If our increasing acclimatization to digital interfacing, hyper-stimulation and sedentary consumption breeds concern over physical atrophy or "turning soft," the result is a yearning for muscular stress and challenge, as well as reconnecting with nature. Whether or not the genders respond to such worries differently is beyond the scope of this chapter, but the generic field in which this fetishization takes place is mostly gendered male. More specifically, the narrative scenarios portrayed assume masculinist subject viewers, regardless of their gender. Protagonists are invariably men, mostly white, who must prove their self-sufficiency and competence over other men, frequently through violence. A sexist division of labor is consistently implied, and women, when they appear at all, are relegated to the sidelines of narrative action. The survival landscape is therefore constructed as a masculinist domain. There, audiences can identify with male heroes who reconstitute themselves in the image of a coherent and able-bodied masculinity, which entails such traits as ruggedness, self-sufficiency, level-headedness and physical dominance.

Within this masculinist domain, the apocalyptic landscape works as a sort of cleansing fantasy that renders the process of masculine regeneration more visible. In this respect, *The Road*'s generic affinity with the Western is pertinent. The film shares not only the Western's emphasis on masculinity and the "ethical" use of violence, but also its penchant for long shots and long takes of frontier horizons. The clearing of infrastructure also seems a necessary precondition to the discourse of masculine regeneration. Clint Eastwood once remarked that the Western remains viable because of the longing for a time when it still seemed plausible that one person could "make a difference," as opposed to today when everything is "so mired down in bureaucracy that people can't fathom a way of sorting it out."[5] Just as Westerns wind us back to a "simpler" time, apocalyptic landscapes project us forward: they clear away civilization's strictures and revive the frontier conditions where "man" can "heroically" invent himself anew. The generic field of this critique is undoubtedly founded upon America's long-standing Frontier Myth. This is plain to see in each text's following of the tripartite narrative scenario described by cultural historian Richard Slotkin: "separation [from civilization], temporary regression to a more primitive or 'natural' state, and *regeneration through violence*."[6] In *Gunfighter Nation*, the third volume of his magnum opus on the Frontier Myth in American history, Slotkin tracks the prevalence of this narrative apparatus in the so-called "male" genres of the Western, War, Detective and Sci-fi genres. Though he doesn't address masculinity specifically, I've argued elsewhere that Slotkin's formula serves as well as a prescription for masculine subject formation.[7] The tripartite scenario provides a roadmap for overcoming adversity, a sort of gender-performative script that, upon completion, delivers the male hero and those who would identify with him into a masculine ideal. I use the Frontier Myth here as a critical rubric to determine whether a film promotes or critiques this gender-performative script by the ways in which it either adopts or deviates from the tripartite scenario.

A second useful rubric is the death-drive psychodynamic. If the Frontier Myth operates on one level, then an injection of trauma takes place on another. Kaplan proposes that the wellspring of trauma future-tense cinema is Freud's death-drive. Indeed, it's hard to ignore the intuitive connection between trauma's compulsion to repeat and audiences' obsessive return to screens showing wide-scale annihilation—as if to master their inner death-drive. In such events the near-future settings are even more effective for their *visceral* as opposed to their *visible* proximity to today. If it's true that the death-drive outwardly manifests through a deluge of doomsday projections and reportage of mass destruction and entropy, then trauma future-tense provides a fantasmatic safe-space where one can die preferentially, in one's "own fashion" as Freud would say."[8,9] But as scholar Rosi Braidotti points out, Freud regarded the vital function of the self as much more desperate and fragile than he could publicly admit in his writings. Against the death-drive, the vital function merely "consists of blocking the flows, storing up energy (capital, profits, fats, money), fixing the subject in sedentary stability."[10] The death-drive pushes relentlessly in the opposite direction, however, aiming at a state of perpetual motion and discharge of energy until all is spent. The vital function of the self or ego is no more than a temporary binding of energy—a wrapper, ever in the process of unwrapping.

Bearing Braidotti's description in mind, we can interpret the literal road in Hillcoat's film as an apt metaphor for Freud's death-drive. What are those scenes of huddling by the campfire, showering in the waterfall and holding out in the bomb-shelter so amply stocked with supplies, if not momentary detours—fleeting respites—from the fatalistic call of the road? What is their rickety shopping cart, which gets ransacked time and again, but a fruitless effort to store up vital necessities? The specter of death is visible from the moment we first see the father's hollow-cheeked figure, and it closes in mercilessly scene-by-scene, pace-by-excruciating-pace, until his final quiescence by the ocean.[11] If, as Kaplan suggests, trauma future-tense cinema projects the death-drive into these scenarios so that one may attain a sense of mastery over it, then the ego/death-drive binary provides us a second rubric to critique the generic field.

It is precisely through both rubrics that we see *The Road* distinguish itself, even as it partakes of the generic field's common themes and iconography. To reiterate, the generic field is a trans-generic cluster of texts that dramatizes the trauma of mass annihilation, clears the diegesis of civilization and infrastructure, stages a tripartite scenario that ends with masculine regeneration through violence and conquers the death-drive through surviving apocalyptic landscapes. Within this context it's immediately apparent how *The Road* eschews the fantasy of masculine regeneration: the father is not regenerated, but utterly undone by the narrative's progression. He is the very image of brokenness and desperation, exhibiting mastery over nothing. In one scene his survival is narrowly sustained by the dumb luck of a passed-over seedpod found in the corner of an abandoned barn. If the death-drive is let loose in other narratives only to be recontained and mastered through the protagonist's reconstitution, *The Road*, by contrast, leaves it to completely unfurl.

Dominick LaCapra's work on trauma, absence and loss is particularly useful here for exploring the ethics of representing traumatic events.[12] In the process of suffering of such events, LaCapra argues for the importance of distinguishing between absence and loss using Freud's concepts of mourning and melancholia. He writes, "When absence is converted to loss, one increases the likelihood of misplaced nostalgia or utopian politics in quest of a new totality or fully unified community."[13] What's at stake is the avoidance of the pitfalls and detours of working through trauma, especially when absence is conflated with loss, or the one is converted into the other. Though the context of LaCapra's writing is the Holocaust and South African apartheid, his versatile model can also be applied to the "crisis in masculinity" rhetoric embedded in the apocalyptic/dystopic generic field. What is perceived in Western contemporary men's experience as *absence*—absence of uncontested privilege, absence of lasting marriage and career longevity, absence of an "essential" character of manliness and virility—gets converted into *loss* as though these things were not only entitlements, but also their possessions in decades past. I submit, in turn, that this generic field participates in a "misplaced nostalgia or utopian politics" by attempting to reconstitute ontologically "coherent" masculinity through Slotkin's tripartite scenario. In other words, late modernity's oppressive conditions traumatize masculinities by their "feminizing" effects, requiring men to *separate* themselves from these strictures, *regress* to a more "natural" state and *regenerate* themselves through some savage trial by fire.

This fantasmatic process of subject formation is certainly not new to cinema, just as today's crisis of masculinity rhetoric is not new. As sociologists of masculinity Michael Kimmel and Stephen Whitehead have both documented, clamor about a "crisis in masculinity" has been heard in almost every generation in the twentieth century.[14] Yet, this doesn't change the fact that this rhetoric persists and remains as convinced of itself as ever. The following passage written by Whitehead in 2002 holds equally well today:

> [A]cross many societies, most notably but not only in the Western world, the idea that men are facing some nihilistic future, degraded, threatened and marginalized by a combination of women's 'successful' liberation and wider social and economic transformations has become a highly potent, almost commonsense, if at times contested, understanding of men at this point in history.[15]

While there may be evidence of structural changes men can use to justify their personal or collective sense of traumatic loss, it is likely this gendered "cultural condition" has more to do with a tendency to essentialize masculinity than with the historical changes themselves. Post-structuralist theory informs us that the self is multiple, unstable and contingent. Glimpsing this knowledge about the self may fill the subject with existential dread about the lack of inner authenticity, precipitating a search for ontological security. For Whitehead this search is always already a "gendered quest:" the "constant engagement in those discursive practices of signification that suggest masculinity" constitutes what Whitehead calls one's "masculine ontology."[16]

So it is that the absence of an inner authenticity, for which many men continue to search, gets taken up and conflated with its loss, generation after generation. The process of conversion between absence and loss, LaCapra maintains, "is also crucial to conventional narrative structure," which transitions from an Edenic beginning of wholeness and unity, through loss, trials and tribulations, only to be recovered at some higher level of insight by the end.[17] LaCapra observes that regeneration through violence also follows this same schema. In the simplest terms, the process is about mastering anxiety. And anxiety is different from fear, Freud tells us, because anxiety has the quality of indefiniteness and the lack on an identifiable object. Anxiety is, furthermore, "the elusive experience or affect related to absence—[a] fear that has no thing (nothing) as its object."[18] Converting absence into loss becomes a way to identify and locate a lost object, which, through seizing upon it, enables one to master their anxiety. But there is a key difference between what is absent and what is lost. In LaCapra's words:

> Paradise absent is different from paradise lost: it may not be seen as annihilated only to be regained in some hoped-for, apocalyptic future or sublimely blank utopia that, through a kind of creation *ex nihilo*, will bring total renewal, salvation or redemption. It is not there, and one must therefore turn to other, non-redemptive options . . . other than an evacuated past and a vacuous or blank, somehow redemptive future.[19]

This speaks to the heart of the gendered fantasy of regeneration through violence that fuels the apocalyptic/dystopic field, a fantasy that rests upon the conflation and subsequent conversion of absence into loss. For LaCapra, absence must be accepted *as absence*, whereas loss, when it truly exists, must be mourned as a process of "working through." When loss is not worked through, it risks being converted into absence, which results in interminable melancholy—what LaCapra calls "acting out."

The Road engages with absence, loss, mourning and melancholy in a more ethically responsible way than other genre films of its ilk. To recapitulate, the generic tendency is to displace the structural absence of coherence of self into a historical loss of essential masculinity, and then project this loss into diegetic landscapes where the lost object can be regained. But *The Road* does not wholly abide by Slotkin's formula: while there is separation and regression, there is no conventional ideal of masculinity regained through violence.

Additionally, its formal structure dictates an unconventional aesthetics of trauma. The father is haunted by reminiscences, but the temporal logic of trauma is somewhat reversed. At times he is haunted by memories of his wife, his house, his horse and the myriad blessings taken for granted in the civilized world. However, it is not the past, but the present—and its ever-traumatizing absence—that stokes these reminiscences. These nostalgic memories are also mingled with more traumatic ones. The latter are of the first years after the unnamed "event," as the family of three struggles to sustain itself. We see their rations steadily diminishing, their belongings becoming firewood—first the furniture, then the piano, then the floorboards—each piece more precious than the last. One fateful evening the wife decides to abandon the family and her image is slowly engulfed by the icy darkness. The intermingling of these contrasting good and bad memories makes a menace of the past that is slightly more bearable than the present. In this way pastness becomes a portrait of loss.

The present, however, is cast as pure absence. One of the most harrowing features of this film's diegesis that further distinguishes it from the generic field is its utter absence of life. There are no birds, insects, plants or even seeds to be found; the world is nothing more than a mute and endless mass of gray sludge. Comparing this post-apocalyptic landscape with those seen in the *28 Days* or *The Walking Dead* series, it is striking what comfort viewers can take in the latter's abundance objects, because such objects are vital to the characters' resuscitation. *The Walking Dead*, for example, pays little heed to the characters' food supply—a structural absence that creates the sense of unlimited supply.[20] In *28 Days Later*, whenever the characters need to stock up, they hit the supermarket and freely fill their carts, depicting the transgressive pleasure of a raiding party. Plenitude and abundance, then, buoy these survivors and revitalize their utopian journey of masculine regeneration forged through a savage war on zombies. In coping with the trauma of post-apocalyptic devastation, Gaia's regenerative capacity is instrumental; it animates a hopeful, forward-looking horizon. By contrast, *The Road* pushes the image of a barren and inert Gaia to the extreme, insisting on the present, which is agonized by the past and bereft of a future. The formal arrangement of its flashbacks pitches the past against the present and temporally converts the real losses suffered by the father into absence, as opposed to the conventional turning of absence into loss. Whereas the latter retains its utopian dimension, the former copes with the experience of historical loss by recasting the world as a place both brutal and desolate where precious signs of vitality are fleeting, if they exist at all.

Even so, the conversion from loss into absence is problematic in another way. According to LaCapra, "When loss is converted into . . . absence, one faces the impasse of endless melancholy, impossible mourning and interminable aporia in which any process of working through the past and its historical losses is prematurely aborted." This is a fitting description for the overwhelming affect clouding *The Road*. LaCapra understands mourning as a form of "working through" and melancholia as a form of "acting out." As such, there are various scenes where the father's process of mourning personal loss is dashed by melancholia's tendency to "act out."

One such scene happens when the father takes his son on a detour to see his childhood home. As we've come to expect, exposure to the elements has left the place in soggy ruin. He shows the boy the place on the mantle where they used to hang their Christmas stockings. When he sees his son's bewilderment, he begins to explain, then stops himself with an air of defeat. How to explain Christmas stockings to one who has no experience of Christmas? Sensing the heaviness of his father's melancholy, the boy voices his concern, saying, "I don't think we should be doing this," and leaves to wait outside. The father remains, almost in a trance. He picks up the couch's seat cushion from the floor, traces the paisley design that has miraculously retained its color and places it squarely on the couch. He sits down on it. From there he looks at the blank television screen while his reflection is momentarily blotted out by a trickle of water running down. He is so traumatically paralyzed by melancholy that the mise-en-scène weeps for him.

In a moment of sensory reengagement, the father becomes possessed by the past. He is not only possessed by his family life, but by the couch and the entire world it signifies that is no longer. The viewer might reflect here on the irony of the couch as a metaphor for late modernity's creature comforts, the very place where they sit and watch their survival programs, kill zombies on the Xbox and identify with fantasies of masculine regeneration. Such scenes of interminable melancholy are nonetheless symptomatic of *The Road*'s conversion of loss to absence; here the unbearable conditions of scarcity and lack provoke a narcissistic identification with the lost object that can never be retrieved. To be clear, this lost object is not the same as the nonexistent lost object central to the generic field—that is, essential masculinity. Stripped of electricity, cable connection and the hundred other things that comprise the home entertainment milieu, the television is a shadow of its former state, and really no longer a television at all. It is precisely such vestigial objects that haunt the father's field of vision, incessantly reminding him of what is at one and the same time lost and absent. Stuck in this impasse, the father becomes narcissistically entranced by the television's former life-world, while the screen itself can only reflect back his own melancholic disposition.

The Road's formal structure juxtaposes scenes like these against certain others in order to construct a temporality of trauma. Scenes of melancholy are interspersed with scenes of mourning where the father more effectively works through his sense of loss. One such scene of mourning happens on a bridge. He decides at long last (it's been five years or more) to shed himself of the two remaining tokens from his marriage. He takes one last look at the wallet photo of his wife and then tosses it into the river. Next is the ring, which he nudges slowly across the concrete rail until it reaches the edge, where he pauses. At this point we witness his most painful reminiscence of the night she left. For all his anguished pleading, she would not change her mind. As he narrates in voiceover: "She was gone, and the coldness of it was her final gift. She died somewhere in the dark. There's no other tale to tell." As he prepares to push the ring over the edge, the frame lingers on his stoic visage. The scene which began with his quiet weeping at the memory of having to hack apart their piano has now transitioned to his cold stamping out of emotion, a lesson remembered from his wife's parting. After this scene he suffers no more *bad* memories.

However, he does still suffer moments of melancholy. The scene on the couch, for instance, comes *after* the mourning on the bridge, indicating one step forward, two steps back. In this way, *The Road* is an exemplar of what LaCapra calls "empathic unsettlement." Because realistically coping with trauma requires that one embrace an "intermediary, or transitional process," LaCapra argues that to expect pure mastery over the past and its definitive closure on one hand, or endless wallowing and the acting out of repetition compulsions on the other, is a confining all-or-nothing logic.[21] Accordingly, *The Road* positions itself between these two extremes, always struggling to work through, sometimes successfully, at other times, not. LaCapra maintains that empathy plays an important role in representations of trauma, but there is a risk that audiences will identify too closely as to claim the experience of the traumatized victim as their own. Empathic unsettlement is therefore necessary to provide the virtual experience of being in the victim's shoes while at the same time distinguishing one's place from the other. This has obvious implications for film viewing, too. Ideally, narratives should "neither confuse one's own . . . position with the victim's nor seek facile uplift, harmonization, or closure, but allow the unsettlement that they address to affect the narrative's own movement in terms of both acting out and working through."[22] Unlike others in its generic field, *The Road* does not exploit its traumatic imagery only to suture viewers through a totalizing narrative. While it relies heavily on stylistic techniques to draw the viewer into an experience of vicarious trauma, identification is unsettled by working against the generic grain. Therefore, we don't identify with the father as we would in a conventional narrative; he is neither victim nor hero, but merely someone who struggles to make do with scarce means.

To put it differently, trauma future-tense cinema tends to hurl the viewer into the future so they can retrieve what is lacking now, deferring awareness of the present crisis through imaginary solutions. *The Road*, on the other hand, projects us into the future only to wring it slowly of hope. The father and son's slog southward to the ocean may seem hopeful at first. The ocean here literally represents in Freud's terms the "oceanic feeling . . . the indissoluble bond of being one with the external world as a whole."[23] This is their goal, their hope and the audience hopes along with them. Will there be some fledgling community ready to receive them? The boy wonders if the ocean will be blue. But as they trudge along, hope's deferral—into the next scene, around the next bend, under the next trap door—is always crushed. And when they finally reach the ocean—heaving, gray and indifferent—they are again robbed by a scavenger. In the relentless churning of hope into hopelessness, the future is rubbed out and the viewer landed back in the unbearable absence of the present.

It is as though Cormac McCarthy and the filmmakers of *The Road* set out to represent a post-apocalyptic world that would make audiences regret they ever enjoyed such imaginings. Such is the film's polemical tone. In lieu of socio-political commentary, it critiques popular culture's propensity to imagine a better world by resetting and starting over with refreshed and reinvigorated heroic masculinities. *The Road* demythologizes this false consciousness with an aesthetic of trauma that leaves viewers no quarter and no hope, forcing acceptance of absence as absence and loss as loss. Masculine subject formation thus appears as a tenuous process wherein the cultivation of dignity is as difficult as it is fragile. The father and son's pathetic struggle to preserve their humanity at all costs is the way Freud envisioned it, as fundamentally opposed by "man's natural aggressive instinct, the hostility of each against all and all against each."[24] Death emerges as the constitutive principle of life. After the final scene, the credits roll for some time and the musical score then gives way to the ambient sounds of a present-day backyard. Birds chirp, neighbors murmur, doors slam, lawnmowers roar. Quickening viewers to the present like this, *The Road* aims to definitively foreclose our escape into the future. The apocalypse, therefore, is no *thing* to wish for; it is neither the place where anxieties stemming from the nothing at our center may be alleviated, nor where utopia may be fantasmatically restored.

Notes

1. E. Ann Kaplan, *Climate Trauma: Foreseeing the Future in Dystopian Film and Fiction*. (New Brunswick: Rutgers University Press), forthcoming.
2. E. Ann Kaplan, "Trauma Future-Tense (with reference to Cuarón's *Children of Men* (2006)," in *Trauma und Film*, ed. Julia Koehne, 364–381, 370 (Berlin: Kadmos Publishing, 2012).
3. Ibid.

4. Ibid., 380.
5. See Kenneth Turan's interview with Clint Eastwood, "A Fistful of Memories: Interview with Clint Eastwood," in *The Western Reader*, eds. Jim Kitses and Gregg Rickman, 249 (New York: Limelight, 1998).
6. Richard Slotkin, *Gunfighter Nation: The Myth of the Frontier in Twentieth Century America*, 12 (New York: Harper Collins, 1992); emphasis in original.
7. See Brent Strang, "'That There Corpse is Startin to Turn!': *Three Burials* and the Postmortem Western," *Cinephile* 5, no. 2 (2009): 39–46.
8. Sigmund Freud, *Beyond the Pleasure Principle*, ed. and trans. James Strachey, 47 (New York: W. W. Norton, 1948).
9. Teresa De Lauretis makes a similar point in her book *Freud's Drive* in which she writes: "In [cinematic] spectatorship, too, the death drive overlays the erotic drive and both converge in the movement of turning round upon the subject to yield the primal pleasure, at once sadistic and masochistic, of seeing (one's) death at the movies," 38.
10. Rosi Braidotti, *Transpositions: On Nomadic Ethics*, 245 (Cambridge: Polity, 2006).
11. Note the stranger's advice to the boy at the end of the film to "stay off the road," implying that it will only bring death.
12. See Dominick LaCapra's chapter "Trauma, Absence, Loss," in his book *Writing History, Writing Trauma*, 43–85 (Baltimore: Johns Hopkins University Press, 2001).
13. Ibid., 46.
14. See Michael Kimmel, "The Contemporary 'Crisis' of Masculinity in Historical Perspective," in *The Making of Masculinities: The New Men's Studies*, ed. Harry Brod, 121–53 (Boston: Unwin Hyman, 1987) and Stephen Whitehead, *Men and Masculinities: Key Themes and New Directions* (Oxford: Blackwell, 2002).
15. Whitehead, *Men and Masculinities*, 50–51.
16. Ibid., 212.
17. LaCapra, *Writing History, Writing Trauma*, 52.
18. Ibid., 57.
19. Ibid.
20. While it's true that food supply does become a central plot concern by Season Four, the fact that it manifests so late in the show's development reveals it's inclusion as only one among several plot elements devised to keep the show moving into uncharted territory.
21. LaCapra, *Writing History, Writing Trauma*, 71.
22. Ibid., 78.
23. Sigmund Freud, *Civilization and Its Discontents*, ed. and trans. James Strachey, 11–12 (New York: W. W. Norton, 1961).
24. Ibid., 82.

CHAPTER 11

Propagation and Procreation: The Zombie and the Child

James Berger

Toward the conclusion of Don DeLillo's *White Noise*, we find the following odd conversation between Jack Gladney and his son:

> "There are more people dead today than in the rest of world history put together . . ."
> I looked at my son. I said, "Is he trying to tell us there are more people dying in this twenty-four-hour period than in the rest of human history up to now?"
> "He's saying the dead are greater today than ever before, combined."
> "What dead? Define the dead."
> "He's saying people now dead."
> "What do you mean, now dead? Everybody who's dead is now dead."
> "He's saying people in graves. The known dead. Those you can count."[1]

The terror DeLillo's protagonist feels goes beyond a fear of his own personal death. It is fear of a world engulfed by death; of death as a force that will overcome life entirely. The dead outnumber us already, that much is clear. But they are under the ground. It feels uncanny to think of them there, and to imagine oneself joining them. Walt Whitman made that effort. "O how can it be that the ground itself does not sicken," he wrote. "Is not every continent worked over and over with sour dead?"[2] And James Joyce, in "The Dead," saw this. "Yes, the newspapers were right: snow was general all over Ireland . . . It lay thickly drifted on the crooked crosses and headstones, on the spears of the little gate, on the barren thorns. His soul swooned slowly as he heard the snow falling faintly through the universe and faintly falling, like the descent of their last end, upon all the living and the dead."[3] These three passages anticipate zombie narratives. The dead are numberless, omnipresent, awful in their power—at least potentially, if they should rise against us. The central fact about zombies is that they propagate.

But why do they propagate, and why do they rise up against us? Why this particular fantasy now? There have been previous fantasies of resurrected dead. In prior times, these were gods. Osiris rose from the dead. So, later, did Adonis. Most famously, Jesus accomplished it, and the goal and end-point of the Christian story is a universal resurrection. In these cases, unlike in zombie depictions, the resurrected person possesses consciousness, and his body is undecayed. The fictive dead return also as ghosts. But ghosts have no bodies and enjoy varying degrees of consciousness and agency. In some modern fiction, we see revenants who seem to be mixtures of ghost and incarnate dead—the Thanatoids of Pynchon's *Vineland* or Morrison's embodied ghost in *Beloved*. In all these cases, whether salvific, benevolent, or hostile, the dead return with motive—to warn or save or avenge. Ghosts are generally signs of some crime or trauma whose effects continue in the present; that is the function of haunting.

But zombies do not haunt. Their rising is inexplicable, without motive or cause. Some narratives invoke a virus or radiation or some such supposed origin. But these "causes" have no real relevance; they are merely pretexts. Then again, though the zombie irruption is causeless, zombie narratives are presumed to *mean* something. The zombies' mindless consumption of flesh is seen as analogous to contemporary consumer culture, and George Romero's work and many scenes in Colson Whitehead's novel *Zone One* certainly facilitate such readings. Or the zombie scenario is an allegory for class war or Hardt and Negri's "multitude" or some other social conflict in which one group is perceived to be mindlessly destructive. Lauro and Embry's "Zombie Manifesto" takes the zombie both as a theoretical epitome of posthumanism (i.e., the posthuman would resemble the zombie and not, say, Haraway's depiction of the cyborg) and as a "stand-in for our current moment, and specifically for America in the global economy, where we feed off the products of the rest of the planet, and, alienated from our humanity, stumble forward, groping for immortality even as we decompose."[4]

All these readings are tenable. The zombie slate is blank enough to take on almost any imprint. But the zombie fantasy is excessive. All apocalyptic fantasies deal in excess, of course, for the end of the world has not actually happened. Yet the excess or hyperbole of most apocalyptic narratives since the end of the Second World War have gestured toward some historical precedent or genuine, extrapolatable possibility: toward Hiroshima or the Nazi genocides; toward ecological disaster, viral pandemic, the breakdown of the modern city, or a fatal collision with some astral body. These end-of-the-world anxieties are tethered to some technological, political, medical, or astronomical possibility. Indeed, we could say that the typical post-apocalyptic scenario of the late twentieth century is distinctive because by the time it had been represented in fiction, it had already occurred in historical reality: the death camp, the nuclear explosion, the urban wasteland.[5]

Zombies are another story. The fantasy of the zombie apocalypse is, simply, the worst thing that can be imagined. It is total, incurable, irreversible; it engages the uncanny horror of seeing one's loved ones transformed into monsters whom you then must kill (again); it necessarily induces complete social breakdown—it is not domination by some superior, malevolent force or totalitarian order, but absolute violent chaos. But beyond all this, the zombie fantasy is both an utter reversal and violation of nature—the dead do *not* return to life, ever—and a horrific fixation on the biological processes of mortality and decay. The zombie is pure, organic materiality, whose process of decomposition has become universal; as, in reality, it is . . . but not everywhere, all at once. Imagine Keats's "living hand, now warm and capable/Of earnest grasping . . . if it were cold/And in the icy silence of the tomb."[6] The fantasy of zombie apocalypse contains nothing pleasurable. In other apocalyptic fantasies, social critique (whether direct or implicit) provides a satisfaction. The prophet of doom, as Nathanael West noted, is happy, for the world deserves what it gets. And whatever mechanisms of destruction arrive to give the world its due, even if the results are the same, we can, if we try, imagine worse. But in its mindless, visceral, putrifying, motiveless, meaningless, chaotic biological yet unnatural end, the zombie end-of-the-world seems to find the limit. Edgar judiciously observes in *King Lear*, "The worst is not/So long as we can say 'This is the worst'" (IV.1.27–28).[7] The zombie scenario, I think, proves this truism wrong.[8] Apocalyptic fantasy is always a mix of anxiety and desire. About whatever desire might be present in zombie fantasies, I will speak of later. With regard to its anxieties, I suggest that they are of no single thing. They are not anxieties about nuclear war or radiation, environmental crisis, race or class conflicts, rapid technological change, the emptiness of consumer culture, the destructive, exploitative character of global capital, or even global pandemic disease (though this might seem the closest direct referent). The zombie fantasy is a pooling of all these anxieties regarding the world's future. It is an incarnation of anxiety about the future *as such*. Can there be a future? Is this a functional category in any sense?

The most relevant historical referent for the current American fascination with zombie narratives is the series of attacks on 9/11. This is not simply because 9/11 was traumatic in itself, though of course it was. In retrospect, we can see this moment as pivotal in a number of ways. First, it marked the end of the brief and illusory "end of history" initiated by the end of the Cold War and Soviet communism—the end, that is, of meaningful ideological conflict and the start of an age of technical tinkering with the triumphant and only workable political and economic model: liberal democratic capitalism.[9]

An apparently relatively stable future was, on 9/11, displaced by chaos and violence. We entered a period of permanent ideological and military conflict and of permanent economic instability. Further, by the first decade of the twenty-first century, the extent and possible consequences of global climate change were becoming apparent. Food, water, and energy shortages seemed suddenly not so distant; likewise, pandemic disease. Political and economic institutions seemed increasingly unequal to these threats and challenges. The genealogies of all these new crises reached back decades, of course. But 9/11 was the inescapable crisis that made these others newly visible and that made the very idea of a human, livable future newly problematic.[10]

In the collapse of the two World Trade Center towers, three thousand people died and most of their bodies were never found. They were incinerated and pulverized in the wreckage. This absence of corpses is characteristic of other modern atrocities. The bodies in the death camps were burned; many of the bodies of those killed by atomic blasts or in firebombings were not recovered; disposal of victims of massacres in mass graves was also common. We should not take this feature as a norm; the wars of the past century produced extreme numbers of quite visible cadavers. Nevertheless, the idea of an event of mass death that somehow results in no corpses became part of the late twentieth-century cultural imagination. In most apocalyptic and post-apocalyptic films of our time—for example, *On the Beach* (1959), *Dr. Strangelove* (1964), *12 Monkeys* (1995), *The Terminator* (1984) and its sequels, *The Road Warrior* (1981), the Roland Emmerich extravaganzas *Independence Day* (1996), *The Day After Tomorrow* (2004), and *2012* (2009), *Armageddon* (1998), and one might name many others—hundreds of millions of people die, and yet there are no bodies. Where are the bodies? At least a few of them? A city's worth? It's very clean, this apocalyptic imagination. There is great pleasure in seeing the famous emblems of our rotten and inadequate civilization blown to bits. Even Hal Lindsey, the noted Christian fundamentalist apocalypticist, exuded this pleasure in *The Late Great Planet Earth* (1971). "Imagine cities like London, Paris, Tokyo, New York, Los Angeles, Chicago—obliterated!"[11] Or, as Henry Miller wrote in *Tropic of Cancer* (1934), "for a hundred years or more the world, our world, has been dying. And not one man, in these last hundred years or so, has been crazy enough to put a bomb up the asshole of creation and set it off. The world is rotting away, dying piecemeal. But it needs the coup de grace, it needs to be blown to smithereens."[12] We imagine the world destroyed because, at some level, we want to see the world destroyed.[13] But where are the bodies? As Whitman's poetic anxiety indicated, the corpses of all our wars, crimes, disasters, and ordinary deaths lie beneath us, rotting. The world's vitality—all the domestic, personal, social, economic, and cultural domains that we (in these privileged realms that consume this culture) regard as normal—how can this be sustained? *"How can it be that the ground itself does not sicken?"* The absence of the dead in the late twentieth-century apocalyptic imagination seems to me akin to the general *denial* of the social impasses, traumas, and crimes that incited the apocalyptic anxieties in the first place. In psychoanalysis, "denial" (or "negation") is a psychic response in which a traumatic event is acknowledged (i.e., it is not repressed) but is presumed to have no continuing consequences or effects. Thus, life proceeds in a room filled, as it were, with cumbersome, symptomatic, spectral elephants. In denial's present form, we first reject the thought that our present social and environmental ills have any histories in which we ourselves might be complicit; then, in a growing state of disorientation and paralysis, we reject any possibility of action toward ameliorating our problems and creating a path toward a future. It has become a commonplace to observe that it is easier to imagine the end of the world than the end of capitalism.[14] Now, in the second decade of the twenty-first century, we Americans seem incapable of conceiving and executing even the most piecemeal reforms.

But presently, throughout popular culture, at least there are zombies. Now we know the whereabouts of the post-apocalyptic dead. They're here, everywhere. At the mall, of course—George Romero showed us that. They're occupying, invading, taking private space and placing it in common; taking public space and making it uninhabitable; dominating the ecosystem. And, as I said earlier, the zombie is without motive. It does not haunt. It is the absolute negation of whatever is conscious, volitional, symbolic, rational, affective, subjective, and social in the human organism. To say a world ending by zombies is meaningless is a severe understatement. Beckett's *Endgame* (1957) shows us "meaningless." The zombie fantasy goes well beyond. It shows us even the *process* of the voiding of meaning. In the Zach Snyder remake of *Dawn of the Dead* (2004), the protagonists, from the roof of their shopping mall, make contact with a man on the roof of another building. They communicate with him by writing messages on whiteboards. Over the course of several weeks, a friendship develops. Finally, the new friend's building is overrun. Bitten, he runs across the roof, writing a final message on his whiteboard: an unintelligible smear of blood—the new world's *logos*. Zombies are the limit case. They are the worst.

And they reproduce. The zombie apocalypse is a story of procreation. It condenses the problem of the future to an opposition between the zombie and the child. The astonishing, horrific fertility of the zombie horde stands as cohort or bookend to the apocalyptic sterility at the center of *Children of Men* (2006). In both cases, the problem of the future is the problem of the child. This focus on procreation has been central to apocalyptic thinking since the

Book of Revelation. The so-called Lament for Babylon (18.1–24) lists the people and institutions that will no longer exist after Christ's final triumph: the political powers that fornicated with the great whore, the merchants and craftsmen who provided the world's economy, then the artists and musicians and all cultural life; finally, we read, "The voice of bridegroom and bride will never be heard in you again" (18.23). This culmination to the list of doomed entities negates procreation both biologically and culturally. Human procreation and sexuality, and the historical continuities they entail, are always embedded in a set of social-cultural relations. Thus, this brief negation is as central to the text's apocalyptic vision as all the battles and destructions, the Lake of Fire, and the New Jerusalem. As long as human biological and social reproduction can take place, the apocalypse is incomplete. Something essential of the old world remains as it is passed on, biologically and culturally, to the child. And the death or absence of the child signifies the end of the human project, the end of *this* world.[15]

It is, of course, a platitude of liberals, conservatives, and pop singers that children are the future. Lee Edelman is astute to question the central role of the child in conventional politics and to criticize an attitude and ideology he calls "reproductive futurism," inherent in heteronormative ideology, to detach social views of the child from the sentimental and the sacred, then to reconfigure *queerness* as a category both traumatic and revolutionary, akin to the Lacanian *real*, that attacks and consumes every normativity. This ideology of procreation that seeks to link one generation to the next and to imagine both a coherent future and an extension of the individual beyond his or her death is, for Edelman, part of a heterosexual/heteronormative suppression of nonproductive sexualities, homosexuality in particular. The child, he writes, "invariably shapes the logic within which the political itself must be thought,"[16] and the ideology of the child is a fantasy of a wholeness, coherence, and historical meaning that does not and cannot exist. Thus, he argues, queerness is not simply a sexual orientation, but a fundamental challenge to the fantasy that governs our social and political lives and institutions; and at the center of our humanity is a nonhuman, biological, thing—nonconscious yet motivated by desire or appetite. But in these terms, does queerness not resemble above all the zombie—that absolute, inhuman other that demolishes any social order present or future? Queerness is the zombie—the living-dead within us that resists any rational understanding. It is also a version of the apocalyptic—the end of this world as an object and home for human consciousness then becomes, in Edelman's genuinely provocative and valuable book, a zombie-like entity, partaking of the zombie's hyberbolic, apocalyptic negativity. To simply romanticize the child and the cultural–biological continuities it bears is to deny the histories that put the future—and thus the child—in question. In that sense, Edelman's decoupling of genetic from cultural transmission, his insistence that abjection, perversity and the death drive be reintroduced to *eros* and that sexuality be separated from fecundity, is an important gesture. It is, in different language, the apocalyptic formula per se. The future, if there is to be one, must be, in Yeats' words, "changed utterly."

Modern apocalyptic portrayals veer through numerous approaches to procreation, from sentimental to critical to radically transformative. In *On the Beach* (1959), the most powerful emotional moment comes with the young couple euthanizing their infant daughter before the nuclear cloud reaches them. The central drama of *The Terminator* involves the prevention or fruition of a pregnancy. The story of *The Road Warrior* is told, we ultimately discover, by the quasi-feral boy now grown up and possessing language. Octavia Butler's post-apocalyptic *Xenogenesis* trilogy (republished as *Lilith's Brood*) is concerned with reimagining human political structures through a new conception of the species itself in terms of biology, sexuality, communication, and culture. Beckett's apocalyptic vision in *Endgame* is replete with distorted or parodically devastated filial relations. Cormac McCarthy's *The Road* (which strikes me as a humorless derivation of Beckett) is entirely focused on the father–son relationship and on the child as conduit for a residue of ethical values. And in Russell Hoban's *Riddley Walker*, we see a partly humorous, partly quite serious set of references to child cannibalism. The question Riddley poses in his final address to us is, what is this persistent urge to "kill the baby"?[17] That question, in every sense, is the question of the future, the question that all these apocalyptic texts are asking. Is procreation possible, and will we devour any offspring we produce? Can a social world be instituted that provides genuine care across generations, or do we produce children only to deprive them of the means of material and cultural subsistence? Are we creating a future devoted to life or to death?

Zombies are the logical, fantastical incarnation of these anxieties. They are the active—impossible but inevitable—presence of what is absent both from our apocalyptic imaginings and our genocidal histories . . . that is, the masses of dead, victims of our crimes, stupidities, eugenic fantasies, and variously motivated revels and revelations of destruction. And they are emblems of our anxieties concerning procreation and futurity, whose morbid fecundity curtails any living outcome.

It is not just that zombie propagation is a reversal of human procreation. In fact, pregnancy and birth are central problematics in several significant zombie narratives. Both versions of *Dawn of the Dead* (Romero's in 1978 and Snyder's in 2004) feature pregnant characters whose fates suggest different attitudes toward the future. Fran, in the earlier version, is one of two characters who escape in a helicopter at the end of the film. It is an ambiguous ending. She and Roger have no sense of where they will go as the tide of zombies rises. Nevertheless, she is alive and her pregnancy intact. Any possible future, however unlikely, will contain her and her child. Her fertility is the film's only signal of such a future. This ending, though, revises an earlier ending (which can be seen on the DVD as a special feature) in which both Roger and Fran commit suicide in the helicopter. The twice-imagined ending whose pivot is not just present, but immanent life, summarizes the whole genre's stake.[18]

Snyder's remake makes the question of pregnancy more focused and intense, and introduces also the issue of gender hierarchy. The pregnant woman's husband is determined that their child be born. Andre's motives for this are mixed. On the one hand, he wants to commit himself and the group to a living, human future. To bring the pregnancy to term would be an act of faith and resistance. On the other hand, the film presents him as gripped (infected?) by certain masculine pathologies. He is quite possessive about Luda, and his wish that she bear their child seems more driven by some personal, masculine need for paternity and ownership—the wish to reproduce himself, with Luda merely the vessel for that reproduction. When Luda is bitten, Andre keeps this fact hidden from the group, telling them only that she is ill and that he will take care of her in private. He ties her to a bed in order to keep her alive until she gives birth. Unfortunately, Luda dies during labor and becomes a zombie. They then are discovered, and there is shooting. Luda is killed, Andre is killed. The baby is born. It is, of course, a zombie. Ana, the film's protagonist, enters the room, discovers the infant and kills it.

In keeping with the genre's requirements, the scene presents us with something close to the worst that can be imagined. The newborn zombie, the merging of two antithetical modes of biological reproduction, certainly approaches that limit. It's possible to take the scene as camp, but if that defense is denied—if the scene is taken straight, as I believe is intended—the scene is intolerable. The death drive and its appetites triumph before the attachments of love and care can even begin. But we are not permitted to dwell just on the hideous oxymoron of undead new life. The ugliness of the living—the captivity of the dying woman, the unfeeling and arrogant drive toward paternity—is equally insupportable. On the whole, I would say that Snyder's *Dawn* is relatively mild in its critique of American culture and ideology; not nearly as persistent as Romero's original in its parallels between zombies' consumption and consumer society. But in this scene, patriarchal domination and reproduction are presented clearly as homogenous with zombie reproduction. Andre deserves the child he engenders.

The problem of the child is explored at greater length in the TV series *The Walking Dead* (2010–). After a first season devoted mainly to the unfolding of the zombie horror, the breakdown of all social order, and the frantic efforts of a small group to survive, the second season focuses on children and reproduction. In the opening episode, Sophia, the 12-year-old daughter of Carol, runs into the woods during a zombie attack. The search for Sophia becomes one of the central plot elements for the remainder of the season. The search takes on both real and symbolic significance for the characters. It soon is apparent that the girl will not be found. It would be impossible for her to survive on her own in a wild, zombie-infested terrain. But the group perseveres, putting themselves in danger and claiming that they *will* find her, that this is certain. The characters' hope is infectious. Any viewer who is invested in the show deeply wants Sophia to be found, is aware of how improbable this outcome is, and yet maintains that double hope of the reader of fiction: first, that in realist terms (from inside the perspective of the narrative), she might survive; and second, from an external view, hoping that perhaps the writers might conceive of some miracle . . . and knowing that the miracle of Sophia's survival would be gratifying in one moment but disappointing in the next, since it would represent the writers' condescension to the viewers' sentiment at the expense of the narrative's logic. The search for Sophia thus stages a metanarrative drama. We are forced to judge whether the pleasure of seeing Sophia alive would justify the violation of verisimilitude and genre. All of us—characters and viewers—know she must be dead. And all of us hope with desperation that she is not. The fact of her being a child is what makes the hope a desperate one. She must survive because we cannot bear the thought of her death. We cannot bear the thought of her terror and helplessness before her death. We—both characters and viewers—cannot bear to think of our collective failure to protect her.

When Sophia, now a zombie, walks out of Hershel's barn in episode 7, a future which had been obvious but denied now is present. Zombie propagation negates human procreation. Rick kills Sophia as her mother collapses.[19]

But at this point, we know that Rick's wife, Lori, is pregnant. Their son, Carl, a boy about Sophia's age, has just recovered from a gunshot wound (an accident, the bullet was intended for a deer); his wounding and recovery parallels the plot of Sophia's disappearance and death. Now the couple discusses whether to bring a new child into the broken, futureless world. Even earlier, when Carl's life was in jeopardy, Lori had wondered whether it might be better if he died. "Maybe this isn't a world for children anymore. Maybe this is how it's supposed to be. Why do we want Carl to live in this world; to end up just another animal who doesn't know anything except survival?" Rick responds, "I don't accept that; I can't accept that." But why? Rick's only explanation is that once, on briefly coming to consciousness, Carl talked about seeing the deer and how beautiful and alive it was. "He talked about the deer,

Lori," Rick says. "He talked about the deer." But it was through the deer that he was wounded. Otis shot the deer; the bullet passed through the deer and injured Carl. Later, Otis is killed by zombies as he and Shane get antibiotics from an infirmary. In fact, Otis is sacrificed; Shane shoots him and gives him to the zombies in order to escape with the medicine that saves Carl. Still later, as Shane grows increasingly violent and erratic, Rick is forced to kill him. Carl then shoots his reanimated corpse. The season presents circles of predation, both human and zombie, with the attempts to protect children at their centers. The child is of no value in a world of zombies. He or she needs protection, eats and can't fight. When Rick and Lori reluctantly give Carl his own gun, he is effectively no longer a child. He has left the past, slid back from the future, and now lives in the present. Sophia is gone, and Carl *the child* is gone too.

After the catastrophe at Hershel's farm that ends season two, after the group finds their next refuge, a prison, clears it out, and settles in, Lori resolves to have the baby. Then, in episode 4, there is, unsurprisingly, more calamity. Lori is isolated with Carl and Maggie in an area of the prison full of zombies just as her labor begins. The baby won't come out. She'll need a C-section, but there is no anesthetic. Lori knows where to cut—she has a scar from a previous C-section when Carl was born. She knows she won't survive the birth, but that the child must. She says goodbye to her son. Maggie must cut her open and pull out the baby. This, in a state of horror, she does. The baby is healthy. Carl then must shoot his dead mother in order to prevent her reanimation.

This hideous scene—the violent birth of the child and death of the mother—strangely reinstalls the generational and procreative norms that Sophia's death had wrecked. The child is meant to bury and mourn (and, in a zombie narrative, prevent the reanimation of) the parent, not the reverse. As his uncle tells Hamlet, the "common theme" of both nature and reason is "death of fathers . . . from the first corse till he that died to-day" (I.2.104–105). This summation is, of course, far too simple an application for either drama, ignoring, as it does, murder ("foul and most unnatural" [I.5.25]) and the return of revenants. But with the recovery of Carl and the birth of his sister, a future of some human shape becomes available again to be hoped for. Their survival challenges the zombie negation. It marks out a social space that can at least be imagined to extend beyond the lifespans of the adult inhabitants, as it could not if the surviving cast contained no children.

In demarcating this social space and its possibility of temporal extension, the children's survival allows for the unfolding of the central drama of season three: the question of the possibility of a social order under conditions of unceasing crisis, trauma, and loss—we might say, in contemporary political terms, in a state of terror. The question here, as in so many apocalyptic/post-apocalyptic narratives, is, can a coherent, just society be formed at all? And what, in this state of terror that the zombie narrative envisions, is the role of violence in creating and defending a social order, its future, and the children who symbolize that future?

Season three of *The Walking Dead* presents two possible social models: the consensus-driven, quasi-democratic group lead by Rick, and the authoritarian, quasi-fascist group lead by the Governor.

What would be its forms of leadership and hierarchy? What potentials might be found for democratic, egalitarian governance? What would be the place of force or violence in a just society? And can a *just* society survive under conditions of terror, or must justice and democracy be subordinated to the urgencies of survival? There is not space here to examine these questions and their expositions in zombie narratives, but I will close by sketching out a few directions for argument and then return to the problem of the child. Season three of *The Walking Dead* presents two social models. Though Rick declares early in the season that their group "is not a democracy," the group is generally consensus-driven, and by the end of the season it has moved toward an explicitly democratic form of governance. In contrast, the group led by "The Governor" is unquestionably authoritarian. Though at times, his dictatorship appears benevolent, The Governor *governs*. All decisions are his and anyone whose authority might threaten his is killed. This is a typical post-apocalyptic dichotomy. The question is, will a democratic structure prove too weak, diffuse, and undisciplined to triumph over either the nonhuman zombie threat or its more coordinated authoritarian human counterpart?[20]

One key distinction between the two groups lies in how they regard violence. Or rather, what appears to be a distinction turns out in large part to be a commonality. Both groups rely on violence to protect themselves against others (human or zombie) and against perceived threats from within the group. (Rick, after much provocation, finally does kill Shane). When the group is in danger, there is no law; there is only force. The post-apocalyptic situation is always a "state of exception" or emergency, as Giorgio Agamben describes it, in which legal, constitutional apparatus is suspended. The real difference between democratic and authoritarian violence, as the show presents it, seems to reside in the attitude with which the violence is performed. Rick's group usually (there are some exceptions) performs violence against living people reluctantly, only if there is no other way. In the Governor's group, violence is often sadistic and is performed without misgiving. Violence is even a form of spectacle, as the Governor stages bizarre gladiatorial events featuring captive zombies. This difference produces—I assume is intended to produce—differing responses in viewers. One sympathizes with the use of violence by the democratic group; it is necessary, justified. One is sickened by the gratuitous, pathological violence of the authoritarian group.

Yet, on the whole, the groups are equally violent, and both rely on violence to survive. One of the post-apocalyptic gambits is that restrictions on violence are eased. One can do . . . *anything*, as long as the deed is not openly sadistic and can be justified in terms of survival. I would argue that ultimately Rick's group prevails over the Governor's because it is more efficient in the use and direction of its violence. It does not waste its violence by turning against its own or in displays of sadism and perversity. Or at least not as much.[21]

These differences point back, I believe, toward differing psychic responses to trauma and loss—and are reflected again in attitudes toward children. When finally, after weeks of searching, the zombie Sophia walks out of the barn, there is no question what must be done. Hershel had tried to maintain his dead family there, hoping eventually a cure would be found. But after they are all killed (at Shane's instigation), and after he has seen firsthand a zombie riddled with bullets continue to live, he accepts that the dead must die, that they will never be living people again. If people must be killed twice in order to die, so be it. Indeed, in real life, the dead must always die twice: first, biologically, and then through the process of mourning so that their active presence in the mind can be put to rest and life for the living can continue.[22]

Sophia is shot. Her corpse then is buried and she is mourned. The Governor, however, keeps his dead daughter dead-alive in a secret closet. She has been cleaned; she has been dressed in clean, pretty clothes. She wears also a straitjacket and is chained by the neck and hooded. The Governor visits her every day, removes her hood, plays music for her and strokes her hair (scenes which are among the program's most difficult to watch, among many very difficult scenes). He cannot accept or work through her loss, and this incapacity structures his life, his style of governance, his perversity. The omnipresence of death, and the particular death of the child, produces here a denial of death. The Governor has created his little town of Woodbury with its clean streets and facade of normality—a triumphal merging of nostalgic past and utopian future that seeks to elide the horror of the present—based on the hope of reviving his daughter. When she is killed—emphatically—by Michonne, his sense of the future crumbles and his leadership decisions become increasingly flawed.

In the zombie narrative, there are always more dead than living, always more dead "now dead" (as in DeLillo's phrase) than at any time in history. But this is always true. What animates the dead in these stories, and what sets the figure of the child as their counterpoint, are the broad and deep anxieties about the future—about the possibility of a future—that characterize this historical moment.[23]

Notes

1. Don DeLillo, *White Noise* (New York: Penguin, 1985), 266.
2. Walt Whitman, *Leaves of Grass* (New York: Modern Library, 2001), 459.
3. James Joyce, *Dubliners* (New York: Dover, 1991), 153.
4. Sarah Juliet Lauro and Karen Embry, "A Zombie Manifesto: The Nonhuman Condition in the Era of Advanced Capitalism," *boundary 2* 35 (2008): 85–108, 93. Jose J. Ramirez suggested the connection of zombies to Hardt and Negri's multitude. Jose J. Ramirez, "Shadows of the Multitude: Zombies, Collectivity, Globalization" (paper presented at the Northeast Modern Language Association convention. April 2011).
5. An exception may be the invasion of aliens from space. Even here, though, evocations of colonial invasion are often unmistakable. We certainly have seen visitors with superior technologies dominating and destroying the traditional lives of less technically advanced civilizations. See my *After the End* for a more extended argument regarding the historical, traumatic contexts of apocalyptic imaginings. James Berger, *After the End: Representations of Post-Apocalypse* (Minneapolis: University of Minnesota Press, 1999).
6. John Keats, *Selected Poems* (New York: Penguin, 2007): 237.
7. William Shakespeare, *The Complete Works of Shakespeare* (London: Wordsworth Editions, 2007).
8. This is the premise, I think, of Daniel Drezner's tongue-in-cheek political science treatise about geopolitical responses to a hypothetical zombie outbreak. When he tries to imagine the most catastrophic and destabilizing international crisis that could occur, one that would test most severely the capacities of all existing approaches to cross-border catastrophe, the conclusion he reaches is zombies.
9. This of course is Francis Fukuyama's well-known and problematic argument. The "end of history" turned out to be quite brief. Francis Fukuyama, "The End of History?" *The National Interest* 17 (Summer 1989): 3–18.
10. I recall writing shortly after the turn of the millennium, in a somewhat lighthearted spirit, of what a dud (in millennial, apocalyptic terms) the year 2000 had turned out to be. It could not even pull off its much-anticipated Y2K computer glitch. Not that I was especially optimistic, that's not my temperament; but as a scholar of apocalyptic sensibilities, I could find little to say. It turned out I was writing a year too soon. James Berger, "Twentieth-Century Apocalypse: Forecasts and Aftermaths," *Twentieth-Century Literature* 47 (2000): 1–10.
11. Hal Lindsey, *The Late Great Planet Earth* (Grand Rapids, MI: Zondervan, 1970), 166.
12. Henry Miller, *Tropic of Cancer* (New York: Grove, 1961), 26.
13. This element of desire explains also, I think, the grim enjoyment of Doomsday Preppers and survivalists. If the catastrophe does not come, these people are merely cranks; if it does they are vindicated prophets.
14. The origins of this quote have not definitively been identified. Žižek attributes it to Jameson. Slavoj Žižek, "Spectre of Ideology," in *Mapping Ideology*, eds. Slavoj Žižek and Nicholas Abercrombie, 1–32 (p. 1) (London: Verso, 1994), but does

not cite a Jameson text. One might refer, for example to *Archaeologies of the Future: The Desire Called Utopia and Other Science Fictions* (London and New York: Verso, 2005), 199. But here, Jameson begins his comment with, "As someone has observed," with the implication that it wasn't him. An anonymous blogger named "Qlipoth" makes a strong case that H. Bruce Franklin was first to utter something like that phrase. http://qlipoth.blogspot.com/2009/11/easier-to-imagineend-of-world.html

15. *The New English Bible with the Apocrypha* (New York: Oxford University Press, 1971), 317–336.
16. Lee Edelman, *No Future: Queer Theory and the Death Drive* (Durham and London: Duke University Press, 2004), 2.
17. Russell Hoban, *Riddley Walker* (Bloomington: Indiana University Press, 1998), 220.
18. *Dawn of the Dead*, Dir. George Romero. Laurel Group. 1978; *Dawn of the Dead*. Dir. Zach Snyder. Warner Bros. 2004.
19. *Walking Dead*. AMC TV series, 2010–2013.
20. Claire Curtis argues that one primary impetus within apocalyptic narratives, one reason to clear the slate of the existing order, is to imagine new forms of social order—to reimagine the social contract in a newly formed state of quasi-nature. The move to question and rethink social structures is certainly an important piece of the apocalyptic picture, and we see it played out in the zombie narratives under discussion. My criticism of Curtis concerns her lack of attention to the libidinal and traumatic components of apocalyptic thought, the precise forms of enjoyment and anxiety they produce and derive from. Claire P. Curtis, *Postapocalyptic Fiction and the Social Contract: 'We'll Not Go Home Again'* (Lanham, MD: Lexington Books, 2010).
21. These parables of violence seem allegories of contemporary geopolitical narratives. What is it that distinguishes the violence of liberal democracies—seen as necessary, and justifiable—from the insane, sadistic violence of terrorists and dictators?
22. See first, of course, Freud's articulation of these issues in "Mourning and Melancholia." In Lacanian psychoanalysis, we see the notion of the "second death," which refers to the symbolic as opposed to the biological closing of life. As Dylan Evans explains, "the first death is the physical death of the body, a death which ends one human life but that does not put an end to the cycles of corruption and regeneration. The second death is that which prevents the regeneration of the dead body." Dylan Evans, *An Introductory Dictionary of Lacanian Psychoanalysis* (London: Routledge, 1996), 32. This is an especially useful concept in analyses of post-apocalyptic narrative. Cf. Slavoj Žižek, *The Sublime Object of Ideology* (New York: Verso, 1989), 132–134; *Looking Awry: An Introduction to Lacan Through Popular Culture* (Cambridge: MIT Press, 1989), 22–23; and my *After the End: Representations of Post-Apocalypse* (Minneapolis: University of Minnesota Press, 1999), 42–43. See also the early twentieth-century anthropologist Robert Hertz's analysis of traditions of double burials: the first just

after death; the second a reburial of the bones after the flesh has completely disintegrated. While there is still flesh, the corpse retains dangerous powers. Robert Herz, *Death and the Right Hand* (Glencoe, IL: Free Press, 1960).

23. It should be clear that in this essay, I am concerned exclusively with what I would call "pure" zombie narratives; that is, narratives in which the zombies are entirely other, without language, consciousness, etc. My argument does not consider variants of the genre in which zombies are partially rehumanized—*Land of the Dead, Warm Bodies*, for example. The urge to imagine the *tout autre* is countered by the urge to bring the other back toward the same and the known. To imagine the limit is necessarily to imagine the other side of the limit. But then the radically other must be imagined anew, somewhere past the new limit. In *Warm Bodies*, for instance, a small group of zombies begins to recollect their humanity. At that point in the film, who should turn up but a contingent of some sort of *ur*-ombies, entirely skeletal and malevolent, against whom the living and the now only partly undead make an alliance.

Afterword (Afterward)

Barbara Gurr

As a sociologist, I often wonder of what use I'll be after the apocalypse (which I and my loved ones will, of course, be capable enough and righteous enough to survive). After all, I imagine in the first few months at least there won't be much need for a thorough understanding of Marxist theory or stratification or most of the other sociological paradigms I've spent so much of my life learning and loving. Or perhaps I'm wrong, and sociologists will lead the renaissance. Still, I fear my current skill set doesn't bode well for my post-apocalyptic value. I'll have to figure out how to skin a deer fast so I won't get voted off the island. Assuming there are deer. But as a sociologist, I like to think I'll be somewhat useful after we get our feet back under us, defeat the aliens (or learn how to live with them), and start to rebuild some sort of civilization (hopefully with coffee). Perhaps, along with the historians and the anthropologists and the cultural theorists who contributed to this book, the sociologists will be able to offer some insights for a better future. Or maybe that's just more of the hubris that will get us destroyed in the first place.

The contributors to this book have argued in different ways that the apocalypse and particularly what comes after are enduring cultural fascinations, but they are also adaptable; consider, for example, the figure of the zombie, examined in several chapters here not only due to the zombie's enduring and increasing popularity in film and TV, but also because its function as a cultural signifier is almost infinitely flexible: zombies have been used to critique everything from capitalism and race relations (*White Zombie*, 1932) to heteronormative procreation (Berger, Chapter Eleven, this volume). Similarly, interstellar aliens in popular culture have represented Cold War fears (*Invasion of the Body Snatchers*, 1956), immigration fears (*District 9*, 2009), and the dangers assimilation, miscegenation, and hybridity represent to racial purity (*Alien Nation*, 1988 and its follow-up TV show on Fox from 1989–1990, as well as several follow-up TV movies; *Defiance* on SYFY, 2014–present; *Falling Skies* on TNT, 2011–2015). Disease, nuclear war, and even wrathful angels (TNT's *The Last Ship*, 2014–present; the CW's *The Hundred*, 2013–present; SYFY Network's *Dominion*, 2014–present) also continue to provide the precipitating events and at times the symbolic fodder of the apocalypse itself. But in all of these PASF narratives, humans remain, struggling to survive and rebuild. In all of these stories, there is something *afterward*.

An empirical analysis of post-9/11 post-apocalyptic fiction would indicate that the first thing survivors experience after the world as we know it ends is stark terror, mitigated only by grief. There may be paranoia and anger; we may point fingers at each other, or at others; we may turn to authority figures in the State, the Church, the Family, for reassurance (it begins to sound similar to the days and weeks following the 9/11 attacks . . .). Eventually, however, we'll have to eat. We'll have to find someplace to sleep in relative safety. As both Brent Strang in Chapter Ten and Amanda Hobson in Chapter Nine argue, being alone too long might not be good for us either physically or emotionally, and certainly not psychologically. So we will find each other, perhaps form groups for companionship as much as for safety. We may immediately institute certain rules of behavior, as did the survivors in *The Walking Dead*, and certain folks may rise to the top of an apparently inevitable leadership hierarchy, as do the protagonists of *Jericho* and *Falling Skies*; or we may find that the old rules no longer work and new kinds of relationships must be forged, as humans, vampires, and shapeshifters in *True Blood* discovered. But it seems likely, based on the evidence offered by PASF narratives, that societies of some sort will form, or reform.

The end of all we know leaves us with something of a blank canvas, an opportunity for re-creation: what has been is no longer, and our rebirth in the mud and terror of survival may be daunting, but it also carries potential and promise. Yet as the narratives highlighted in this volume demonstrate, rarely are we ever truly free of the past; at the same time that post-apocalyptic stories look forward, speculating on the "what after," they are always already shaped by our histories, embedded in the now *and* the before as much as in the potential future. What ancient habits will we bring with us into the brave, new world after the world ends? Will we continue to be bound by the previous mechanics of our then defunct societies? Or will we imagine something different? After the apocalypse, who, and what, will we be, and what does this reveal about who we are now, about what we believe, about our ambitions and desires and fears? If popular culture both reflects and produces broader cultural values and beliefs, as cultural theorists including the contributors to this book argue, the question of what we build *afterward* carries a unique and profound urgency; the apocalypse, after all, potentially removes any obligation or accountability to past institutions, power structures, and social ideologies, yet popular narratives seem to indicate that we will return to these, or at the very least struggle to be free of their memory. The profound durability of our social, political, and economic hierarchies even in our most imaginative speculations reveals, perhaps, the depths of our current habitus but also offers us the opportunity to consider the *efficacy* of social structures and institutions in our own lives and futures.

The first few years of this century have brought rapid changes to the United States in terms of foreign and domestic policy, natural disasters, technology, the role of the military, our domestic economy and its place in the global system, and our understanding of the global climate and our environmental future. Yet are these changes significantly different than those experienced in the middle of the twentieth century, as the United States struggled with . . . foreign and domestic policy, natural disasters, technology, the role of the military, our domestic economy and its place in the global system, and our understanding of the global climate and our environmental future? Perhaps, indeed, the more things changes, the more they stay the same.

Or, perhaps, the future is indeed in flux. Seventy years after the apocalypse that ended World War II; or five hundred years after the fateful voyage that opened Turtle Island to Europe and precipitated the trans-Atlantic slave trade; or one hundred years after the apocalypse that brought down the twin towers in New York City, if human societies still exist, will our descendant social forms look familiar to us? Should they? Is what we have worth recreating? Are we in the midst of recreating those same social forms right now, regardless of their worth? Perhaps, of all the questions raised by the cultural politics of TV and film in the early twenty-first century, this is the richest: what is the worth of what we have and what we create, not only before and afterward, but right now?

What we carry into the unknown future and what we abandon, by choice or by force, in the dust and rubble of our destruction tells us a great deal about who we are, and who we imagine ourselves to be. Maybe we will rebuild in our own image. Or maybe we'll build something different, afterward. Maybe we can build something different now; we seem to be always working on that anyway, for better or worse. As the contributors here have pointed out, as perhaps the creators of the narratives under consideration in this book are pointing out, what comes afterward, what I have called the politics of the post-apocalypse, is worth speculating on not only for entertainment but perhaps also for enlightenment.

So say we all.

Appendix: What Else Is Out There?

Kirk Lustila

The proliferation of transmedia networks with multiple and often interacting media platforms in the early twenty-first century has changed the way we interact with, produce, and consume stories, including speculative fiction and post-apocalyptic narratives. This appendix offers a brief list of suggested media that include some of the issues under consideration in this book. It would be a virtual impossibility to create a comprehensive list, given the tremendously dynamic and often transitive nature of so much of our media engagements. Nonetheless, this list illustrates what the contributors to this book argue is a growing re-envisioning of the post-apocalypse following the trauma of 9/11, and provides at least a brief acknowledgment of some of the issues that are only briefly considered, if at all, in this book (for example, the role of technology; the increasingly complicated dominance of the military and military ideology in our everyday lives; and the meaning of friendship in survival horror narratives). Although TV and film are included, this list also includes games as well as fan websites and blogs.

Film

9. *DVD. Directed by Shane Acker. Universal City, CA: Focus Features, 2009*

A CGI film that follows a group of homunculus as they seek to fulfill their deceased creator's wish of saving all life from complete extinction by working together to defeat one of their creator's previous creations; a man-made, sentient war machine that was responsible for the total annihilation of all forms of life on the planet. The film is a mashup of fantasy and sci-fi thematic elements, and presents a lifeless world devastated by technology that can only be saved by the group of mystical, alchemical homunculus, each said to possess a piece of their creator's soul. Rated PG-13 for violence and scary images.

28 Days Later. *Directed by Danny Boyle. London, 2002*

This British post-apocalyptic film is widely credited with reinvigorating the zombie genre and stars, among other Christopher Eccleston (the ninth doctor of the *Doctor Who* series). In this narrative, zombies are created by a highly contagious virus. Survivors try desperately, and often fail, to find sanctuary. Rated R for violence and language.

28 Weeks Later. *Directed by Juan Carlos Fresnadillo. Los Angeles, CA: 20th Century Fox, October 9, 2003*

Sequel to 2002's *28 Days Later*, the film portrays an American-led resettlement mission of Great Britain following a 28-week quarantine. The quarantine was due to an outbreak of an engineered virus that caused infected people to lose any semblance of humanity and become extremely aggressive, violent, and cannibalistic beings of rage. The discovery of infected survivors and a failure to maintain quarantine initiates a catastrophic failure of the resettlement mission, which US forces respond to with progressively more destructive and violent attempts at containing the outbreak. Morality is tested with the choices leaders make and how far they go in order to prevent an apocalyptic threat from spreading. Rated R for strong violence and gore, language, and some sexuality and nudity.

Children of Men. *Directed by Alfonso Cuarón. Universal City, CA: Universal Pictures, 2007*

Film adaptation of the 1992 novel of the same name, this film takes place the UK in 2027 and portrays a world that has experienced 18 years of human infertility. Civilization and society as is collapsing, and the UK represents the last stable nation with a government that still functions. Social and civil unrest are on a rise with increasing number of people seeking entrance into the UK yet capitalism still exists, like the commercialization of a suicide industry. The protagonist is given guardianship of the last known pregnant woman alive, and tasked with guaranteeing her safe passage to a group working to cure human infertility while ensuring she does not fall into the hands of government agents or insurgent forces. The film includes apocalyptic and dystopian themes, showing the extent that people will go to see that the status quo is maintained while humanity itself is heading toward extinction. Rated R for strong violence, language, some drug use, and brief nudity.

Dawn of the Dead. *Directed by Zach Snyder. Universal City, CA: Universal Pictures, 2004*

A film that portrays a group of survivors after the sudden and rapid destabilization of society due to the dead rising and turning into violent, voracious undead creatures. The survivors barricade themselves within a commercial shopping mall in an attempt to wait out the undead threat. The setting of the movie allows the survivors to still experience some semblance of a normal life thanks to the amount of commercial goods within the confines of the mall. The survivors are forced into drastic action, however, once the supplies ultimately run out. Rated R for pervasive, strong horror, violence and gore, language, and sexuality.

Equilibrium. *Directed by Kurt Wimmer. Santa Monica, CA: Miramax Films, 2002*

The film is set in 2072 and portrays a world recovering from a third world war. A totalitarian, surveillance-state government maintains order by requiring all citizens to take doses of a drug that suppresses emotion, bans and destroys any material that might be emotionally stimulating, and executes any "Sense Offenders," people who refuse to take the emotion suppressing drug. The protagonist is an enforcer of the society's laws, and when he inadvertently misses a dose of the drug and begins experiencing emotion, he finds himself questioning the morality of the choices he has made in the name of maintaining order. Rated R for violence.

Television Shows

Adventure Time. *Created by Pendleton Ward. Burbank, CA: Cartoon Network Studios, 2010*

An animated television series follows the adventures of a human boy, and his best friend and adoptive brother, a dog with magical powers to change shape and grow and shrink at will. The two live in the post-apocalyptic Land of Ooo, about a thousand years after a "Great Mushroom War," which essentially was a nuclear holocaust. Since the show takes place after the bombs fell, the world is full of magic that has surfaced once again. Evidence of the nuclear holocaust is only hinted at, sometimes limited to things like buried cars in background scenes. Appropriate for viewers ages 10 and up.

Jeremiah. *Created by J. Michael Straczynski. Beverly Hills, CA: MGM, 2002*

American–Canadian television series that is loosely based on the comic book series of the same name by Belgian writer Hermann Huppen. The show takes place in 2021 in a post-apocalyptic future where 15 years prior a virus had killed most of the world's adult population that was above the age of 13. Both the event and the virus itself are referred to as "The Big Death" and "The Big D." The story's main protagonist is looking for a place called "Valhalla Sector," a place that his father, who researched viruses prior to the outbreak, had mentioned as a possible refuge shortly before disappearing into the chaos of "the Big Death." The story unfolds as various survivors work with and against one another in order to survive in a world that is otherwise absent of parental guidance. Rated mature for nudity, sexual content, violence, and language.

The 100. *Created by Jason Rothenberg. Burbank,*
CA: Warner Bros. Television, 2013

An American post-apocalyptic drama television series that is set 97 years after a devastating nuclear war wiped out civilization on Earth. Survivors live aboard space stations that orbited Earth before the war started, and have banded together to form one massive station named "The Ark," where roughly 2,400 people survive and are led by democratically elected officials. All crimes are punishable by death unless the perpetrator is under 18 years of age. A hundred juvenile prisoners are sent to the surface after the station's life support systems begin to fail. The 100's mission is to determine if Earth is habitable again. The 100 struggle to form a community as they confront the dangers of the surface world and threats from within their ranks while the remaining survivors aboard the station face the reality that their time aboard the station is running out. Rated for teenage audiences, includes violence, frightening scenes and images, and some sexual content.

The Last Ship. *Created by Hank Steinberg. Los Angeles,*
CA: Platinum Dunes, 2014

An American post-apocalyptic drama television series that is based on a novel of the same name by William Brinkley. A viral outbreak has decimated the world's population, killing over 80% of humanity. A US Navy guided missile destroyer and her crew were unaffected by the virus, and the show follows their efforts at finding a cure so the virus can be stopped and humanity can be saved. Appropriate for viewers ages 14 and above, includes violence, disturbing images, and some language.

Revolution. *Created by Eric Kripke. Santa Monica,*
CA: Bad Robot Productions, 2012

An American post-apocalytpic drama television series set in a near future in which virtually all technology has stopped working due to an event known as "the Blackout." North America has been divided into several warring factions and the show's two seasons focus on both individual lives and the larger battle for dominance over land and supplies. Appropriate for ages 14 and above with some sexuality, graphic violence, and language.

Video Games

Beyond Good and Evil *(PlayStation 2 version). Developer:*
Ubisoft/publisher: Ubisoft, 2003

An action-adventure video game that follows the adventures of an investigative reporter who works to reveal a planet-wide alien conspiracy. It takes place in 2435 on a mining planet located in a remote section of the galaxy, and the world itself combines modern elements with those of science fiction and fantasy, such as spaceships and anthropomorphic animals living with humans. A military dictatorship has come to power and has promised to defend the populace; however, they seem unable to stop the alien invasion despite public assurances, and an underground resistance movement fights them because they believe the dictatorship is in league with the aliens. Rated teen for comic mischief and violence.

Deus Ex: Invisible War *(PC version). Developer: Ion Storm/publisher: Eidos Interactive, 2003*

Sequel to 2000's *Deus Ex*, it is a cyberpunk-themed first-person action role-playing video game that takes place in 2072, twenty years after Deus Ex. The world is being rebuilt after a catastrophic event called "The Collapse," a period of war and economic depression during which new factions rose to power and prominence. Remaining cities have regulated themselves into city-states. Following a terrorist attack that destroys the city of Chicago, the player assumes the role of a trainee from a specialized academy, and their support is sought by several organizations. As the player progresses, they learn of conspiracies which could change the world if brought to fruition. The game was designed to allow the player a choice in both plot and gameplay, with branching plot lines and emergent gameplay elements. Rated mature for blood and violence.

Gears of War *(Xbox 360 version). Developer: Epic Games/publisher: Microsoft Studios, 2006*

The first game in a series of military science fiction third-person shooters, it focuses on a squad of troops as they wield attempt a last-ditch effort to save the remaining population of their planet from an unstoppable subterranean enemy that has been overrunning and destroying entire cities with massive numbers of soldiers and their use of bestial monstrosities. The player assumes the role of a former prisoner and war-hardened soldier who is tasked with leading his squad toward success.

Half-Life 2 *(PC version). Developer: Valve Entertainment/publisher: Valve Entertainment, 2004*

Sequel to 1998's *Half-Life*, it is a single player first-person shooter video game and takes place 20 years after the events of *Half-Life*. The game's setting is a dystopian alternate history of Earth where the planets resources and population are being harvested by an oppressive multidimensional empire whose technology far exceeds that of humans. The players' protagonist is a MIT graduate with a PhD in theoretical physics—considered to be one of gaming's greatest characters that just so happens to not have a single line of spoken or test dialogue—who works with scientists and resistance forces against the oppressive alien force. Rated mature for blood, gore, and intense violence.

Homefront *(Xbox 360 version). Developer: Kaos Studios/ publisher: THQ, 2011*

A first-person shooter video game set in a near-future alternate reality of a United States occupied by a Korean invasion force. In the 2020s tensions between North Korea and the global powers due to the country's nuclear capabilities, the formation of the Greater Korean Republic (GKR), and a global oil supply decrease due to a nuclear war between Iran and Saudi Arabia ultimately brought about a surprise attack and invasion of the continental United States by GKR forces. GKR forces seized much of the US Pacific Coast and areas in the Midwest, dividing the nation along the Mississippi River, an area now irradiated after nuclear strikes. Players portray a US resistance fighter living in an occupied Colorado, working with others against occupying forces while aiding a scattered US military. Rated mature for blood, strong language, and violence.

Kingdom Hearts *(PlayStation 2 version). Developer: Square/publisher: Square, 2002*

An action role-playing game, the first game in the Kingdom Hearts series and the result of a collaboration between Squaresoft and the Walt Disney Company. The game combines elements from Disney with those from Square's *Final Fantasy* series. The story follows a young boy's quest to save iconic Disney worlds and characters before they are destroyed by a malevolent Darkness and enemies called Heartless, the same foes that were responsible for the destruction of his own world. Rated acceptable for all ages.

Metal Gear Solid 2: Sons of Liberty *(PlayStation 2 version). Developer: Konami Computer Entertainment Japan/publisher: Konami, 2001*

An action-adventure stealth game that revolves around a terrorist seizure of an environmental disaster clean-up facility off the shores of New York City, constructed to clean up an oil spill caused by a tanker sinking two years prior. The group of terrorists call themselves the "Sons of Liberty" and demand a ransom in exchange for the President of the United States, and will create an environmental disaster by destroying the facility if their demands are not met. As the story progresses, the motives and identities of many of the enemies and allies change and the player uncovers a conspiracy constructed by a powerful secret organization that could shift the balance of world power. Rated mature for blood and violence.

Metro 2033 *(Xbox 360 version). Developer: 4A Games/publisher: THQ, 2010*

A survival horror first-person shooter video game loosely based on the 2005 Russian novel *Metro 2033* by Dmitry Glukhovsky. The game takes place in the ruins of a post-nuclear Russia, the result of a 2013 nuclear war that destroyed or damaged most surface structures and left severe radiation across the surface. Survivors were forced to move underground into metro stations, away from the deadly effects of radiation. Surface radiation heavily mutated animals, and turned them into aggressive and deadly beasts that make surface travel incredibly dangerous. The story follows a young survivor as he tries to save his home from the apparent threat of the Dark Ones, otherworldly beings that live on the surface and are believed to be a threat that could wipe out the last remaining survivors in Moscow.

Warcraft 3: Reign of Chaos *(PC version). Developer: Blizzard Entertainment/ publisher: Blizzard Entertainment, 2002*

This is a high fantasy real-time strategy video game, the third set in the Warcraft fictional universe. The game takes place in the fictional world of Azeroth, a world populated by humans, dwarves, elves, orcs, and other mystical creatures. Several years prior, a demon army intent on Azeroth's destruction had corrupted the Orcs so that they may be used to attack Azeroth. Ultimately the Orcs were defeated and Azeroth was at peace until a new threat emerged. Not content with defeat, the demon army brought forth undead hordes that would sweep across Azeroth, and would bring about a shift in power relations between the races of Azeroth. Rated teen for blood and violence.

Websites and Blogs

Motherboard *at http://www.motherboard.vice.com*

While this website as a whole does not focus closely on speculative fiction, the post-apocalypse, post-9/11, or race, gender, or sexuality, it does offer numerous critical essays that consider these matters, including examinations of feminist science fiction; cyberfeminism; gender, race, and gaming; and gender and technology.

QueerSciFi *at http://www.queerscifi.com*

This is largely a clearing house for queer scifi writers and fans; it lists books, topics, and authors, and also provides space for ongoing dialogue as well as fan fiction.

The Apocalypse Blog *at http://www.apocalypseblog.com*

This fictional blog, written in real time, tells the story of a young woman surviving an apocalyptic bombing in her city. The main character must survive acid rain, possibly zombies, and other post-apocalyptic dangers. Some adult themes.

Scavenger of the Dead *at http://www.scavengerofthedead.com*

Similar to *The Apocalypse Blog*, this is an online serial story written in blog form. Some adult themes and violence.

Notes on Contributors

James Berger is Senior Lecturer in American Studies and English at Yale University. He is author of *The Disarticulate: Language, Disability, and the Narratives of Modernity* (2014), *After the End: Representations of Post-Apocalypse* (1999), and editor of Helen Keller's *The Story of My Life: The Restored Edition* (2003). He is also author of a book of poems, *Prior* (2013).

Robert A. Booth is a socio-cultural anthropologist who holds a PhD from the University of Connecticut. His research focuses on issues of identity politics and national identity in Europe, societal memory—especially in "memory institutions" such as museums—and how that memory is used in public discourses about social trauma and human rights. Additionally, he has long held an interest in science fiction television, film, and literature.

Mary C. Burke is a Lecturer in Sociology and Gender, Sexuality, and Women's Studies at the University of Vermont. Her research and teaching interests include gender, sexuality, social movements, and science studies.

Barbara Gurr is an Assistant Professor in Residence in the Women's, Gender and Sexuality Studies Program at the University of Connecticut. She is the author of *Reproductive Justice: the Politics of Healthcare for Native American Women* (2014). Her research and teaching interests include settler colonialism, race, gender, sexualities, and popular culture. She also likes cat videos and piña coladas.

Andrea Harris has a dual appointment in the English Department and the Women's Studies Program at Wright State University in Dayton, Ohio. Her area of focus within women's studies is gender and violence. She has designed and taught multiple courses on representations of women in media. Her newest course explores the significance of gender within contemporary zombie film and television.

Amanda Hobson is an administrator at Ohio University in the Department of Residential Housing. She received a Master's of Education focused on feminist pedagogy and English literature. Currently, Hobson is a PhD student in Interdisciplinary Arts at Ohio University, whose areas of study are aesthetics and film. Her research concentrates on the construction and portrayal of gender and sexuality in transnational socio-cultural history, mainly using the vampire and the paranormal as a cultural lens.

Sarah L. Jirek is an Assistant Professor of Sociology at Westmont College. Her research and teaching focus on social inequalities, gendered violence, crime victims and offenders, trauma recovery, life transformation, post-traumatic growth, and how social systems, organizations, and helping professionals can play a more effective role in facilitating positive life change.

Maura Kelly is an Assistant Professor of Sociology at Portland State University. Her research and teaching interests include gender, sexuality, and work.

Melissa F. Lavin is an Assistant Professor of Sociology at SUNY Oneonta. She has researched extensively in the areas of sex work and drug use. Her areas of expertise include but are not limited to crime and deviance, social inequality, gender, sociological psychology, and pop culture. Her work appears in the *Journal of Deviant Behavior* and *Humanity and Society*.

Brian M. Lowe is an Associate Professor of Sociology at SUNY Oneonta. He is currently working on a project regarding mediated representations and spectacular morality.

Kirk Lustila has been an avid consumer of science fiction and video game media for more than two decades. They studied history and women's, gender, and sexuality Studies before graduating from the University of Connecticut in 2014. They spend most of their time looking for one of those elusive living wage jobs.

Michelle Meagher is Associate Professor of Women's and Gender Studies at the University of Alberta, Edmonton, where she teaches courses on gender and representation, feminism and popular culture, and feminist art. The main focus of her research is on understanding and cultivating the relationships between feminist theory and feminist art, with particular interests in bodies, embodiment, and aging. Her work on these topics appears in journals including *Hypatia*, *Feminist Theory*, *Feminist Studies*, and *Body and Society*.

Stacy Missari is an Assistant Professor of Sociology and internship coordinator at Quinnipiac University. Her research and teaching focus on the relationship between gender, sexualities and inequality, in particular the relationship between sexual subjectivity and inequality and women's contraceptive decision-making.

Tracey Raney is Associate Professor of Politics and Public Administration at Ryerson University in Toronto, Canada. Her research includes popular culture and politics, nationalism and national identities, women and politics, social policy, and Canadian politics. Her work has been published in journals including the *Canadian Journal of Political Science, International Journal*, and the *Journal of Canadian Studies*.

Brent Strang is a PhD candidate in Stony Brook University's Cultural Analysis and Theory Program. His dissertation is a cultural study of the remote control device. He has published in *Journal of Visual Culture* and *Cinephile*, and has a forthcoming chapter in *The Western in the Global South*.

J. Sumerau is an Assistant Professor of Sociology at the University of Tampa. Zir teaching and research focuses on the interrelation of gender, sexualities, religion, and health in the interpersonal and historical experiences of sexual and religious minorities.

Index

9/11, 5, 6, 8, 113, 151–152, 166, 169; apocalypse on, 7; and TV/film, 15, 18, 25, 26, 99; and Muslim(s), 25, 27, 30

African-American, 63
alien/s, 21, 24, 27, 37, 38, 42, 165, 172–173; invasion, 2, 21, 36, 38, 41, 43, 88, 99, 161, 173
allegory, 46, 53, 88, 92–93, 97, 150
anxieties, 2, 6, 12, 19, 23, 26, 46, 51, 53, 55, 99, 114, 139, 147, 150–155, 160; about immigrants, 23, 24, and gender, 10, 45–46, 51; and race, 10, 23
anxiety, 20, 24, 27, 36, 39, 55, 138, 144, 151–152, 162

capitalism, 22, 77, 100, 108, 138, 151, 153, 165, 170
class, 7–8, 24, 26, 27, 59–64, 68, 72, 75–76, 81, 90, 119–120
conservative, 6; gender roles, 8, 36, 125, 127; ideologies, 2, 9, 11, 48, 23, 41, 46, 48, 52, 91, 92, 93, 114, 126, 128; masculinity, 136; values, 9
contagion, 17, 19, 20–21, 27
controlling images, 73–75, 80
cyberfeminism, 108, 175
cyborg(s), 49, 108–109, 150

death-drive, 140–141, 148, 155–156
disempowerment, 60, 102
dystopian film, 24, 26, 59, 61
dystopian future, 68

empowerment, 101–103, 105, 107
enabling conditions, 72
essentialism, 101, 103, 105–107, 109
essentialist, 125

family, 4, 36, 40–41, 47, 52–53, 87, 93–94, 112, 128, 144–145, 166
femininity, 47–51, 55, 65, 79, 102–105, 107–108, 135
feminism (see also cyberfeminism; second wave feminism; third-wave feminism; pre-feminist; post-feminism), 45, 51, 56, 101, 102, 108
feminist, 3, 47–48, 51–52, 55, 100–103, 105, 108, 109, 175; scholars, 60
feminize/d, 49–50, 103, 121, 133; de-, 80; hyper-, 120
feminization, 129
feminizing, 73, 142
frontier, 31–35, 36, 37, 39, 40–41, 139–140

gay, 8, 73, 89, 90, 91–94, 95, 96, 113, 122
gender dichotomy, 102, 105, 106–108
gender performance, 34, 53, 103
god, 33, 34, 35, 43, 54, 91, 127–128, 133, 150

hero/es, 32, 40, 75, 100, 126, 130, 131–132, 146; action, 101–102, 103; female, 47, 52–53, 103, 106; feminized, 103; male, 138, 140; masculine, 49; post-feminist, 46

heroine, 62; action, 103; post-feminist, 152
heteronormative, 40, 65, 67, 96, 154, 165
heteronormativity, 67, 68, 88, 89, 91
heterosexual, 3, 31, 33, 35–36, 38, 42–43, 53, 66, 67, 71, 90, 100–101, 103–105, 118–119, 121, 154; masculinity, 35, 41, 81
heterosexuality, 41, 70, 81, 90
hierarchy, 8, 27, 40, 101, 103, 107–108, 118, 130, 156, 159, 166
horror (see also survival horror), 4, 17, 21, 36, 99, 100, 105, 108, 123, 151, 157, 158, 160; film, 19–20, 21–22, 99, 133, 136
human rights, 5, 88, 91

identity, 39–41, 50, 123, 135; American, 32–35; collective, 32, 40, 42; gender, 46, 49, 51, 55; sexual, 90, 96
immigration (see also immigrants), 11, 17, 23–24, 33, 35, 113, 138, 165
immigrants, 22–25, 32
invasion, 2, 21, 36, 41, 161, 173, 174

lesbian, 8, 90–91, 94, 96, 113, 122
liberal, 48, 55, 151, 154, 162

magical negro, 74
masculinity, 31–32, 35–36, 53, 55, 74–75, 77, 81, 103, 105–107, 120–121, 125–136, 138–140, 142–143, 145; female, 47–50; hegemonic, 9, 11, 32, 33, 38, 41, 118, 119–120, 121, 125–126, 128, 130–136; perceived crisis in, 137–138, 142
mourning, 142–143, 145–146, 160, 162

Native America, 32, 36–38
Native American, 32, 34, 36–38, 42–43, 44, 76, 108

patriarchal, 40, 49, 52, 77–79, 92, 101–104, 105–108, 118, 127–130, 134, 156; essentialism, 103, 105–106; gender dichotomy, 105–106; hetero-, 2, 4
patriarchy, 43, 46, 78, 118–119, 125, 128
people of color, 4, 8, 35, 43, 61, 63, 64, 69, 73, 74, 126
post-9/11, 10, 12–13, 24–25, 30, 32, 39, 43, 123, 175
post-feminism, 45, 47, 101
post-feminist, 60, 49, 50, 51, 52, 55, 103
post-gender, 46–48, 51, 61
pre-feminist, 52, 53, 55–56

queer, 3, 12, 35, 43, 89–90, 93, 96–97, 121; (gender), 66; -ness, 154; scifi, 175; sexuality, 89; resistance, 89–90. 97

rape (see also sexual violence), 18, 106–107, 127–128, 130–131
regeneration, 109, 137, 139–141, 143–145, 162
religion, 28, 87, 91, 127–129, 136
reproduction (biological), 2, 108, 128, 154, 156–157
reproduction (of culture), 2, 38, 72, 154
reproduction, technological, 54
Romero, George, 19, 22, 99–100, 150, 153, 155, 156

same-sex marriage, 91, 93, 94
second wave feminism, 48, 55, 101
settler colonialism, 32, 34, 36–37, 38, 42–43
sexuality, 2–3, 6–9, 12, 34–35, 60–61, 63–68, 87–89, 91, 93, 95–96, 103, 114, 118–119, 123, 134, 154–155, 170–172, 175; female, 90; masculine, 80; queer, 89; women's, 80
sexual violence (see also rape), 61, 73, 130
survival horror, 1, 100, 169, 174

terrorist/s, 5, 6, 23, 26, 99, 113–114, 162, 173, 174
third-wave feminism, 101
transgender, 122
trauma, 6, 12, 17, 51, 137–142, 144–147, 150, 153, 158, 160, 169
trauma future-tense, 138, 140–141, 146

traumatic, 17, 59, 137–138, 141–142, 144, 146, 151, 153–154, 161, 162

video games, 3, 72, 100, 172–175

white supremacy, 8, 10
white supremacist, 10, 119

Printed by Printforce, the Netherlands